A fundamental question for theology is the question how we are to understand the claims that we make about God. The only language we can understand is the language we use to talk about human beings and their environment. How can we use that language to talk about God while respecting the infinite difference between God and humanity?

The traditional answer has been to appeal to the concept of analogy. However, that appeal has been interpreted in widely different ways. This book aims to clarify the question and this answer by an analysis of the concept. It begins with an exploration of the way the concept was evolved by Aristotle out of Greek mathematics as a technique for comparing "things that were remote"; followed by a critical examination of three very different classical accounts of the way religious language works: those of Thomas Aquinas, Immanuel Kant and Karl Barth. The book finally investigates the way in which analogy could be applied to answer the question initially posed—how is it possible to use human language to talk about God. This is a question of fundamental significance for the whole of religion and theology, concerning as it does our whole understanding of what we mean when we talk about God.

Roger M. White is Senior Fellow of the Department of Philosophy, The University of Leeds, UK. He is also the author of *The Structure of Metaphor*, 1996, and *Wittgenstein's Tractatus Logico-Philosophicus: A Reader's Guide*, 2006.

Transcending Boundaries in Philosophy and Theology

Series editors:
Martin Warner, University of Warwick
Kevin Vanhoozer, Wheaton College and Graduate School

Transcending Boundaries in Philosophy and Theology is an interdisciplinary series exploring new opportunities in the dialogue between philosophy and theology that go beyond more traditional "faith and reason" debates and take account of the contemporary reshaping of intellectual boundaries. For much of the modern era, the relation of philosophy and theology has been conceived in terms of antagonism or subordination, but recent intellectual developments hold out considerable potential for a renewed dialogue in which philosophy and theology have common cause for revisioning their respective identities, reconceiving their relationship, and combining their resources. This series explores constructively for the 21st century the resources available for engaging with those forms of enquiry, experience and sensibility that theology has historically sought to address. Drawing together new writing and research from leading international scholars in the field, this high profile research series offers an important contribution to contemporary research across the interdisciplinary perspectives relating theology and philosophy.

Talking about God
The Concept of Analogy
and the Problem of Religious Language

ROGER M. WHITE
The University of Leeds, UK

ASHGATE

Published by
Ashgate Publishing Limited
Wey Court East
Union Road
Farnham
Surrey, GU9 7PT
England

Ashgate Publishing Company
Suite 420
101 Cherry Street
Burlington
VT 05401-4405
USA

www.ashgate.com

British Library Cataloguing in Publication Data
White, Roger M.
    Talking about God: the concept of analogy and the problem of religious language. – (Transcending boundaries in philosophy and theology)
    1. Language and languages – Religious aspects. 2. Analogy (Religion) 3. Language and languages – Religious aspects – Christianity. 4. God (Christianity) – Knowableness.
    I. Title II. Series
    210.1'4–dc22

Library of Congress Cataloging-in-Publication Data
White, Roger M.
    Talking about God: the concept of analogy and the problem of religious language / Roger M. White.
      p. cm. – (Transcending boundaries in philosophy and theology)
    Includes bibliographical references and index.
    ISBN 978-1-4094-0036-3 (hardcover: alk. paper) – ISBN 978-1-4094-0042-4 (pbk.: alk. paper) – ISBN 978-1-4094-0363-0 (ebook) 1. Analogy (Religion) 2. Knowledge, Theory of (Religion) 3. Philosophical theology. 4. God – Christianity. I. Title.
    BT55.W47 2009
    210–dc22

2009046524

ISBN 9781409400363 (hbk)
ISBN 9781409400424 (pbk)
ISBN 9781409403630 (ebk)

Mixed Sources
Product group from well-managed forests and other controlled sources
www.fsc.org Cert no. SA-COC-1565
© 1996 Forest Stewardship Council
FSC

Printed and bound in Great Britain by
MPG Books Group, UK

Dedicated to the memory of Donald Mackinnon,
who first helped me to appreciate the depth of the question of analogy

Contents

Abbreviations

BT	Aquinas, *Commentary on Boethius' "de Trinitate"*
Cat.	Aristotle, *Categories*
CD	Barth, *Church Dogmatics*
CJ	Kant, *Critique of Judgment*
Conflict	Kant, *The Conflict of the Faculties*
CPR	Kant, *Critique of Pure Reason*
CPrR	Kant, *Critique of Practical Reason*
dAn.	Aristotle, *de Anima*
dP	Aquinas, *de Potentia Dei*
dV	Aquinas, *de Veritate*
EE	Aristotle, *Eudemian Ethics*
FQA	Barth, *Anselm, Fides Quaerens Intellectum*
G&C	Aristotle, *de Generatione et Corruptione*
HA	Aristotle, *History of Animals*
Meta.	Aristotle, *Metaphysics*
Mete.	Aristotle, *Meteorologica*
NA	Cajetan, *The Analogy of Names*
NE	Aristotle, *Nicomachean Ethics*
Origin	Darwin, *The Origin of Species*
PA	Aristotle, *Parts of Animals*
Pölitz	Kant, *Lectures on the Philosophical Doctrine of Religion*
Poet.	Aristotle, *Poetics*
Pol.	Aristotle, *Politics*
PostA	Aristotle, *Posterior Analytics*
R2	Barth, *The Epistle to the Romans* (2nd edition)
Religion within ...	Kant, *Religion within the Boundaries of Mere Reason*
Rhet.	Aristotle, *Rhetoric*
SCG	Aquinas, *Summa contra Gentiles*
ST	Aquinas, *Summa Theologiae*
Top.	Aristotle, *Topics*

Preface

In this book I am concerned with one question only: "How is it possible to use human language to talk about God?" and with the answer that is most frequently given to that question: "Words that are used both of God and of creatures are used *analogically*"; or rather, I am concerned with a set of answers to that question, since the claim that the words are used analogically has been interpreted in widely different ways. Even the word "analogy" has itself been highly unstable, changing its meaning from author to author and sometimes seeming to be little more than a loose synonym for "similarity".

Although the book is concerned with just one question, it is a question that is of fundamental significance for the whole of religion and theology, concerning as it does our whole understanding of what we mean when we talk about God. Unless we give a proper answer to this question, we are liable to lapse into more or less gross anthropomorphism or idolatry, and atheist opponents of religion to attack a straw man.

I begin by examining the emergence of the concept of analogy in Greek thought, which is where virtually all the concepts involved in the subsequent debate over analogy had their origins. Initially the basic idea of analogy was within Greek mathematics, where the importance of analogy first became apparent. Later thinkers, especially Aristotle, showed what could be done when one extended the ideas of the Greek mathematicians beyond mathematics. These early discussions of analogy were marked by a clarity and precision that unfortunately was frequently absent from the later theological discussions.

Against this background I then undertake a study of the theological application of analogy in three thinkers who have addressed the question that concerns me— Thomas Aquinas, Immanuel Kant and Karl Barth. This cannot be considered as a history of the application of analogy in theology—that would require consideration of a far wider range of authors—and my purpose in examining these three in detail is not historical. These three have been chosen as having presented three of the weightiest and most worked out accounts of the application of analogy to the problem of religious language—and have done so in strikingly different ways. Although I do not attempt to disguise my belief that it is Barth who has come closest to the truth, I do not attempt to decide between them. Rather, these three have been chosen because between them they bring out the issues at stake here.

My other reason for not deciding between them is because that would be a theological task, whereas my aim is primarily philosophical, aiming at conceptual analysis. These three authors between them serve to bring out the full potential of analogy, and hence serve to show us what that concept really is, and its power in aiding us to see what is involved in using language to talk about God.

In the course of writing this book, I have benefited from discussions with a number of colleagues at Leeds University, to whom I am grateful for their comments. I would mention in particular, Geoffrey Cantor, Angelo Cei, Jamie Dow, Stig Hansen, Malcolm Heath, Greg Radick, Scott Shalkowski and Kevin Ward. But my largest debts are to three people: first, my wife Gabrielle, who has given me support and help throughout the project; second, Martin Warner, who, as one of the editors of this series, has read and made extensive comments on the whole manuscript of this book; and third, Jon Hodge, with whom I have had many discussions of the issues raised, and who has similarly made detailed comments on my discussions of Aristotle and Aquinas. Between them, they have enabled me to introduce many improvements into the book.

Analogy and Talking about God

The Problem of Religious Language

A religion such as Christianity could not exist without the possibility of talking about God. And, indeed, a theistic religious community could not exist without a complex network of places where God is written about or spoken of: most fundamentally there is the Bible, but there is a vast range of other situations that are vital to religion but which could not exist without talking of God: creeds, sermons, liturgies, private prayers, theological debates and informal conversations between believers, etc. In all this diversity, there is one thing that plainly runs through the whole language in which the talk is of God. God is spoken about using language in such a way that it is primarily the language that is appropriate for speaking about a human being. God is described *as though* He were a human being. If we just consider the Bible, whether the Old Testament or the New Testament, there are frequent passages in which: human organs—mouth, eye, hand, arm and so on—are ascribed to God; in which God is given human cognitive capacities—knowing, seeing, hearing, even smelling;[1] in which God speaks; in which human offices such as king, father or judge are assigned to God; in which God has the same kind of moral characteristics, such as justice, patience and compassion, that we ascribe to human beings, and perhaps most strikingly of all, in which God is described as an emotional, even passionate, being, who can be loving, jealous, angry and compassionate.

There is a clear and obvious incongruity here: no one believes God to be a human being, or even a being that could have the kind of attributes of a human being that the Bible ascribes to Him. At its simplest, no one will conceive of God as a material being, with material attributes, but there is clearly a range of ways in which we talk about human beings where it would be completely absurd to talk about God in the same way. Human beings are finite, limited, fallible and corrupt. Without prejudging the extent or nature of the mismatch, we may regard *each* of the ways of talking about God mentioned in the last paragraph—even the "moral" attributions—as under the suspicion of involving a completely inadequate language for doing so. The problem perhaps stands out at its sharpest if we consider the ascription of emotions to God: there is a long theological tradition, possibly largely under the influence of Plato, that forbids the ascription of emotions to God. However, not only does the ascription of such emotions look completely

---

[1]   *E.g.* in Gen. viii, 21. Perhaps most remarkably, God is talked of as changing His mind or repenting of His decisions (*e.g.* Gen. vi, 7).

uneliminable from the Bible, we cannot help but talk and think about God in emotional terms. It is simply humanly impossible, for example, to give thanks to a being without thinking of that being as capable of emotions. One can be grateful to a dog that saves your life, but not to a hospital life-support system.

At the same time, this use of "human" language in talking about God is inevitable. If we are to use language at all to talk about anything whatsoever, we have no alternative but to use language in a way that is intelligible to us as human beings. Every way of talking that could be grasped by a human being must be such that it could be learnt by a human being, and explained to a human being: we simply cannot step outside the human condition and use language in a way that transcends the limits of our comprehension. The language we can understand is, in the last resort, the language that we learn at our mother's knee, a language that is concerned with human beings, their empirical environment and their relation to that environment. No matter how sophisticated and abstract the subsequent developments of that language may be, to retain comprehensibility for us, it must still retain its links back to those starting points, in no matter how complicated a way. The language we use to talk of God must therefore be a language that relates to our experience. Therefore we cannot say for example that the Bible adopts a pictorial, or popular, way of speaking, but that there is a strict way of speaking that can, when necessary, be used by theologians who are careful to free their language from every trace of anthropomorphism. *Every* use of language, if it is to retain a content that is intelligible to us, must have its roots in and be explicable in terms of the language we all understand. If we coin a special vocabulary to mark off the difference between the divine and the human, we still do it in human terms: thus if we say that God is omnipotent or omniscient or omnipresent, as it stands the language seems only to say that God does on a global scale and in a complete way what human beings do locally and in a fragmentary manner.[2] Not even adopting the most rigorous *via negativa* can do more than testify to the dilemma that confronts us here: either it seeks to retain some content to its talk about God, in which case the basic problem remains, or it reduces language about God to talking about something-I-know-not-what about which nothing can be said.[3]

---

[2]   Karl Barth, *Dogmatics in Outline*, p.46: "When attempts were later made to speak systematically about God and to describe His nature, men became more talkative. They spoke of God's aseity, His being grounded in Himself; they spoke of God's infinity in space and time, and therefore of God's eternity. And men spoke on the other hand of God's holiness and righteousness, mercifulness and patience. We must be clear that whatever we say of God in such human concepts can never be more than an indication of Him; no such concept can really conceive the nature of God. God is inconceivable."

[3]   "There is no way from us to God—not even a *via negativa* not even a *via dialectica* nor *paradoxa*. The god who stood at the end of some human way—even of this way—would not be God" (Barth, "The Problem of Ethics Today" (1922), in *The Word of God and the Word of Man*, p.177).

Equally it does not help to appeal to the concept of metaphor here, and say that all the language in the Bible is to be understood metaphorically. Unless we know what it is to interpret such metaphors, this takes us no further forward, and unless this claim is accompanied by a properly worked out theory of metaphor it is unclear what that amounts to. But finally, we can only make sense of the idea of talking metaphorically about God against the background of our knowing what it is to talk literally about God. There are undoubtedly many claims in the Bible that are unmistakably metaphorical, such as "The Lord is my shepherd, I shall not want; he makes me lie down in green pastures. He leads me beside still waters" (Psalm xxiii, 1–2), but we lose all touch with what it amounts to to say that *such* passages are metaphorical, unless we can differentiate them from other texts that are not to be so taken. Our concern is, therefore, how is it possible to make claims that are *literally* true of God?

This, then, is our problem: the only language we have for talking about God is our human language, the language we use for talking about human beings, their relationships and their relationship with their physical environment. If we are to talk about God at all, it is inevitable that we use such language. But at the same time we are forced to acknowledge that such a use of language is inappropriate and completely inadequate.[4]

On the ceiling of the Sistine Chapel, Michelangelo depicts the creation of Adam, showing God as a bearded man who is airborne with a finger stretched out to a recumbent Adam. We respond with great immediacy to the painting as it presents itself, but no one will interpret this image "naturalistically". There is the picture in the foreground, but to arrive at its meaning we have to penetrate beneath the surface. What is the relation between the painted scene that we see and respond to and its meaning that could not be depicted at all? There has always been an understandable suspicion, witnessed in the Second Commandment, of any attempt to give a pictorial representation of God. But we do not escape the suspect nature

---

[4] "*As ministers we ought to speak of God. We are human, however, and so cannot speak of God. We ought therefore to recognize both* our obligation and our inability, and by that very *recognition give God the glory*. This is our perplexity" (Barth, "The Word of God and the Task of the Ministry (1922), in *The Word of God and the Word of Man*). Barth is not merely talking here of the inadequacy of the words we use in speaking of God, but also of the larger problem laid upon the ministry of talking in God's name, without being able to give proper account of one's authority for so doing. However, the inadequacy of all human words in the sense that interests us was definitely a part of what Barth has in mind here. A major part of what was called "dialectical theology", at least as practised by Barth, was a deep concern with the necessity for speaking about God, coupled with an awareness that anything we said was inappropriate to its subject matter. This was a dialectic that could never be resolved in a higher synthesis, but only acknowledged. I will look at Barth's account of religious language in detail later, but I have cited him three times in these opening paragraphs because of all modern theologians he was perhaps the one who was most deeply conscious, and helped to make us conscious, of the depth of the problem that confronts us here.

of what we do by only using words: here too we have the words in the foreground, to which we respond immediately, but the meaning in the background. How are we meant to construe the relation between the words, for all their inevitable inappropriateness, and their meanings?

We may clarify the concern of the present study by considering the following familiar passage:

> In the beginning was the Word, and the Word was with God, and the Word was God. He was in the beginning with God; all things were made through him, and without him was not anything made that was made. In him was life, and the life was the light of men. The light shines in the darkness, and the darkness has not overcome it.
>
> There was a man sent from God, whose name was John. He came for testimony, to bear witness to the light, that all might believe through him. He was not the light, but came to bear witness to the light. The true light that enlightens every man was coming into the world.
>
> He was in the world, and the world was made through him, yet the world knew him not. He came to his own home, and his own people received him not. But to all who received him, who believed in his name, he gave power to become children of God; who were born, not of blood nor of the will of the flesh nor of the will of man, but of God.
>
> And the Word became flesh and dwelt among us, full of grace and truth; we have beheld his glory, glory as of the only Son from the Father. (John i, 1–14)

If we wish to interpret a rich and subtle text such as this, we need to explore the language used here at a number of different levels. Most simply, we can enquire into the translation from New Testament Greek into English: words such as "ἀρχή" and "λόγος" have a range of connotations that are not captured by any English words, and ask such questions as whether "ἀρχή" should be given the temporal significance that "beginning" inevitably carries with it in English. What is the force of "κατέλαβεν" in verse 5? Equally, at the level of translation, we must ask "What is the precise significance of 'θεὸς ἦν ὁ λόγος'; does this have Trinitarian overtones, or is it, on the contrary, evidence of a subordination of the Son to the Father?" We may locate this passage in earlier uses of the idea of a divine Logos in Greek philosophy and theology; and we may seek to interpret this passage as part of the larger project of understanding the fourth gospel and its theology; and so on. But behind all these obviously necessary and deeply important enquiries, there is a more fundamental question. With the exception of the word "θεὸς" every word used in this passage has an everyday familiar use in talking about human affairs, and unless they had this familiar use, we would not be able to understand the passage at all. But if we tried simply to give the words merely that everyday use, the whole passage would collapse into absurdity. What then is the relation between the everyday use of the words, a use that is indispensable for any understanding of what is being said here, and the use that these words acquire through being put in the context in which John places them for talking about God and His relation to the world?

This last question is a more fundamental question in the sense that it is the answer to this question that provides the framework within which we can properly address those other questions. But it is also a fundamental question for the whole of theology and religion: without an appropriate answer to such questions, we simply do not know what we are talking about when we make and discuss theological claims. We will either mean nothing at all, or interpret these claims in a grossly unsuitable way, importing more or less hidden anthropomorphisms into our thinking. It should be noticed that this question is as much addressed to the atheist opponents of religious belief as to its adherents. It is, if anything, even more frequent for atheists attacking religious beliefs than for believers to construe claims about God in a crudely anthropomorphic way.[5]

The questions we are concerned with here raise both theological issues and issues in the philosophy of language. Although these issues cannot be wholly separated, the primary aim of the present study is to explore the *philosophical* questions that arise here. "How is it possible for us to use words that initially have one set of meanings to specify for us a different set of meanings?"; "How can we use words that have an everyday use rooted in our everyday empirical experience of the world in such a way as to communicate, in a way that remains intelligible to us, a reality that transcends that everyday experience?"; and "How can we use an essentially anthropomorphic language in such a way as to remove every taint of anthropomorphism from the claims we make about God?" That is to say, the *philosophical* questions that arise here are all concerned with the question of the *possibility* of an account of the way language works here giving a coherent description of the way in which human beings can intelligibly think and talk about God.

This question is not entirely separable from the *theological* question, which concerns the *actual* way that such language works, and when we look at the answers given to our question by Aquinas, Kant and Karl Barth, it will become very clear that the very different answers they give to what I am calling the philosophical question reflect deep differences in their respective theologies. Thus, as I read Barth, he bases his whole account of the possibility of our being able to speak appropriately about God upon the idea of human beings being created in the image of God, and upon his particular understanding of what that amounts to. This account is further coloured both by his refusal to allow natural theology any status in theological discussion and by his answer to the epistemological question, "How is it possible to recognize the image of God?"

---

[5]   If I understand Anselm correctly, the aim of *Proslogion* Chapters 2 and 3 was not to put forward an "ontological argument", but to present an argument designed to show that "the fool who has said in his heart there is no god" didn't know what he was talking about: that whatever he thought he was denying, it could not be the God in whom Anselm believed.

However, although it is in this way impossible altogether to avoid raising theological issues, and although my own standpoint is a specifically Christian one and, to be specific, my own theological position is closer to that of Karl Barth than to any of the other authors I shall discuss, it is my aim not to beg any theological questions in what follows. I regard my task as primarily a philosophical one, but not as an essay in metaphysics. It is rather one of conceptual analysis, of what Ralph McInerny called "the logic of analogy".[6] As a result, it cannot be my aim to offer a complete theory of the role of analogy in religious language: that would require a full discussion of the theological issues involved. The following study is, rather, a prolegomenon to such a theory, aiming to discover what it does and does not make sense to say here, and what conceptual constraints should be put on such a theory.

Analogy

The answer most frequently given to the questions I have just been raising has been in terms of *analogy*. The near-unanimity among theologians who have discussed these questions in giving this answer is, however, deceptive. The word "analogy" has historically refused to stay with one fixed meaning and has proved highly slippery, being understood by different people in very different ways. In everyday usage, it is often little more than a synonym for "similarity", and even amongst theologians and philosophers of religion there is extraordinary diversity: for instance, both Aquinas and Kant give their accounts of religious language by saying that words are said of God and creatures by analogy, but as we shall see, they understand the word "analogy" in such different ways that there is virtually no overlap in their understanding of what saying that amounts to. Aquinas and Kant are, however, both highly conscious of the way that they are using the language of analogy and careful in their explanations of that language, and as a result it is possible to spell out precisely what they mean. By contrast, in the case of a number of authors the concept of analogy is left at an unexplained level, or given highly intuitive and unclarified characterizations, such as "partial similarity" (whatever that means), or "similarity in dissimilarity".[7]

---

6   *The Logic of Analogy*. However, as the subtitle of his book indicates, he is primarily concerned to interpret what Thomas Aquinas understood by "analogy" (*analogia*), whereas I am following the original Aristotelian use of the word.

7   Sometimes, as in Erich Przywara, with the gloss from the Fourth Lateran Council, "*maior dissimulitudo in tanta similitudine*" ("with a greater dissimilarity in such similarity"). Przywara himself, however, later complained that he had been misunderstood: "My dear friends from Karl Barth through Söhngen and Haecker to Balthasar have obviously never understood that according to Aristotle '*analogia*' means 'a relation between two X's'" (*In und Gegen*, p.278). When I come to look at Barth, one of the major difficulties in interpreting the debate that Przywara is referring to here does indeed lie in disentangling

ἀλλὰ πῶς δὴ λέγεται; οὐ γὰρ ἔοικε τοῖς γε ἀπὸ τύχης ὁμωνύμοις. ἀλλ'ἆρά γε τῷ ἀφ'ἑνὸς εἶναι; ἢ πρὸς ἓν ἅπαντα συντελεῖν; ἢ μᾶλλον κατ'ἀναλογίαν; ὡς γὰρ ἐν σώματι ὄψις, ἐν ψυχῇ νοῦς, καὶ ἄλλο δὴ ἐν ἄλλῳ. ἀλλ'ἴσως ταῦτα μὲν ἀφετέον τὸ νῦν· ἐξακριβοῦν γὰρ ὑπὲρ αὐτῶν ἄλλης ἂν εἴη φιλοσοφίας οἰκειότερον.

But in what way are different things called "good"? For they do not seem to be called by the same word by chance homonymy. Possibly they are all called "good" because they derive from one good, or all contribute to one good. Or perhaps they are called "good" by analogy: for as sight is good in the body, so is reason in the soul, and similarly another thing in something else. But we should perhaps leave this question on one side for the moment, since it really belongs to another branch of philosophy.[8]

One of Aristotle's major concerns was the fact that many philosophically interesting words were "said in many different ways",[9] where, although it was not by chance that the same word was used on two different occasions, there were significant differences between the two uses.[10] In this passage from the *Nicomachean Ethics*, he identifies two basic patterns for ways in which this can occur. The first of these, which has been called by G. E. L. Owen "focal meaning",[11] will be a major concern when we come to look at Aquinas. Here we have a primary use of the word to apply to one thing, and secondary uses where we call other things by that word because of their relation to that thing: thus, to use one of Aristotle's own examples, in the case of the word healthy, we straightforwardly describe cows as "healthy", but we also talk of a climate as "healthy", but only because, say, it promotes health in cows. The second is what Aristotle meant by "said by analogy": here an analogy was a four-term relation following the pattern "A is to B as C is to D". A clear case

---

how exactly the word "analogy" is being understood. But, even in Przywara's own case, it is difficult to pin down in a work like *Polarity* how the word is being used and, if I am not mistaken, in *Analogia Entis*, his whole account of what Aristotle meant by analogy rests on a crucial misinterpretation of uses of the word "analogy" in *Meta.*, IX 1048a 39 and 1048b 7, which explains what he means by his obscure phrase just quoted: "according to Aristotle '*analogia*' means 'a relation between two X's'" (see, *e.g.*, *Analogia Entis*, pp.29, 115). I shall be looking at the passage from Aristotle's *Metaphysics* just referred to, including Przywara's misunderstanding of it, in Chapter 3.

[8]   *NE*, I 1096b 26–31.

[9]   I deliberately do not follow the frequent practice of translating this "used with many different senses", since the examples that Aristotle has in mind are cases where our normal criteria for sameness and difference in the sense of words leave us in the lurch. The cases he has in mind are ones in which (1) we apply the same word to two different things; (2) it is not by chance that we apply the same word; but (3) the criteria for the correct application of the word are significantly different in the two cases.

[10]   Without prejudging whether "ambiguity" is the right word, we may say that the concern here is the same as that of Russell when he talked of "systematic ambiguity".

[11]   "Logic and Metaphysics in Some Earlier Works of Aristotle".

of a word "said by analogy" is the word "wing" as said of both a bird's wings and a butterfly's wings. A butterfly's wings and a bird's wings are radically different morphological structures, but we call them both "wings", because a butterfly's wings are to a butterfly as a bird's wings are to a bird.[12]

Aristotle uses the word "analogy" (ἀναλογία) exclusively to refer to the second of these cases, and devotes far more attention to analogy than to focal meaning. The one crucial exception to this is when at *Metaphysics IV* (1003a 33–35) he proposes that "being" is used according to the first of his two patterns of a word being said in many ways, giving to "focal meaning" a key role in the whole of his metaphysics. This passage was central to mediaeval discussions of "analogy". In those discussions, philosophers and theologians came to use the word "*analogia*" as a generic term, for any case where a word was used in different ways, but where it was not by chance that the same word was used. In this way, Aristotle's two cases came to be regarded as two species of the genus *analogia*, the first of his cases, which is the one that Owen called "focal meaning", being called "the analogy of attribution", or "being said *per prius et posterius*", the second, "the analogy of proportionality", with sometimes yet other species of the genus being proposed. As we shall see when we come to look at Aquinas, mediaeval theologians paid far more attention to the so-called analogy of attribution than to that of proportionality.

I do not myself regard this way of treating "analogy" as a generic term as useful or helpful: the two main "species" of "*analogia*" function in such different ways that it can only create the possibility of confusion, at least in the mind of the reader, to use the same word to cover such different phenomena. Obviously when I discuss Aquinas I shall fall in with his way of speaking, but for the rest, and throughout this book, unless in talking about other authors I explicitly signal the fact that a deviation is necessary, I shall stay with Greek usage, and follow Aristotle in reserving the word "analogy" for its original use to designate the four-term relation "A is to B as C is to D". This simple relation turns out to be so rich and complex as to deserve full exploration in its own right. One of the most central questions I shall be addressing is "How far is this type of analogy, the analogy of proportionality, capable of providing the key to the way religious language is to be understood?"

It is important throughout the discussion of the role of analogy in theology to be clear precisely which question one is addressing. It is possible to appeal to analogy both in discussions of metaphysics and epistemology as well as in discussions of the use of language. That is to say, we may ask "*Is* there an analogy between God and the world?" or "May we *argue* by analogy from the creation to God?" as well as asking "When we talk about God are we *using our words* by analogy with our use of those words in talking about creatures?" Even though this necessarily involves talking at various points about the metaphysical and epistemological questions raised by the concept of analogy that have bearings upon the linguistic

---

[12]   It is in precisely the same way that we talk of the wings of an aeroplane.

issue, this present study is primarily concerned with the *linguistic* issue—whether, say, language about God rests upon the words used being used on the basis of an analogy with their everyday use, and what it amounts to to say that it does.

The different questions mentioned in the last paragraph are intertwined: for example, many will maintain that an affirmative answer to the linguistic question is only possible on the basis of an affirmative answer to the metaphysical question. Even so, these are different questions, and confusion can easily result and has resulted, unless one keeps clear in one's mind which of these questions one is asking. Because of the close interrelationships between these different questions, it frequently happens, both in mediaeval and in modern discussions, that the same form of words can be used to pose quite distinct questions and the disputants talk at cross purposes. To take just one example, when Karl Barth declared "I regard the *analogia entis* as the invention of Antichrist",[13] it looks very much as if, under the influence of discussions with Erich Przywara, he was concerned with an *epistemological* issue—whether an analogy between God and the world made possible a *knowledge* of God independently of revelation. When Barth's Roman Catholic critics, beginning with Gottlieb Söhngen, argued that Barth's *analogia fidei* presupposed an *analogia entis*, they were concerned with a metaphysical understanding of the idea of an *analogia entis*—whether there *was* an analogy between God and the world. As a result, the whole discussion becomes at the very least confusing and difficult to follow.

What I wish to do in the present book is first to explore the concept of analogy in its own right, independently of its theological use. After first examining the mathematical background to the concept of analogy, I shall do this largely by examining its use in Aristotle, who, more than any other writer, showed the full potential of the concept as an all-purpose tool of research and as the key to making comparisons between "genera that are remote".[14] In the present context, we are obviously most interested in his use of analogy in explaining the use of language involved when the same word is applied to two things that belong to different categories, but I shall set this in the context of his wide-ranging explorations of the concept of analogy and the uses to which it can be put.

In the following chapters, I shall look at three of the most significant accounts of religious language that give to analogy a fundamental role in that account—those of Thomas Aquinas, Immanuel Kant and Karl Barth.[15] As noted above, however,

---

[13]   *CD* I/1 xiii.

[14]   *Top.*, I 108a 6ff.

[15]   In the case of Barth, it is frequently unclear how precisely he would spell out what it means: in a question and answer session held in the Princeton University chapel in 1962, Barth replied to the question that concerns us as follows: "Question: How can we explain the covenant of God with man analogically, and what type of analogy would you consider appropriate for an evangelical theology? Answer: What is meant in theology by analogy? I would say an analogy is a created picture, an image, which involves both similarity and dissimilarity. In the picture or image—if we have eyes to see—the original is itself mirrored."

they all understand the word "analogy" in different ways. In fact, of the three, only Kant rigorously adheres to the use of the word that I am myself adopting.

This is clearly not intended as a history of appeals to analogy in the context of discussions of religious language: that would require a very different kind of study from the one I am undertaking, bringing in a large number of philosophers and theologians, ranging from Maimonides, say, to Erich Przywara. Instead I am concentrating on these three accounts, since they are to my mind three of the weightiest attempts to answer the questions that concern me here. By concentrating in this way, I shall have the opportunity to explore in detail the strengths and weaknesses of each of these accounts. The three accounts are surprisingly different, and each in very different ways illuminates the issues that concern us.

Each of these accounts, at least as they stand, seem to me to have significant weaknesses: Aquinas ties his account to a set of highly dubious metaphysical principles;[16] Kant's account only makes sense against the background of his idiosyncratic account of religion and as a result although he offers us a meaningful account of religious claims, it is an extremely attenuated one; and Barth's account seems to me to suffer from considerable conceptual unclarities and technical inadequacies at least in the exposition of his position.[17] But at the same time, each of these accounts has a richness and subtlety and contains insights that far outweigh the difficulties I find in them. For that reason, they may serve to provide us with three very different models of the way in which appeal to analogy may help us to make sense of religious language. I am therefore using them to help us orient ourselves and gain an understanding of both the possibilities of using analogy to explain religious language, and the difficulties that need to be overcome if we are to do so.

I shall then turn to the question of the nature of analogy and the possibilities of using it to provide an account of the significance of religious language, and its capacity to retain the meaningfulness of such language while ridding it of any taint of anthropomorphism. I shall not be here presenting my own theory of religious language: to do so would involve settling specifically *theological* issues that lie beyond the scope of the present study. This book is, rather, a prolegomenon to such a theological enquiry, aiming to clarify the *conceptual* tools necessary for the conduct of such enquiry.

I believe, however, that what he calls the "*analogia relationis*" can best be interpreted in terms of the original Aristotelian concept of analogy that I am myself following.

[16] We should distinguish the question whether the specific metaphysics adopted by an author in their account of religious language is defensible from the question whether an account of religious language should commit theology to a specific metaphysics at all. I myself believe that it is a bad idea to think of a religion as tied to a specific metaphysics, but here I am concerned with the dubious nature of the metaphysical principles Aquinas actually appeals to in support of his account of the analogy of names.

[17] What I have in mind when I talk of "technical inadequacies" is best illustrated by the long footnote in *CD* II/1 discussing Quenstedt's account of analogy (pp.237–243) which I shall return to in Chapter 6.

Chapter 1

The Mathematical Roots of the Concept of Analogy[1]

The origins of the concept of analogy are to be found in Greek mathematics. Although the concept becomes transformed in the hands of Plato and Aristotle, they were both inspired by the achievements of the mathematicians to take their ideas and to seek to extrapolate those ideas beyond their mathematical confines. What we shall be concerned with are both the continuities and the discontinuities between the mathematical and the non-mathematical concepts of analogy. Both Plato and Aristotle were clearly concerned to explore and exploit the potential for taking the mathematical concept and extending it more widely, and hence their interests tend to highlight the continuities between the mathematical and the non-mathematical uses of analogy.[2] Whereas when we come to look at Kant's use of analogy in his account of religious language, we shall find that he assigns an equally crucial role to the discontinuities between the two cases.[3]

Incommensurable Magnitudes

The original mathematical interest in the analogical formula, $A/B = C/D$, was among the Pythagoreans in the context of the theory of musical harmony. What concerns us, however, is the way that this formula would eventually become one of the basic ideas of Greek mathematics as a result of developments that had their origins in the Pythagorean theory of relative magnitude, a theory that is encapsulated in the slogan "all is number".[4]

---

[1] It should be noted that in discussions of Greek mathematics, it is usual to translate the word ἀναλογία as "proportion". However, for our purposes, I will use "analogy" throughout, to keep the continuity with the rest of this book. Aristotle himself uses the same word both in contexts where he is discussing the mathematical theory of proportion and in contexts where "analogy" is the obvious translation.

[2] Occasionally, as at *NE*, V 1131b 3–11, Aristotle appears not fully to appreciate that there are discontinuities, and applies parts of the *mathematical* theory of analogy outside mathematics, where it is difficult to make sense of his so doing.

[3] Above all, that, outside mathematics, we can no longer use analogy in such a way that, given three terms, we can *calculate* the value of the fourth.

[4] In what follows, I am restricting my attention to those ideas in the history of Greek mathematics that are directly relevant to my present project. For a good general history of

since it seemed clear [to the so-called Pythagoreans] that all other things have their whole nature modelled upon numbers, and that numbers are the ultimate things in the whole physical universe, they assumed the elements of numbers to be the elements of everything, and the whole universe to be a harmony or number.[5]

Without speculating as to the full import of the slogan, one thing that it certainly meant was that you could give a complete theory of the relative magnitude of two lengths A and B, by citing two positive whole numbers m and n, such that:

$$m \times A = n \times B$$

It would be anachronistic to interpret this as meaning that you could cite a rational number (n/m) that gave the relative magnitude of A and B: the only numbers that are acknowledged here are the positive whole numbers (1, 2, 3, 4...) and this formula must instead be interpreted *geometrically*: if you perform the geometrical constructions of extending A to m times its original length and B to n times its original length, you would obtain two lines that were the same in length. If this theory of relative magnitude had been correct, then you would have been able, in principle, to give a complete mathematical description of the universe using only the natural numbers.

This simple vision was, however, shattered by the discovery of "incommensurable magnitudes"—that is to say, cases of two magnitudes A and B where it could be proved that it was impossible to cite two whole numbers p and q such that $A/B = p/q$: specifically that the Pythagorean theory of relative magnitude could not give an answer to the question, "What is the relative magnitude of the hypotenuse of a right-angled triangle and one of its sides?" The elegant proof of this may be thought of as the starting point for modern mathematics, leading ultimately to the development of modern number theory. At the time, however, it would initially be perceived as the discovery of a crisis in the foundations of Pythagorean mathematics.

Consider a right-angled isosceles triangle, with hypotenuse of length H, sides of length S. Then, by Pythagoras' Theorem:

(1) $H^2 = 2S^2$ or $H^2/S^2 = 2$

Suppose H and S are commensurable. Then there exist two whole numbers p and q, without any common factors, such that $H/S = p/q$. Therefore, $H^2/S^2 = p^2/q^2 = 2$. Or, in other words:

---

the development of Greek mathematics in this period, the reader may consult B. L. van der Waerden, *Science Awakening*.

[5]   Aristotle, *Meta.*, 985b 34–986a 4.

(2) $p^2 = 2q^2$

Now the square of an even number is even $[(2a)^2 = 4a^2]$, and the square of an odd number is odd $[(2a + 1)^2 = 4a^2 + 4a + 1]$. Hence from **(2)**, p is even and $= 2r$, say. Therefore

(3) $(2r)^2 = 4r^2 = 2q^2$

From which it follows that

(4) $2r^2 = q^2$

Hence q is also even, so that p and q are both divisible by 2, contradicting our assumption that p and q have no common factors. Hence, by *reductio ad absurdum*, the hypotenuse of a right-angled triangle and one of its sides are incommensurable.[6]

As it stands, this proof shows that it is possible to specify two lines such that there was no answer within a Pythagorean framework to the question as to their relative magnitude. The mathematical challenge was therefore to replace the Pythagorean theory of magnitude by a new theory that would be equally applicable to both commensurable and incommensurable magnitudes.

Euclid Book V, Definitions of Ratio and Analogy

The two mathematicians who made the most significant contributions to this question were Theaetetus, who may have been responsible for the contents of Euclid Book X, and Eudoxus of Cnidus, who will principally concern us, and who is usually thought to be responsible for the contents of Book V.[7] It is the battery of

---

[6]   This proof is usually ascribed to Hippasus of Metapontum. All reconstructions of the early history of mathematics are necessarily to a greater or lesser extent conjectural, and it is sometimes disputed whether this was the actual original proof of the existence of incommensurable magnitudes, proposing, say, that some of the tests for incommensurability to be found in Euclid X might have been employed to show the irrationality of $\sqrt{2}$. Although the precise details of the history are irrelevant to our present study, I would just say that it is far more plausible to me that the elegant proof given here should have been the one actually used. This proof is one that someone might easily stumble upon when, say, trying to work out the relative magnitude of the hypotenuse and side of a right-angled triangle, whereas the far more complicated tests for incommensurability given in Euclid X look as if they have been developed at a time when people were already familiar with the concept of incommensurability.

[7]   Proclus, writing in the fourth century AD, says that Euclid "collected the theorems of Eudoxus, perfected many of those of Theaetetus, and completed fragmentary works left by others". Although the reliability of late testimony for Eudoxus' responsibility for the

definitions at the start of Euclid Book V that not only mark the high point of Greek mathematics but also explain why the simple formula "A is to B as C is to D" contained within itself a rich complexity, such that it would inspire philosophers such as Plato and Aristotle to explore the question "How far can you extrapolate this formula beyond its mathematical confines to produce an all-purpose tool for scientific research?" In this chapter we are simply looking at this formula as it is used within mathematics.

The relevant definitions from Book V are:

3. Ratio is a mutual relation of two magnitudes of the same kind to one another in respect of quantity.
4. Magnitudes are said to have a ratio to one another, when the less can be multiplied so as to exceed the other.
5. The first of four magnitudes is said to have the same ratio to the second, that the third has to the fourth, when any equimultiples whatever of the first and third being taken, and any equimultiples whatever of the second and the fourth, if the multiple of the first be less than that of the second, the multiple of the third is also less than that of the fourth, and if the multiple of the first be equal to that of the second, the multiple of the third is also equal to that of the fourth, and if the multiple of the first be greater than that of the second, the multiple of the third is also greater than that of the fourth.
6. Magnitudes which have the same ratio are called proportionals (analogous). When four magnitudes are proportionals (analogous), it is usually expressed by saying, the first is to the second as the third is to the fourth.
7. When of the equimultiples of four magnitudes, taken as in the fifth definition, the multiple of the first is greater than the multiple of the second, but the multiple of the third is not greater than the multiple of the fourth, then the first is said to have a greater ratio than the third has to the fourth; and the third is said to have to the fourth a less ratio than the first has to the second.
8. Analogy, or proportion, is the similitude of two ratios.

The first point about this set of definitions is that, in Definition 4, what it is for two magnitudes to have a ratio to one another is not explained as in the Pythagorean account so as only to fit the case of commensurable magnitudes, but in such a way that a pair of incommensurable magnitudes can fit the definition just as easily as a pair of commensurable magnitudes.

The crucial definition is, however, Definition 5, the "equimultiples" definition. This can be stated more clearly in modern notation, as follows: given four

---

contents of Book V can be, and has been, challenged, for my present purposes I will accept this traditional ascription. It certainly makes sense of many of Aristotle's remarks about analogy if we assume that he was familiar with much of the contents of Euclid Book V.

magnitudes, A, B, C and D, the ratio of A to B is the same as the ratio of C to D if and only if the following condition is satisfied:

$$(\forall m)(\forall n)\,((m \times A > n \times B \rightarrow m \times C > n \times D)$$
$$\&\,(m \times A < n \times B \rightarrow m \times C < n \times D)$$
$$\&\,(m \times A = n \times B \rightarrow m \times C = n \times D))$$

where the quantifiers range over the natural numbers.

This powerful definition has obvious affinities with nineteenth-century definitions of real numbers. The manoeuvre that Eudoxus employs here is basically the same as that which Dedekind employs when he gives his "Dedekind Cut" definition of a real number, where, in effect, you define a real, or irrational, number by dividing the rational numbers into two sets, those that are less than or equal to the irrational number, and those that are greater. But it is important, both from the point of view of the history of mathematics and for our purposes, to see that describing Definition 5 as defining the irrational numbers is completely anachronistic.[8] The idea of the system of irrational numbers belongs to a later stage of mathematical development than was achieved by the Greeks.[9] They are still thinking *geometrically*, and this definition is not the definition of the value of a number, but is simply the definition of when we should say that the relative magnitude of one pair of lines was the same as the relative magnitude of another. For the Greeks, its importance lay in the fact that it is equally applicable to commensurable and incommensurable magnitudes.

What concerns us, however, is not the details of the mathematics, but the basic strategy that lies behind giving a definition such as this. Let us suppose you have two magnitudes, A and B, that are incommensurable. Then, *ex hypothesi*, you cannot give a closed arithmetical formula that specifies their relative magnitude. That was the basic challenge that had shown the inadequacy of the original Pythagorean

---

[8]   The difference in mathematical approach is illustrated by the following quotation from R. Dedekind ("Continuity and Irrational Numbers", pp.9–10): "the way in which the irrational numbers are usually introduced is based directly upon the conception of extensive magnitudes—which itself is nowhere carefully defined—and explains number as the result of measuring such a magnitude by another of the same kind". Along with the footnote: "The apparent advantage of the generality of this definition of number disappears as soon as we consider complex numbers. According to my view, on the other hand, the notion of the ratio between two numbers of the same kind can be clearly defined only after the introduction of irrational numbers."

[9]   Whether the Greek mathematicians actually ever proposed anything that would constitute a theory that could be considered a real number theory depends to my mind on the following quotation from Aristotle (*PostA*, I 85a 38, 39): "Demonstration concerning what is actual and which is infallible is superior to demonstration concerning fictions, which is fallible. Now universal demonstration is of the latter kind: (to engage in it is to reason well illustrated by the idea that analogy is what corresponds to some definition of an entity which is neither line, number, solid, nor surface, but an analogy apart from all these)."

theory of magnitude. What was required to meet that challenge was a fundamental change of perspective on the question, "What is it to specify the relative magnitude of two lengths?" Instead, that is, of attempting directly to specify a value for A/B, what one can do is specify the conditions under which one relative magnitude was the same as or different from another relative magnitude. In this way we arrive at the following idea—an idea that is perfectly exemplified by Definition 5—*we can give an account of the relative magnitude of two quantities A and B, which is equally applicable both to the case where they are commensurable and where they are incommensurable, by giving a general specification of the truth conditions of A/B = C/D.*[10]

It is in Definition 5 that we encounter in its initial form the idea that gives to the analogical relationship its potential power: where two entities A and B cannot be directly compared ("are incommensurable"), we can nevertheless compare them indirectly by introducing a third and fourth entity, and comparing the relation of A to B with the relation between the third and fourth. In this way, although we cannot give a closed arithmetical formula to express the ratio of the hypotenuse of an isosceles triangle to one of its sides, we can give a formula that tells us when that ratio is, or is not, the same as the ratio of a second pair of lines.

A Universal Theory of Magnitude

One of the most important features of the definitions we have just looked at is their universal applicability to any kind of extensive magnitude whatsoever. Although it is natural to read Euclid as primarily concerned with spatial lines and lengths, the definitions just as they stand can be applied to give an account of the relative magnitude of two volumes, two times, or two numbers, *etc.*:

> Again the law that analogies alternate ["if $A:B::C:D$, then $A:C::B:D$"] might be thought to apply to numbers *qua* numbers, and similarly for lines, solids and times: indeed it used to be proved for each separately. A single proof would of course suffice for all, but they lacked a term for the property the numbers, lengths, solids and times had in common, and hence gave separate proofs. Now the law is proved universally; for the property did not belong to them *qua* lines, or numbers, but *qua* having a particular universal property.[11]

---

[10]   The step that it appears the Greek mathematicians did not take was to convert this account into an irrational number theory. To undertake that step one needs to perform a Fregean abstraction upon the formula A/B = C/D, transforming it into "the number that gives the value of the ratio of A to B is the same number as the number that gives the value of the ratio of C to D".

[11]   Aristotle, *PostA*, I 74a 18.

As Aristotle says here, we now have a single, universal, theory of magnitude, dispensing with the need to develop a theory of magnitude first for lengths and then for times, reduplicating one's efforts by forcing one to prove what is essentially the same theorem twice over.

What this implies is that one can now use the mathematical theory of analogy (proportion) to allow one to operate at a level of abstraction that transcended each of the particular mathematical sciences. In this way, one could simultaneously respect the particularities of the particular sciences, but at the same time develop general mathematical theories that could be applicable by analogy *mutatis mutandis* to each of those particular sciences:

> Of the first principles used in the demonstrative sciences, some are peculiar
> to one science and some are common, but only analogically common, being
> used only in so far as they fall within the genus to which the particular science
> is dedicated. Peculiar principles are, *e.g.* the definition of line, or straightness,
> common principles are such as that "when equals are taken away from equals,
> the remainders are equal". Each of these latter truths need only be assumed to
> be true for the particular genus under consideration: for a principle of this latter
> sort will have the same force even if not assumed generally, but applied by the
> geometer only to magnitudes, and by the arithmetician only to numbers.[12]

It is here, with the possibility of using analogy to construct a theory of magnitude that transcended each of the particular sciences, that I believe that we have an initial intimation of the way in which eventually, once we extend analogy beyond its mathematical confines, analogy can be used to provide an account of how the same language can be used to talk both of God and of humanity, without thereby automatically lapsing into gross anthropomorphism.

Cross-Categorial Comparisons

For all its vagueness, Definition 3 of Euclid V, "Ratio is a mutual relation of two magnitudes of the same kind to one another in respect of quantity", is clear on one point: the whole of the subsequent account of ratio and analogy (proportion) is predicated on the assumption that we can only talk of the ratio of two magnitudes if the magnitudes are of "the same kind"—we may talk of the ratio of two lengths to one another, or of two times, or of two volumes, but not of the ratio of a length and a time. However, if we consider the extension of the concept of analogy beyond its mathematical confines, whether we are thinking of many of Aristotle's secular employments of analogy or, which interests us most, the possibility of its theological use, this condition is simply not met. Therefore, while still remaining for the present within the mathematical employment of analogy, I must now look

---

[12] *PostA*, I 76a 40.

at the question "How far does analogy provide us with a way to compare things that are not 'of the same kind'?"

This question can be answered straightforwardly by looking again at Definition 5, which, in modern notation, ran:

> Given four magnitudes A, B, C and D, the ratio of A to B is the same as the ratio of C to D if and only if the following condition is satisfied:

$$(\forall m)(\forall n)\,((m \times A > n \times B \rightarrow m \times C > n \times D)$$
$$\& \,(m \times A < n \times B \rightarrow m \times C < n \times D)$$
$$\& \,(m \times A = n \times B \rightarrow m \times C = n \times D))$$

It is a necessary condition for applying this definition that A and B should be magnitudes "of the same kind", so that we can compare a multiple of A to a multiple of B. It is similarly a necessary condition that C and D should be of the same kind. *But there is no reason to suppose that A and C should be of the same kind.*

This definition can readily be applied, for example, to the case where A and B are spatial distances, but C and D are times. In fact nothing is simpler than comparing the relative magnitude of two distances and the relative magnitude of two times. If it were impossible to make such heterogeneous comparisons the whole of science would be crippled. For instance, if we wish to say that two bodies are travelling with the same velocity, we can only do so by comparing the relative distances covered by the two bodies with the relative time that they take to travel that distance. Thus if body A travels distance d_1 in time t_1 and body B travels distance d_2 in time t_2, then the velocity of A will be the same as the velocity of B if and only if $d_1/d_2 = t_1/t_2$.

It is precisely with this possibility of establishing analogical relations between heterogeneous elements that we see how it is that analogy enables us to make comparisons between entities that are "remote"—things that are so different in kind or category that straightforward comparisons are impossible.

Trans-Categorial Alternation?

Although many of the definitions and theorems concerning analogy in Euclid Book V carry over straightforwardly in the way just outlined to the case where A and B are one kind of magnitude and C and D are a different kind of magnitude, there is one basic theorem where it appears impossible to extend beyond the case where all four terms are of the same kind. This is the idea that "analogies alternate":

> Euclid V, Definition 13:
>
> *Permutando* [ἐναλλάξ], or *alternando*, by permutation or alternately; when there are four proportionals, and it is inferred that the first is to the third, that the second is to the fourth.

That is to say, A/B = C/D → A/C = B/D.

The reason that this principle appears to be restricted to the case where A, B, C and D are all of the same kind is clear: the original explanation of a ratio assumed that there could only be a ratio between two terms of the same kind. Hence if A and C are not of the same kind, say, we cannot talk of the ratio "A/C". In fact, if we restrict our interpretation of analogy so as to conform to Euclid V, Definition 8, any attempt to alternate an analogy between heterogeneous magnitudes will typically result in nonsense.[13]

Nevertheless, when we come to look at the use of analogy outside mathematics, one of the main differences that we shall encounter is that the conditions laid down in Definition 8 of Book V, that analogy is a similarity of two ratios, and in Definition 3, that a ratio can only be between magnitudes of the same kind, are typically not observed. That is to say, whereas within mathematics the formula "A is to B as C is to D" will typically require A and B to be of the same kind, in the non-mathematical applications of analogy, the formula "A is to B as C is to D", it is typically only A and C that are to required to be of the same kind. So the question arises can we significantly alternate analogies when we are constructing analogies across categories, or between things that are different in kind?

This may seem an arcane question, but I believe it can be shown to play a crucial, if unrecognized, role in the use we make of analogy in religious language, where we are par excellence concerned with analogical comparisons between "things that are different in kind".[14] I shall return to this point in my final chapter and for now simply raise the question in general and in the abstract.

Aristotle certainly seems to have thought such alternation was possible, since in his discussion of justice as analogy, he writes:

> For analogy (proportion) is equality of ratios, and involves four terms at least …
> and the just, too, involves at least four terms, and the ratio between one pair is
> the same as that between the other pair; for there is a similar distinction between

---

[13]   It is clear that the proof that analogies alternate given in Euclid V, Proposition 16 presupposes that A, B, C and D are all of the same kind.

[14]   To anticipate, the kind of context in which we need to "alternate analogies" is in interpreting parables such as Luke xi, 11–13: "What father among you, if his son asks for a fish, will instead of a fish give him a serpent; or if he asks for an egg, will give him a scorpion? If you then, who are evil, know how to give good gifts to your children, how much more will the heavenly Father give the Holy Spirit to those who ask him!" This parable is based on the analogy God is to human beings as a father is to his children, so that God will give good gifts to those who ask for them, just as a human father gives good gifts to his children. The full force of the parable lies in the words "how much more". But to bring out the force of that we need to alternate the analogy: God is to a human father as human beings are to the father's children, from which we arrive at the conclusion, the greater the giver, the greater the gift, so that God will give the greatest gift of all—the Holy Spirit—to those who ask.

the persons and between the things. As the term A, then, is to B, so will C be to
D, and therefore, *alternando*, as A is to C, B will be to D.[15]

That is to say, Aristotle is here prepared to infer from, for example, "The builder
is to the shoemaker as the builder's produce is to the shoemaker's produce" that
"The builder is to his produce as the shoemaker is to his produce". Admittedly the
paragraph just quoted in which he acknowledges this possibility is the murkiest
passage in his whole discussion of justice, and it is difficult to make full sense
of the detail of what he says, but his remark here serves to pose the question that
interests us here.

Stated in general terms, if A and C are heterogeneous magnitudes, so that we
can no longer talk of the ratio of A to C, we cannot ask "Does $A/B = C/D \rightarrow A/C
= B/D$?". Instead we must replace that question with the more general question:
"Will it, in general, be the case that if $R(A, B) = R(C, D)$, there is a relation R' such
that $R'(A, C) = R'(B, D)$?" That is to say, will we always be able to find a suitable
interpretation for the alternated analogy?

Perhaps the best way to approach this question at this stage is to return to the
case mentioned above of two bodies travelling with the same velocity. There, we
supposed that body A travels distance d_1 in time t_1 and body B travels distance d_2 in
time t_2, then the velocity of A will be the same as the velocity of B if and only if $d_1/
d_2 = t_1/t_2$. We arrive at the concept of velocity by abstraction from that formula, and
may now write that the velocity of $A = d_1/t_1 = $ the velocity of $B = d_2/t_2$. In this way
we represent the velocity of a body as the result of having alternated the analogy
$d_1/d_2 = t_1/t_2$ and explain the meaning of the alternated analogy as having the same
truth conditions as the original.[16] That is to say, within the mathematical sphere we
can indeed alternate analogies in the ways indicated and indeed we need to be able
to do so if it is to be possible to form such concepts as the concept of the velocity of
a body. I shall postpone discussion of the question whether it is as straightforward
a matter to alternate analogies outside mathematics until Chapter 7.

---

[15]   *NE*, V 1131b 3–11.

[16]   It is here that we can see clearly the advantages of real number theory over analogy
theory, and why the theory of analogy was developed into and later replaced by real
number theory, and, with that, real numbers came to replace analogy as the basic notion in
mathematics. Although analogy theory is fully adequate to the task, once one can use real
numbers to specify the magnitude of both a distance and a time, one can short-circuit the
argument in the text and straightforwardly interpret "$d_1/t_1 = d_2/t_2$" in terms of the equality of
two real numbers. Thus, if we have real numbers, $\delta_1, \delta_2, \tau_1, \tau_2$ such that $d_1 = \delta_1$ m., $d_2 = \delta_2$ m.,
$t_1 = \tau_1$ sec. and $t_2 = \tau_2$ sec., then $d_1/t_1 = \delta_1/\tau_1$ m./sec $= d_2/t_2 = \delta_2/\tau_2$ m./sec. But now, $\delta_1/\tau_1 = \delta_2/\tau_2$
is a simple equation asserting the equality of two real numbers. It is with this development
of the theory of analogy into a real number theory that number theory rather than geometry
comes to be regarded as the master science in mathematics.

Analogical Models

Models and Euclid Book VI

One of the most important applications of the analogical relationship is using it to define a particular type of model. Understanding the way such models work is crucial for an understanding of the role analogy plays in human thought: for instance, it explains such ideas as argument by analogy, and it is through the study of such models that we can evolve criteria for deciding whether a particular argument by analogy is a good argument or not.

The starting point for explaining the particular kind of model that can be defined using analogy is Euclid Book VI. It is here that we find the raw materials for defining the simplest of all such models—the scale model.

> Euclid VI, Definition 1: Similar rectilinear figures are those which have their several angles equal, each to each, and the sides about the equal angles proportionals.

Book VI is principally concerned with the properties of *similar* figures, of which the simplest examples are similar triangles. As said in this first definition, it is the idea of proportionality, or analogy, that explains the relevant notion of similarity. Suppose we have two triangles, ABC and A'B'C', such that pairs of corresponding sides are analogous to one another (AB/A'B' = BC/B'C' = AC/A'C'), then the triangles are called similar.[17] This in fact gives us the simplest kind of scale model: one triangle may in this case be considered as a scale model of the other.

The idea of one triangle being similar to another can readily be extended to the case of an arbitrary rectilinear figure being similar to another, and in Proposition 18 of Book VI Euclid gives the simple construction necessary if you wish to construct a rectilinear figure that is a model of a given one: you only need to ensure that every triangle in the original figure is similar to the corresponding triangle in the model. This suffices to give us the general notion of a scale model: a scale model of a given figure (rectilinear or otherwise) is a second figure in which every triangle inscribed in the model is similar to the corresponding triangle in the original figure.

Although if we wish to understand the notion of an analogical model in general we shall need to consider far more complex and subtle cases than the simple case of the scale model,[18] it is worth pausing to consider this case, since we arrive at the general notion by extending ideas that are already present in the idea of the

---

[17] The clause in the definition from Euclid stating that corresponding angles must be equal is in fact redundant, since the equality of these angles is already guaranteed by the second clause of the definition.

[18] This is most obviously true if we wish to appeal to the idea of using the human as an analogical model of the divine: in fact one way of thinking of anthropomorphism

scale model. One of the main concerns of Book VI is to decide which geometrical properties will be held in common by the two similar figures: thus, to give simple examples, we can prove that corresponding angles will be equal,[19] and given that a pair of lines are parallel to each other in one figure, the corresponding pair will also be parallel to each other. On the other hand, corresponding areas will typically not be equal. Let us call those properties that are held in common "properties that are invariant under analogy".

A *valid* argument by analogy will then be one that only infers from the model to the original those properties that are invariant under analogy. It is worth stressing that, at least within the confines of mathematical modelling, we can have valid arguments by analogy since it is frequently said that there could not be any such and that arguments by analogy are at best only probabilistic. The main reason for this widespread view stems largely from a misunderstanding of what an argument by analogy really is.[20] It can also be shown that, provided appropriate conditions are met, there is no reason why an argument by analogy outside mathematics should not be valid. It is precisely the possibility of such arguments that give to models, including the simple case of scale models, their usefulness.

Consider here the case of the Ordnance Survey map that has been produced by triangulation. Here, one produces a scale model of a terrain by producing on paper a network of triangles each of which is similar to the corresponding triangle on the ground. The usefulness of such maps resides precisely in the fact that there are a wide range of topological and geometrical features which the map and the terrain will have in common—properties that are invariant under analogy. Every time, then, that you work out a route, say, on such a map, you are in fact making use of a valid argument by analogy. Suppose, for instance, that you see that these two dots on the map are separated by a blue line, and infer that to go from town A to town B you must cross a river, then you are exploiting the idea that the fact that a line separates two points is a topological property that is invariant under analogy.

---

in theology is to imagine that we can arrive at God simply by "scaling up" the human (possibly to infinity!).

[19]   Euclid VI, Proposition 5.

[20]   The ultimate source of such misunderstanding appears to be Thomas Reid (see *Essays on the Intellectual Powers of Man*, Essay I, Chapter IV). For Reid, an argument by analogy meant an argument that proceeded along the lines: A has a number of properties in common with B (FA & GA & HA & … & FB & GB & HB & …). In addition A has the property K. This gives us reason to believe that B will probably also have the property K. Whatever can be said for or against such an argument, it has nothing to do with the concept of analogy as it had hitherto been understood, and this version of an "argument by analogy" could only have arisen at a time when people were losing sight of how the concept of analogy had been understood, and when it was understood as little more than a near synonym for "similarity".

I shall look next at more complicated forms of modelling than the simple scale model, but the basic principles exhibited by the simple scale-model case remain valid even for the most complex extensions of the idea of analogical modelling.

Analogical Models in General

Despite the usefulness of scale models, the real power of the use of models emerges only when we consider the concept of analogical modelling in its full generality. If we continue to interpret the analogical relationship in terms of ratios, then we may proceed quite straightforwardly along the lines indicated above when we discussed cross-categorial comparisons. Just as we produced a scale model by ensuring that the ratios in the model corresponded to the ratios in the situation that was being modelled, we can do precisely the same thing when the model and the situation modelled are heterogeneous. The most familiar example of doing this is provided by the use of a time line to represent the temporal relations between a set of events. Here, we use spatial relationships to model temporal relationships without any difficulty.

The full potential of such models is, however, not shown by such simple examples, but by the far more complex exploitations of analogical modelling that we find, say, in computer simulations of real-life situations or, most strikingly of all, in James Clerk Maxwell's use of analogical modelling in enabling him to transfer the results of one branch of mathematical physics to an another. He writes, for instance:

> In order to obtain physical ideas without adopting a physical theory we must make ourselves familiar with the existence of physical analogies. By a physical analogy I mean that partial similarity between the laws of one science and those of another which makes each of them illustrate the other. Thus all the mathematical sciences are founded on relations between physical laws and laws of numbers, so that the aim of exact science is to reduce the problems of nature to the determination of quantities by operations with numbers. Passing from the most universal of all analogies to a very partial one, we find the same resemblance in mathematical form between two different phenomena giving rise to a physical theory of light.
>
> The changes of direction which light undergoes in passing from one medium to another, are identical with the deviations of the path of a particle in moving through a narrow space in which intense forces act. This analogy, which extends only to the direction, and not to the velocity of the motion, was long believed to be the true explanation of the refraction of light; and we still find it useful in the solution of certain problems, in which we employ it without danger, as an artificial method. The other analogy, between light and the vibrations of an elastic medium, extends much further, but, though its importance and fruitfulness cannot be overestimated, we must recollect that it is founded only on a resemblance *in form* between the laws of light and those of vibrations. By stripping it of its

physical dress and reducing it to a theory of "transverse alternations" we might obtain a system of truth strictly founded on observation, but probably deficient both in the vividness of its conceptions and the fertility of its method. I have said thus much on the disputed question of Optics, as a preparation for the discussion of the almost universally admitted theory of action at a distance.

We have all acquired the mathematical conception of these attractions. We can reason about them and determine their appropriate forms or formulae. These formulae have a distinct mathematical significance, and their results are found to be in accordance with natural phenomena. There is no formula in applied mathematics more consistent with nature than the formula of attractions, and no theory better established in the minds of men than that of the action of bodies on one another at a distance. The laws of the conduction of heat in uniform media appear at first sight among the most different in their physical relations from those relating to attractions. The quantities which enter into them are *temperature, flow of heat, conductivity*. The word *force* is foreign to the subject. Yet we find that the mathematical laws of the uniform motion of heat in homogeneous media are identical in form with those of attractions varying inversely as the square of the distance. We have only to substitute *source of heat* for *centre of attraction*, *flow of heat* for *accelerating effect of attraction* at any point, and *temperature* for *potential*, and the solution of a problem in attractions is transformed into that of a problem in heat.

This analogy between the formulae of heat and attraction was, I believe, first pointed out by Professor William Thomson in the *Camb. Math. Journal*, Vol. III.[21]

It is here that we see the full potential of analogical modelling within mathematics. Maxwell is indicating the way in which one can use one branch of mathematical physics—the theory of heat—as a model for an apparently entirely different branch—the theory of attraction at a distance, and thereby transfer results from the one theory to the other, while, of course, as Maxwell stresses,[22] being circumspect in transferring only those results that are invariant under analogy.

From our point of view, however, the most significant models—the kinds of model that could have the potential for being used in theology—are those where we replace the definition of analogy in terms of ratio by the more general notion of the relation of A to B being the same as the relation of C to D. For this generalization of the notion of a model, the general definition of a model based on analogy may be given as follows:

Given two sets of objects, $\{a_1, \ldots a_i, \ldots a_j, \ldots\}$ and $\{b_1, \ldots b_i, \ldots b_j, \ldots\}$, and an operation R, if:

---

[21]   "On Faraday's Lines of Force", pp.156–157.

[22]   Ibid., p.156: "we must recollect that it is founded only on a resemblance *in form* between the laws of light and those of vibrations."

$$(\forall i)(\forall j)(R(a_i, a_j) = R(b_i, b_j)),$$

then either of the sets of objects may be regarded as a model for the other.

The most successful uses of such models in the history of science have been in Darwin's use of artificial breeding as a model for natural processes in the wild and in Aristotle's comparative biology that I shall look at in Chapter 2, where, in effect, Aristotle's method consists in using one animal as a working model for another.

Beyond science, however, it is one of the contentions of this book that analogical *models* may play a far more significant rôle in one's account of religious language than is usually allowed for by theologians, who have tended to concentrate simply on the analogical relationship as such and not its extension to the theory of models. I hope to show, for example, that Barth's idea of an *analogia relationis* is best interpreted in terms of analogical modelling.

Two basic ideas have emerged from this survey of the mathematical doctrine of proportion or analogy: firstly, the idea that the analogical relationship provides us with a means for comparing entities that are apparently incapable of being directly compared—that, in Aristotle's phrase, "are remote"—and, secondly, the idea that analogy provides us with the means of using one situation as a model for another. To exploit these two ideas for our theological task, we must see what happens to them once we move beyond the mathematical explanation of analogy in terms of ratios to the more general notion of analogy. To explore that, we shall in the first instance see in the next chapter what happens to the concept of analogy in the hands of Aristotle.

Chapter 2
Aristotle: The Uses of Analogy

It is in the work of Aristotle that the full potential of extending analogy beyond its mathematical basis becomes apparent. Although Plato had recognized the importance of analogy in human thought, Aristotle's writings show us the wide range of the fruitful employment of the concept. However, although Aristotle explored the uses of analogy more deeply than any writer before or since, there is no extended piece of writing dedicated specifically to the concept, at least in those works of his that have survived. There are a number of theoretically significant remarks scattered throughout the *Organon*, but for the most part his understanding of analogy is to be inferred from the extremely varied use that he made of analogy in writings devoted to other topics.

In Aristotle's hands, analogy becomes an all-purpose tool of research, and a major part of the interest of his work in this respect is the way he shows by example the extraordinary power of the concept and the diversity of the uses to which it can be put. Although Aristotle's significance for the theory of analogy has been widely recognized, there does not appear to have been a significant attempt to draw together the different threads in his discussions so as to produce an overview of what his conception of analogy actually was.[1] We may regard Aristotle as providing us with

---

[1]   To my mind, G. E. R. Lloyd, in his book *Polarity and Analogy*, misses the opportunity to provide such a study, mainly because he gives an extremely loose characterization of analogy: "to refer not merely to proportional analogy (*a:b::c:d*) but to any mode of reasoning in which one object or complex of objects is likened or assimilated to another" (p.175). Armed with this definition, he ignores almost all the texts in which Aristotle himself appeals to analogy, in favour of examples of Aristotle making comparisons that are not called analogies by Aristotle. This is particularly striking in the case of his discussion of Aristotle's biological writings. As we shall see, Aristotle's use of analogy in biology is perhaps his most sophisticated application of the concept. Lloyd, however, only briefly outlines that use, before saying "the subject which I wish to consider here is not Aristotle's search for, and analysis of, the likeness between different groups of animals, so much as his comparisons between animals and other things" (pp.365–366). There is no reason to suppose that Aristotle himself would consider these latter comparisons to be *analogical* comparisons at all. Two texts should, however, be mentioned here: Richard Whately, *Elements of Rhetoric* and Mary Hesse, "Aristotle's Logic of Analogy". However, despite the fact that Whately's account of analogy is clearly deeply influenced by Aristotle, his book is not intended as an exposition of Aristotle, and even if in a broad sense it can be regarded as an interpretation of Aristotle, Whately was not offering the kind of examination of Aristotle that I have in mind. Hesse is primarily concerned with Aristotle's use of analogy in metaphysics, which, although important, is only part of what needs considering here.

a series of case studies of the ways in which analogical comparisons can be used. What I propose to do in this chapter, therefore, prior to turning in the next chapter to the main topic of this book—the *linguistic* application of analogy—is to survey some of these case studies.

Because of the heterogeneous nature of Aristotle's uses of analogy, it is inappropriate to present them in one single overarching narrative. At the same time, there is one theme that recurs throughout: there are two different ways of comparing two things: the first involves a direct comparison between the two, and the second, which is by analogy, involves an indirect comparison, where the comparison depends upon the introduction of a third and fourth term. The way in which the contrast between a direct and indirect comparison is drawn varies from topic to topic. Thus, in the case of justice, the contrast is between "arithmetical" equality and "analogical" equality; in the biological writings, the contrast is between organs of animals that "differ by the more and the less" and organs that are "related only by analogy;" and in the case of metaphor, on the one hand metaphors based on a transfer from genus to species, or from species to genus, or from species to species, and on the other hand metaphors based on analogy.[2]

Roughly speaking, direct comparisons are made by simple inspection of the properties of the things to be compared. Typically, such comparisons are obvious, and, as a result, little can be learnt from them. By contrast, the indirect, analogical, comparisons are seen as the philosophically interesting comparisons and can appropriately be drawn between things that have no obvious properties in common, and that are "remote". The analogical comparisons are always governed by the formula "A is to C as B is to D", or more explicitly, "$R(A, B) = R(C, D)$", where we compare A and B by introducing a third and fourth term, C and D, and a relation R, where the way in which C, D and R will be specified will depend on the discipline being studied.

By looking at the range of cases in which Aristotle appeals to analogy, in all their diversity, we may hope to get some feel for the concept of analogy and what it is able to do for us. The examples I shall look at are: the contrast in Aristotle's biological writings between parts of animals that differ by "the more and the less" and parts of animals that are related by analogy; the claim in the *Rhetoric* that the successful metaphors are the ones based on analogy; the claim in the *Nicomachean Ethics* that justice is analogy; the role of analogy in the state in the *Politics*; argument by analogy; and the use of analogy in metaphysics. There is considerable variety in the way analogy is used in these different cases and perhaps the only theme to unite them is the idea that analogy enables us to make comparisons between phenomena too "remote" to be compared directly. Many of these uses of analogy are left by Aristotle at a programmatic level, where it would require detailed work to flesh out the details: what interests us in such cases is primarily the programme. It is only really in the case of the biological application that Aristotle not only

---

[2]   *Poet.*, 1457b 6–9.

outlines a programme but carries it through in detail. Because of this, it is the case that deserves most detailed attention in what follows.

Analogy in Biology

Method in Biology

We find the richest and most masterly application of analogy in Aristotle in his biological writings.[3] This is, of course, not to deny that he makes a large number of what can appear to us gross mistakes.[4] These mistakes are understandable in the writings of a pioneer working with an extremely limited empirical set of data and at a time when no one had any understanding of the precise functions of organs like the kidneys, spleen or heart.[5] However, what we are concerned with is the highly sophisticated *method* for biology that he evolves in the *Parts of Animals*.

There are a number of features that give to Aristotle's biology a distinctly modern flavour: its quest for teleological explanations,[6] its attempt to understand animals through an understanding of their parts, and its use of comparison. Although Darwin praised Aristotle as a meticulous observer, it may well be such features that earned Darwin's admiration for Aristotle.[7] Aristotle's biology is essentially a comparative biology, where the technique of comparison was based on a contrast between parts of animals that "differ by the more and the less" and those that are "related by analogy".[8] That contrast provides the key to his biological method.

---

[3]   *Cf.* Charles Darwin's famous letter to William Ogle (February, 1882) in reply to the gift of Ogle's translation of the *Parts of Animals* (Francis Darwin, *The life and letters* ... III, pp.251–252): "My dear Dr. Ogle,—You must let me thank you for the pleasure which the introduction to the Aristotle book has given me. I have rarely read anything which has interested me more, though I have not read as yet more than a quarter of the book proper. From quotations which I had seen, I had a high notion of Aristotle's merits, but I had not the most remote notion what a wonderful man he was. Linnaeus and Cuvier have been my two gods, though in very different ways, but they were mere schoolboys to old Aristotle".

[4]   *E.g.* the brain as an organ of refrigeration.

[5]   It is also easy to underestimate the large number of accurate observations he makes and the extent to which his method does lead to many results that stand up today, since many of the things that Aristotle discovered for the first time now seem obvious to us. (For example, Pliny the Elder's claim that Aristotle first identified the class of insects and coined the name for an insect [ἔντομον] is entirely credible, since the way he applies analogy in biology would naturally lead directly to the discovery and identification of such a class.)

[6]   Admittedly, Aristotle would resist the evolutionary interpretations of such teleological explanations that a modern biologist would give.

[7]   *Cf.* Allan Gotthelf, "Darwin on Aristotle".

[8]   *E.g.*, *PA*, I 644b 8–16: "Now it is practically by resemblance of the shapes of their parts, or of their whole body, that the groups are marked off from each other: as e.g. the groups Birds, Fishes, Cephalopods, Testacea. Within each of these groups, the parts do not

The task that Aristotle sets himself in his biology is to discover the "causes" of animals being the way they are, where, in contrast to his predecessors, he makes clear that he is giving priority to "final" causes, rather than to questions of the material origin of animals.[9] He is addressing such questions as "Why does an animal have the parts it does?", "Why do those parts take the form they do?" and "How do those parts co-operate so as to create a living being?" The answers that he seeks are teleological in form, along the lines of "A giraffe has a long neck in order to browse tall trees". The task is to make sense of animals being the way they are, with the background "metaphysical" assumption, which will inform his whole enquiry, that "nature does nothing in vain" or that "nature does everything for a purpose".[10]

Animals and plants are for Aristotle paradigm cases of substances—that is to say systems of parts that are organized in such a way that the continued existence of the whole is dependent upon the cooperation of the parts. The principle of organization of those parts—the way they are put together so as to produce a creature that is alive—is the "soul" or "form" of the animal. Given the nature of the enquiry he is engaged in, Aristotle stresses that for him "the student of nature should concern himself with the soul rather than the matter of animals".[11] Given this conception of animals and plants, Aristotle's question about the "causes" of the parts of animals becomes the question "how do these parts enable this animal to continue to exist—to successfully live out its life?".

We then start out with a range of things that animals need to be able to do in order to live successfully. For this we need to begin with an open-ended set of activities:

> For many of the same attributes are present in many different kind of animals, for example, sleep, respiration, growth, decay, death, and in addition any remaining affections and dispositions such as these. (I add this because at the moment it is permissible to speak unclearly and indefinitely about these things.)[12]

Given this range of things that an animal must be able to do to live, we may for any member of the range identify a part of the animal as the part that enables it

---

differ so far that they correspond only by analogy (as a man's bone and a fishbone) that is they differ not structurally, but only in respect of bodily quantities, e.g. by being larger or smaller, softer or harder, smoother or rougher, and so forth, or, to put it generally, they differ 'by the more and the less'."

[9]   *PA*, I 640a 1–641a 14.

[10]   See, *e.g.*, *PA*, I 641b 11.

[11]   *PA*, I 641a 29–30. *Cf.* II 651b 24: "no animal has saw-teeth as well as tusks; for nature does nothing without purpose or makes anything superfluously".

[12]   *PA*, I 639a 19–23. *Cf.* I 645b 33–35, where he gives the list "generation, growth, copulation, waking, sleeping and locomotion, and any other such things as are found in animals".

to do those things, dividing parts into the "uniform parts" (blood, serum, marrow …) and the non-uniform parts built up out of these, which are the *organs* of the animal.[13] In this way parts of animals are specified by their function,[14] in such a way that leads Aristotle to deny that an amputated hand, or the hand of a corpse,[15] is still a hand: it is essential to a hand that it should actually function as such.

The question as to the "causes" of the parts of animals thus becomes the question "why do the parts of animals have the structure that they have in order to discharge their functions?". This question will be pursued by Aristotle in a systematic series of comparisons between corresponding parts of different animals, noting similarities and differences between these parts. Similarities will provide a guide to what is important to such a part for it to discharge its function, and differences a guide to the way different parts have been adapted to different animals' ways of life and environments.

It is here that the concept of analogy plays a crucial role in Aristotle's biology.[16] As I have already said, there are two different ways in which the parts of animals may correspond. They may either "differ by the more and the less" or "be related (only) by analogy". The idea of "differing by the more and the less" stems from Plato.[17] Two things "differ by the more and the less" if they are basically the same, with it being possible to specify all the differences between them using nothing but comparatives.[18] Thus in the case which now concerns us—that of animals—we may consider the organs of two different species of bird. The beak of one bird will be basically the same morphological structure as the beak of the other, but longer, straighter and more pointed, say. Whereas, if we compare the organs of a bird with those of a fish, in a large number of cases, we are dealing with functionally equivalent but morphologically quite distinct structures, where the differences are too great to be specified simply by "the more and the less".

In the latter case, the organs are related only by analogy:

> Once again, we may have to do with animals whose parts are neither identical in form nor yet identical apart from differing by the more or the less: but they are the same only by analogy, as, for instance, bone is only analogous to fish-bone, nail to hoof, hand to claw, and scale to feather; for what the feather is in a bird, the scale is in a fish.[19]

---

[13]   *PA*, II 647b 23: τὰ ὀργανικὰ μέρη ("instrumental parts").

[14]   *PA*, I 645b 16.

[15]   *E.g.*, *Mete.*, 389b 31–390a 2. Compare also *Poet.*, 1451a 33–35: "If something's presence or absence makes no discernible difference, it is not a part of the whole." Although Aristotle is here talking about the parts of a tragedy, it is in a context where he is clearly thinking of a tragedy by analogy with a substance.

[16]   Here one must include reproducing itself as part of a successful living out of its life.

[17]   See Plato, *Philebus*, 24a–25d.

[18]   *Cf.* James Lennox, "Aristotle on Genera, Species, and 'the More and the Less'".

[19]   *HA*, I 486b 18–22.

In what follows, I assume that by "being related by analogy", or "being the same by analogy", Aristotle means that the two parts are functionally equivalent: that is to say that the "R" in "R(A, B) = R(C, D)" is to be interpreted as meaning "A performs a similar function for B as C does for D". This has been disputed by James Lennox.

Since the point seems crucial for an understanding of Aristotle's whole project in biology, it is worth going into this. Lennox writes:

> *Analogous likeness*: comparable, but differently designated features of different kinds. …
>
>   We might imagine that by analogous likeness Aristotle has in mind that while the parts are structurally different, they play functionally similar roles in their respective animals (cf. Le Blond 1945: 178). But Aristotle never says that this is his point, and the examples here do not require it. Fish spine is similar to bone both in terms of texture and position; and scales are all over the outside of a fish's body, just as feathers are all over the outside of a bird's—they are comparable in ways that are independent of understanding their bodily function.[20]

Here I believe Jean-Marie Le Blond to be clearly right[21] and Lennox's alternative account to be unsustainable:

1. Lennox's criteria for "analogous likeness" do not seem to have anything to do with the concept of *analogy*. Being "differently designated" is at most an accidental feature of the examples. The other similarities mentioned, such as sharing a texture are precisely the common features that are established by the kind of direct comparison that Aristotle characteristically contrasts with analogical comparisons.[22]

---

[20]   Aristotle, *Parts of Animals*, p.168. Lennox is commenting on *PA*, I 644a 16–22: "those animals that differ by degree and the more and the less have been brought together under one kind, while those that are analogous have been kept apart. I mean, for example, that bird differs from bird by the more or by degree (for one has long feathers, another short feathers), while fish differs from bird by analogy (for what is feather in the one is scale in the other)". However, in Aristotle's *Philosophy of Biology*, Lennox writes (p.179): "Lungs and gills, which are both used for cooling on Aristotle's understanding, are analogous structures (PA I.5 645b8); as are bone and cartilage (PA II.8 653b32ff.) In distinguishing extensive kinds from one another, this term usually refers to a relationship between structures which at a very abstract level perform a similar function for their possessors, but do so by very different means, and are not structural variations on a common theme, i.e. are not open to more/less comparison." This seems exactly right. Since both his commentary of *The Parts of Animals* and Aristotle's *Philosophy of Biology* were published in the same year, it is impossible to tell which is Lennox's final position.

[21]   *Cf.* also Le Blond, *Logique et Methode chez Aristote*, p.221.

[22]   It looks very much as though Lennox is heavily reliant on *PostA*, II 98a 20–23 where Aristotle cites precisely the kind of features of analogically related items that Lennox

2. It is difficult to read a number of passages such as *PA*, I 645b 6–10[23] in any other way than as equating being related by analogy with being functionally equivalent.

3. Since the parts of animals are for Aristotle always identified as the parts they are in functional terms, it is natural to assume that the corresponding parts of different animals will also always be *functionally* corresponding parts.

4. Aristotle's whole project is to discover why animals and their parts are the way they are. The only comparisons between animals that could possibly further that project are comparisons between functionally equivalent parts.[24]

5. When Aristotle does mention a similarity where there is no functional reason for that similarity, he dismisses it as biologically irrelevant. The horned serpents of Thebes are said to have horns "only metaphorically" (*HA*, II 500a 3–6).

6. In his biological writings, Aristotle is engaged in a systematic, scientific, study.[25] If you are to use analogy in such a study, you need a uniform interpretation of the analogical formula—the "R" in R(A, B) = R(C, D) must have the same value throughout the study. The only clearly available candidate for this formula that fits all the contexts in which Aristotle talks about analogy in his biology is "A performs the same function for B that C does for D".

Aristotle first applies the distinction between "differing by the more and the less" and "being related only by analogy" to divide the animal kingdom into nine "largest families" (μέγιστα γένη)—birds, fish, insects, cephalopods, *etc.*, the basis for the division being that if you take any two animals within the same family the corresponding parts of the animals differ only by the more and the less. The corresponding parts of two animals belonging to different families, however,

---

appeals to. However, Lennox is not reckoning with the underlying logic of the discussion in the *Posterior Analytics*, and what Aristotle says at 98a 20 is best read as giving typical *symptoms* of things being related by analogy and not *criteria* for them being so related, let alone a definition of what analogy is.

[23] "Now I have already said that there are many features common to many animals, either identically (such as feet, wings, scales and affections similarly), or else common by analogy. (I call by analogy such cases as some animals have a lung, while others have no lung, but something else that corresponds to a lung; some have blood, while others its analogue, having the same power [τὴν αὐτὴν ἔχον δύναμιν] for them that blood has for the blooded.)"

[24] The apparent exception to this is Aristotle's inclusion of decay and death at 639a 20 among the attributes to be investigated. But it is only an apparent exception: the investigation of function will include the investigation of loss of function.

[25] *PA*, I 644b 15–18: "We have said then ... in what way the study of these things might proceed methodically and with greatest ease. Further about division we have said how it is possible by following it to grasp things in a way that is useful."

show far greater differences, and so they are related only by analogy—by being functionally equivalent.[26] Thus if we consider birds from two different species, they both have beaks, eyes, feathers, wings, skeletons, *etc.*, and both lay eggs. If we compare any of these corresponding parts, it will be possible to describe all the differences between them using the method of the more and the less. By contrast, if we compare the corresponding parts of a fish and a bird, the differences will typically be much larger, and no longer capable of being specified solely in terms of the more and the less, and we have to rest content with the analogical correspondence.

Against this background, Aristotle seeks to explain the parts of animals by comparing them with the parts of other animals: the similarities between corresponding parts giving a guide to what is essential, or at least useful, for a part to discharge its function, and the differences to be explained by showing the way that they reflect differences between the ways of life or environments of the animals to be compared. If the comparison is between parts that differ by the more and the less, these will reflect fine-tuning of an animal to its particular way of life. (Birds of prey, unlike birds that eat seeds, have hooked beaks.[27]) Comparisons between parts that are related by analogy are potentially most instructive, precisely because the differences between the corresponding parts are greater.

In the *History of Animals*, therefore, Aristotle works systematically through the parts of animals amassing a large database of the similarities and differences between those parts in different animals, while in *The Parts of Animals* Books II–IV he gives a series of attempted explanations of such differences and similarities.

The Method in Practice

One can understand the method best by seeing how it is applied.[28] I shall here look at two examples.

In the first passage, we start out from the extraordinary nature of the elephant's "nostril", or trunk, when compared with other animals. Aristotle's task, having

---

[26]   *PA*, I 644a 11–644b 14.

[27]   *PA*, III 662b 1–5.

[28]   Compare with what follows Cuvier's comment on Geoffroy's "Principle of unity of composition": "we take care not to regard this as a unique principle; on the contrary it is only a principle subordinated to another, much higher and more fruitful, to that of the conditions of existence, to the agreement of the parts, to their coordination for the role that the animal has to play in nature; that is the true philosophical principle from which flow the possibilities of certain resemblances and the impossibility of certain others; that is the rational principle from which that of the analogies of plan and of composition is to be deduced, and in which, at the same time, it finds those limitations that some wish to ignore … This is the object of a special science that is called comparative anatomy, but which is far from being a modern science, for its author is Aristotle" (quoted from Le Guyader, *Geoffroy Saint-Hilaire*, pp.142–143).

registered the differences of the trunk from other noses, is to seek to give the reasons for those differences. There are here two comparisons at work —a comparison with the breathing organ of the elephant and that of other mammals, and an analogical comparison between the trunk and the hand.

> For the most part, there is very little variation in the organ of smell among the viviparous quadrupeds … In the elephant this part is unique in its extraordinary size and nature. Using its nostril as though it were a hand, the elephant conveys food, both solid and liquid, to its mouth, and it uses it to uproot trees by winding it round them. In effect it puts it to all the uses to which a hand is put. The reason for this is that the elephant has a double character, both as a land-animal and as a water-animal. It needs to gets its food from the water, but at the same time must breathe, being a blooded land-animal. However, because of its great size, it cannot move rapidly from water to land, as do some other blooded vivipara that breathe. Thus it needs to be equally at home on land and in the water. In the same way, then, that divers are sometimes equipped with an instrument for breathing, giving them access to air from the surface while they are under water, so that they may remain for a long period under the sea, nature has provided the elephant with its elongated nose. Whenever they cross deep water, they lift their trunks up to the surface and breathe through it. For, as I have already said, the elephant's trunk is actually a nose. Now it would not have been possible for the nostril to discharge all these functions if it had not been soft and pliable. For then its sheer length would have prevented it from feeding, in the same way that the horns of certain oxen do, so that they are obliged to walk backwards while grazing. Thus it is soft and flexible, and because it is such, nature has, in her usual way, exploited this by assigning to it an extra function as well as its primary one—it performs the function of forefeet. In polydactylous quadrupeds, the forefeet do not merely support the animal; they serve as hands. But elephants (which, having neither a cloven hoof nor a solid hoof, must count as belonging to this group) are so huge and heavy that their forefeet are reduced to mere supports; and, indeed, because they move so slowly and bend with such difficulty, they are quite unfit for any other purpose. A nose, then, is given to the elephant for breathing, in the same way that one is given to every lunged animal; this is at the same time elongated and capable of being coiled round things, because the elephant spends so much of the time in the water, and takes time to move onto dry land. And since the forefeet are unable to fulfil the normal function of forefeet, nature, as I said, assigns to this part the rôle of discharging the function that should have been performed by the forefeet.[29]

What Aristotle attempts to do in this passage is to make sense of the elephant's nose by relating it back to two features of the elephant—its size and its character as "both a land-animal and a water-animal". The argument throughout is

---

[29]   *PA*, 658b 27–659a 37.

straightforward and intelligible. Because the elephant is a land-animal that spends long times in the water, and needs to breathe when fording deep stretches of water, its breathing organ must be such as to enable it to do so, particularly since its size makes it cumbersome and ill-fitted for bobbing in and out of the water like an otter. Hence it is provided with a long flexible tube for a nose, like the "instruments for breathing" that divers are provided with. But at the same time, because of the bulk of the elephant, its forelegs need to be like pillars, and hence ill-suited to discharging the task of forearms, and although technically polydactylous, the elephant is thus not provided with proper hands. Hence the trunk which is already elongated and flexible is adapted to serve as the analogue of a hand.

What we see in this explanation is the way in which Aristotle, starting out from the difference between the nose of the elephant and that of other animals, seeks to explain that difference by showing how it reflects a variety of other facts about the elephant, which taken together make sense of the trunk. It is worth stressing the nature of the facts that are appealed to in the course of this attempt to spell out the "causes" of the trunk: there are facts about the elephant's environment and life-style—its life in and near water, facts about the elephant as a whole—its size and cumbersomeness, and facts about the relation of this "part" to the other "parts" of the elephant—the unsuitability of the forefeet to fulfil the function of hands necessitating that the trunk take over that function. In this way, we can see how the "cause" of the trunk is given by showing the place of the trunk within the total economy of the elephant—its place within the organization of its parts that enables the elephant to live out its particular life cycle—and the difference of the trunk from other noses is seen to reflect the differences between the elephant and its life, considered as a whole, and other animals and their lives.

In the second example, of the crab, we find the same patterns of explanation: Aristotle starts out from the differences which emerge from the comparison of the eyes of widely diverse animals, highlighting those which need to be explained—the absence of eyelids, the hardness of the eye, the mobility of the eye, and the "fluidity" of fish eyes. We then trace in turn the "causes" of these features by showing how they relate to the animal's other parts and life-style. It is because the crab has a hard skin that it cannot have a functional eyelid; it is because it has no eyelid that the eye must be hard—must itself take over the function of the eyelid; it is because the eye is hard that the eyes are made mobile, to compensate for the reduction in acuity brought about by the hardness of the eye, and so on.

> There are many differences between the eyes of Fish and Insects and hard-skinned Crustacea, although none of them have eyelids. As far as the hard-skinned Crustacea are concerned, there could be no question of eyelids, since using an eyelid depends upon rapid movement of the skin. To make up for the lack of this protection, they have hard eyes—it is as if the eyelid were incorporated in the eye itself and the creature saw through it. But since vision is necessarily dimmed by the hardness of the eye, Nature has endowed Insects (and to an even greater extent, Crustacea) with moveable eyes, in the same way that quadrupeds have

been supplied with moveable ears—in this way they can turn towards the light and catch its rays, and so see more clearly. But Fish have fluid eyes. The reason for this is that they move about a lot and have to be able to see for considerable distances. When land-animals look over such distances, they look through the air, which is sufficiently transparent; but Fish are moving in water, which forms a hindrance for clear vision. But the water contains far fewer objects to injure the eyes than does the air; hence the fish do not need eyelids, and have fluid eyes to counteract the opacity of the water. Since they have no need of eyelids, Nature, which does nothing in vain, has given them none.[30]

A set of explanations is offered for the "fluidity" of fish eyes, and for the lack of eyelids in fish—in this case, in terms of the fish's environment, and the consequent need to see under water. Once again we see a complex of explanations of the differences of the eyes of various creatures from those of other creatures by showing how those differences reflect differences in the place of the eyes within the total economies of the creatures.

What is instructive about both these examples is that in explaining one part of an animal—the elephant's trunk, the mobility of the crab's eye—Aristotle is led to compare and explain other parts of the animal simultaneously—the legs of the elephant being like pillars, the thickness of the crab's skin. Here you are making sense of the animal by not just a single comparison but by a set of interrelated comparisons. You seek to understand what is revealed in one comparison by locating it in a nest of comparisons, so that you are potentially comparing the whole economy of one animal with that of another. In that way, although Aristotle himself never talks in this way, he is using analogy to treat one animal as a model—and indeed a *working* model—of another animal.

Metaphors Based on Analogy

In the *Poetics*, Aristotle divides metaphors into four classes:

> Metaphor is giving to something the name of something else, proceeding either (i) from genus to species, or (ii) from species to genus, or (iii) from species to species, or (iv) by analogy.[31]

He goes on to explain that a metaphor by analogy is one formed according to the following pattern: suppose A:B::C:D, then we call A either "C" or "the C of B". This is a familiar kind of metaphor, illustrated by Aristotle with such examples as "calling old age 'the evening of life'", because old age is to life as evening is to day. However, although he devotes significantly more space to metaphors by analogy

---

[30] *PA*, II 657b 30–658a 10.

[31] *Poet.*, 1457b 6–9.

than to the other three types of metaphor within the *Poetics*, his examples do little to suggest the creative power of this type of metaphor. It is a striking feature of the *Poetics* discussion that almost all the examples, including the metaphors by analogy, are boring.

However, when we look at the somewhat desultory discussion of metaphor in *Rhetoric* III, a central claim is that the successful (εὐδοκῖμος = "thought well of") metaphors are those based on analogy.[32] The *Rhetoric* is a practical work and as such does not offer a theoretical account of such metaphors, Aristotle being content to refer back at *Rhetoric* 1405a 6–8 to the *Poetics* definition and classificatory scheme as presupposed to what follows. What he does offer is a series of brilliant metaphors, beautifully illustrating his claim that metaphors based on analogy are the most successful ones. Indeed, in the case of one of the very few examples of metaphor that is not by analogy—"calling a good man 'square'"—he introduces the example specifically as an example of a wooden metaphor, commenting, "This is metaphor, for both are perfect; but, it does not signify activity [= 'is lifeless']",[33] to contrast it with the "witty sayings that stem from metaphors by analogy, and make one see things".[34]

Although Aristotle cites these as examples of metaphors by analogy almost none of them conform to the pattern for such metaphors that he had given in the *Poetics*, and it is not immediately obvious what the analogical relationship is that Aristotle claims underlies these metaphors. He only spells out the analogy for one example and I shall first look at that to reconstruct how the use of analogy in the formation of metaphors can be extended beyond the simple examples of metaphor in the *Poetics* to the subtle and complex metaphors of the *Rhetoric*.

> [Homer's] fame derives from the way he brings things to life in all his work. Thus, e.g., "Then the impudent stone rebounded back to the plain", "the (bitter) arrow flew", "some [sc. of the spears] stood in the ground, still straining to gorge themselves on flesh", and "the javelin eagerly pierced his breast". In all of these something is animated and made actual, for being "ruthless" and "straining" etc. constitute actuality. He applied these epithets by a metaphor by analogy: for, as the stone is to Sisyphus, so is the impudent one to the one he offends.[35]

On the basis of the *Poetics* account, this explanation of the analogical scheme would lead one to expect that the boulder would be called "the impudent boy" or

---

[32]   *Rhet.*, III 1411a 2.

[33]   *Rhet.*, III 1411b 25.

[34]   *Rhet.*, III 1411b 22–24.

[35]   *Rhet.*, III 1411b 31–1412a 6. Aristotle's interpretation of Homer is questionable here: is the boulder, as Aristotle would have it, someone utterly lacking in respect, or is it a pitiless torturer? Since for *my* purposes nothing hangs on this, I have uniformly made the boulder impudent.

whatever; but that is not what happens. The stone is not called "the impudent boy", but is talked about as if it were an impudent boy, cocking a snook at Sisyphus.

In other words, the supposed transferred name, the word "impudent", does not refer to one of the four terms of the analogical scheme. It is, instead, an adjective that naturally describes one of those terms. This looks a slight difference but, properly understood, means that we are now dealing with a metaphor that, if interpreted in the way Aristotle suggests, cannot be adequately handled by the apparatus of transferred names. There is here a shift, from the *Poetics* conception where on the basis of an analogical scheme "A:B::C:D" we call A "C" or "the C of B", to a conception where on the basis of such a scheme, we talk about A *as if* we were talking about C.

How far Aristotle recognized the difference between the examples in the *Rhetoric* and those in the *Poetics*, and how he would have justified the claim that some of his more complex examples were metaphors by analogy, it is impossible to say. Consider for example:

> And Lycoleon, defending Chabrias: "not even showing respect for the bronze statue which supplicates for him over there"; this, when spoken, was a metaphor, but not for all time, but it made one see things.[36]

It is unlikely that Aristotle would have had a worked out theory for such complex metaphors by analogy to replace the simple *Poetics* account.[37]

Let us take another of his examples and sketch out how regarding it as a metaphor based on analogy can explain its rich complexity.

> You, as one free to roam at large.[38]

This is one of the initial examples that Aristotle uses to show the way in which metaphors based on analogy succeed in producing life (ἐνέργεια) and "make us see things", by contrast with the lifeless "A good man is square". In this, it succeeds brilliantly. Aristotle merely cites this example without any explanation, presumably assuming an audience who will recognize the context without which it is unintelligible and not even recognizably a metaphor. But, in context, the metaphor involves an extraordinarily rich and imaginative comparison. The quotation comes from Isocrates' *To Philip*, §127. Isocrates appeals to Philip of

---

[36]   *Rhet.*, III 1411b 5–8. (The circumstances are that Chabrias had previously defeated Agesilaus, and a statue been raised in his honour by the Athenians, as a memorial to his services to the state. Now he is on trial for alleged misconduct leading to the loss of Oropos. Reflecting the way he had fought the decisive battle against Agesilaus, the statue depicted him kneeling, holding an outstretched spear.)

[37]   My book *The Structure of Metaphor* may be regarded as offering one way in which such a theory could be developed.

[38]   Cited by Aristotle at *Rhet.*, III 1411b 29.

Macedon to unite the Greeks and lead an expedition against Persia, the common enemy of all the Greek states. Isocrates sees the other Greek leaders as tied up with local politics and narrow rivalries between the different states. Philip, however, not only has the power, but is capable of the larger view. Isocrates expresses the contrast by means of the metaphor we are now concerned with:

> While it is only natural for the other descendants of Heracles, and for men who are under the bond of their polities and laws, to cleave fondly to that state in which they happen to dwell, it is your privilege, as one free to roam at large, to consider all Hellas as your fatherland.[39]

The word I have here rendered 'one free to roam at large' (ἄφετος) is the word used for animals that had been dedicated for sacrifice to the gods: as such, they were sacred and it was forbidden to use them as beasts of burden or to circumscribe their freedom in any way.

Despite the immediacy of impact of this comparison, Isocrates has used high metaphysical wit to combine a complex range of ideas into a single image. The initial point of the comparison is the greater freedom enjoyed by Philip, by virtue of his cosmopolitan outlook against the other Greek leaders with their narrower preoccupations, being compared to the freedom of the sacrificial animal. But that initial comparison suggests and is enriched by a whole series of other comparisons: for example, that the cosmopolitan outlook, being able to adopt the larger view, is a higher calling, is like being dedicated to the gods; or, that being bound up with the narrow concerns of nationalism is like being an animal confined to working its master's fields; or, that a Persian expedition, by comparison with local politics and rivalries, is a great enterprise and not petty "nationalistic" politicking, is "roaming at large".

The interesting question is "Why is this metaphor to be regarded, and why indeed is it regarded by Aristotle, as a metaphor based on analogy, and not as a metaphor based on a transference from species, along the lines 'Philip is called ἄφετός because both he and the cow are unconstrained'?" The simple answer is that if we do regard it as such a metaphorical transfer from species to species, we fail to explain how the metaphor succeeds in encapsulating in a single word the rich complex of ideas that I have just outlined. How, then, does seeing the metaphor as one based on analogy help to explain the way in which the metaphor succeeds in generating that complex of ideas? To be sure, if we look at the simple examples that Aristotle uses in the *Poetics* to illustrate the idea of a metaphor based on analogy ("the shield is called 'the cup of Ares'"[40]), it is difficult to find an answer to that question and we must take Aristotle as having implicitly gone beyond the limitations of the *Poetics* account.

---

[39]   Isocrates, *To Philip*, p.323.
[40]   See *Poet.*, 1457b 16–23.

For all the insight into metaphor displayed in the *Rhetoric*, much in Aristotle's account is left at an intuitive level. To develop his desultory remarks into a theory of metaphor we need to introduce a notion that he never explicitly recognized—that of an analogical model. To make sense of Aristotle's claim that such metaphors are based on analogy we must return to the notion of such models.

We see this metaphor as an invitation to use the situation of the sacred cow in a village as a model for the situation of Philip in Greece: we construct such a model by setting up informally a series of analogical relationships between the elements in the one situation and the elements in the other, along the lines: Philip is to the other Greek leaders as a sacred cow is to the other cows in the village; Philip's ability to adopt a cosmopolitan perspective is to the other Greek leaders' being embroiled in local rivalries and politics as the sacred cow's freedom to roam at will is to the other cows' restriction to their own fields, and so on. By a thoroughgoing application of a series of analogies such as these, we make the village a model for the whole of Greece.

In this way a complex and successful metaphor such as this achieves such things as the following: it gives a single, graspable, image for the complex political situation in Greece, and so, as Aristotle says, "it makes one see the situation",[41] and, precisely because the setting up of the model involves the multiple use of analogy, the metaphor can be seen as an invitation to explore the one situation by following up the different possible avenues of thought suggested by the different analogies, thereby giving one a way of seeing ever fresh aspects of the political situation that Isocrates is discussing. This is, I suggest, the best way to make sense of Aristotle's claim that it is such metaphors that "bring things to life and signify 'activity' [ἐνέργεια]".[42]

Justice as Analogy

The basic theme that runs through the whole treatment of justice in the *Nicomachean Ethics*, Book V, is that justice is analogy. Perhaps of all Aristotle's applications of analogy, this is the one that stands in greatest need of development: although the basic idea here is attractive, attempting to see what it means in practice is, as we shall see, fraught with difficulties. The claim that justice is analogy is a general thesis, applicable to all forms of justice—distributive justice, criminal justice[43]

---

[41] *Rhet.*, III 1411b 24.

[42] *Rhet.*, III 1411b 25. Compare with this account, the discussion of metaphor in Max Black, "Models and Archetypes" (pp.236–239). Although Black's remarks here would stand in need of considerable development to be presented as a theory of metaphor, this account strikes me as greatly superior to that in his far more famous article, "Metaphor".

[43] The most explicit treatment of criminal justice as analogy is, however, not to be found in Aristotle himself, but in the *Magna Moralia* (1194a 29–1194b 3). Although this

and justice of exchange (fair trading)—but, for our purposes, I shall concentrate mainly, as does Aristotle himself, on the case of justice of exchange.

> Justice is therefore a sort of analogy. For analogy is not only a property of arithmetical quantity, but of quantity in general, analogy being equality of ratios, involving four terms.[44]

> But in the interchange of services, justice in the form of reciprocity is the bond that maintains the association: reciprocity that is on the basis of analogy, not of equality. The very existence of the state depends upon analogical reciprocity; for men demand that they should be able to requite evil with evil—otherwise, they feel that they are in the position of slaves—and to repay good with good without which no exchange can occur, and it is exchange which binds them together.[45]

> Now analogous requital is effected by diagonal conjunction. *E.g.*, let A be a builder, B a shoemaker, C a house and D a shoe. It is required that the builder shall receive from the shoemaker a portion of the product of his labour, and give him a portion of the product of his own. Now if analogous equality between the products be first established, reciprocation occurs, and the requirement indicated will have been achieved; if not, the bargain is unequal, and trade does not continue.[46]

The problem Aristotle addresses throughout the discussion of justice is: if we think of justice as involving a form of fairness or equality, how can we make sense of establishing equality between two incommensurable entities? We agree that blackmail and rape are serious crimes, but may be at a loss to say which is more serious, or how much more serious is one than the other. A system of punishment demands, however, that we map crimes on to a single linear scale—the graver the crime, the more severe the punishment.

Similarly, in the case of trading of goods and services, while boots, chickens, houses and legal services are valuable commodities, we may be at a loss to say how many chickens a farmer should give a lawyer for a piece of legal advice, or for representation in court. If, however, there is to be an exchange of goods, and if there is to be such a thing as a fair exchange, then we must be able to map heterogeneous goods onto a single linear scale, so that we can assign a price to goods, introducing money to represent a common measure of their value. In line with Aristotle's general approach to the question of comparing heterogeneous entities, we replace the impossible task of direct comparison that asks "How much

---

work is universally supposed not to be by Aristotle, the Aristotelian influence is obvious throughout.

[44]   *NE*, V 1131a 30–33.
[45]   *NE*, V 1132b 32–1133a 2.
[46]   *NE*, V 1133a 5–13.

of each is worth this much of the other?" with a task of indirectly comparing the goods that asks instead "How many chickens are to the farmer as this house is to the builder?"[47] The further question that this gives rise to is, of course, how precisely we are to interpret such a formula—what meaning are we to attach to the "... are to ... as ... is to ..." part of the account. Unless we can answer this question, we have said almost nothing in saying that justice depends upon establishing analogical equality.[48] A plausible answer is in terms of the cost to the farmer and the cost to the builder: if the cost to the farmer to rear n chickens is the same as the cost to the builder to build one house, then giving n chickens for building a house is a fair exchange.

This would be simple and straightforward if the notion of "cost" were simple and straightforward. We should then be able to explain the analogical equality of products as the arithmetical equality of costs to the producers. If we could simply interpret "cost" as the time it takes to rear chickens or build houses, then we should have a simple measure for determining what was a fair exchange. It is at this point, however, that the difficulties with Aristotle's proposal arise. We think of "cost" in far more complicated terms that cannot easily be reduced to a single measure: we include in the cost of doing X such factors as how much hard labour is involved, how much training is required to be able to do X, how risky or even dangerous an enterprise is involved in trying to do X, what skill is required and so on. The trouble we encounter at this point is not simply that we arrive at a complicated account of "cost", but that the elements that enter into our calculations appear almost as difficult to compare as the original goods that we were seeking to balance. Do we pay more, or less, for something that requires great skill than one that requires hard work? If the costs can themselves be incommensurable, then, following Aristotle's line of argument, making the costs to the two producers of the goods equal can only mean making them analogically equal. It is certainly not obvious how that is to be done, particularly if we are to avoid an infinite regress of analogy upon analogy.

---

[47] *Cf.*, for example, *EE*, VII 1241b 33–35: "Since there are two kinds of equality— arithmetical and analogical—there will also be different species of justice, friendship and partnership."

[48] Consider, for example, the unfortunate way in which the author of the *Magna Moralia* (1194a 32–36) interprets the claim that justice is analogy in the case of criminal justice: "Justice between slave and free is not the same. For if a slave strikes a freeman, he justly receives, not blow for blow, but many blows. But this kind of justice too is by analogy: as the freeman is in rank to the slave, so is the reprisal he may take to the injury sustained." Here, punishment is proportioned to social status. We can of course give a more acceptable interpretation of the idea that criminal justice is based on establishing analogical equality: *e.g.*, by saying that the severity of the punishment is to be proportioned to the harm done to the victim. Both are, however, possible ways of interpreting the idea that the punishments for different crimes must be made analogically equal, so that the claim that justice is analogy does not, in itself, give us a way to adjudicate between them.

This may indicate that there are limits to the extent to which we can give a fully rigorous account of our intuitive ideas of justice as fairness. In the present case, Aristotle seems to acknowledge that the problem may be theoretically insoluble, but that practice gives a reasonable solution:

> Money, then serves as a measure which makes things commensurable, and so reduces them to equality. Without exchange, there would be no association, without equality, no exchange, and without commensurability, no equality. Although, strictly speaking, things so different cannot become commensurable, in practice our demand gives a sufficiently accurate common measure.[49]

Here, we allow the marketplace to determine what is an acceptable value for goods, in the belief that although the problem is theoretically intractable, market forces will in practice deliver justice of exchange: "if not, the bargain is unequal, and trade does not continue".[50]

There are cases where Aristotle's account looks insightful and highly attractive. Thus, if you and I both want life insurance and I am twice as likely to die in the next year as you, it seems just that I pay twice as much for the insurance as you do, and, what is more that is the result that the market will tend to deliver. Here, analogy or proportionality will not only be just, it will also be what actually happens. In general, however, while market forces will certainly tend to produce a market equilibrium, Aristotle may be unduly optimistic in thinking that the resulting distribution of costs of goods is in fact a just distribution.

Analogy in the State

Closely related to, but clearly differentiable from his claim that justice is analogy, is Aristotle's concern in the *Politics* with equality in the state. Here, once again, the claim is that if we wish for equality within the state—social equality—the equality to be aimed at is not "arithmetical" equality, but "analogical" equality. Given the programmatic nature of Aristotle's claim here, we can treat this use of analogy on his part much more briefly than the cases we have looked at so far.

> Party strife is everywhere due to inequality, where unequal classes do not receive analogous power (for a lifelong monarchy is an unequal feature, if it exists among equals); for, generally, the motive for factious strife is the desire for equality. But there are two kinds of equality: arithmetical equality, and equality according to worth: by arithmetical equality, I mean that which is equal in number or dimension, by equality according to worth, analogical equality; e.g., 3 is greater than 2, and 2 than 1 by an arithmetically equal amount, but 4 is

---

49   *NE*, V 1133b 16–20.
50   *NE*, V 1133a 13.

greater than 2 and 2 than 1 by an analogically equal amount, since 2 and 1 are equal parts of 4 and 2—namely halves.[51]

Aristotle's contention is that it is a necessary condition for political stability in a state that analogy should be maintained throughout. By this, he means the following: every state depends for its existence upon the cooperation of a number of different classes of people—the artisans, the rulers, the military, *etc.*—and the smooth running of the state requires that every class should have the power, influence and wealth that is appropriate. This does not entail actual equality between the different classes but it does entail analogical equality: that is to say, the wealth of the artisan class is to the role of the artisans within the state as the wealth of the rulers is to the role of the rulers within the state, *etc*. If this analogical equality breaks down—that is, if one section of society lacks its due power and influence—the result will be civil unrest and even civil war.

It is a criterion for judging the satisfactory nature of a constitution how far it is conducive to the preservation of such analogical equality. In particular, this thought lies behind Aristotle's opposition to democracy: a democratic constitution would put too much power in the hands of one class of society, namely, the poor who formed the majority in the society and this would lead to an unacceptable redistribution of wealth.[52] The point here is not so much whether he was right or wrong about this particular application as the principle lying behind it: that a society depended upon a complex balance of the interests of a diverse range of classes within a society. The claim that he makes for political theory is that such a balance cannot be expressed by a simple notion of arithmetical equality, and instead we need to resort to an application of analogical equality.[53]

It is even clearer here than in the claim that justice is analogy that there are severe limits to the extent to which we could give a precise theoretical algorithm for calculating the proportions involved. Finding the right values for analogical equality would inevitably be an empirical matter, based on the idea that we have arrived at analogical equality when we have a stable and smooth-running state, and departed too far from the ideal level of equality when we have instability and even civil war.

---

[51] *Pol.*, V 1301b 27–36.

[52] Cynically one suspects that Aristotle was influenced in his thinking by the fact that under such redistribution he would be one of the losers.

[53] If one were fully to work out Aristotle's idea of the preservation of analogy within the state, his position could be best expressed by saying that in the stable state the distribution of power and influence among the different classes within the state would be a model of the roles of those classes in the state.

Argument by Analogy

There has been a tendency in recent centuries to follow Thomas Reid's lead in presenting arguments by analogy as a particular type of what we now call argument by induction.[54] However, while not actually containing the word "analogy", Aristotle gives us an excellent example of argument by analogy that brings out how different such arguments are from what are now called arguments by induction:

> Having discussed those proofs which are special to particular branches of rhetoric, we have still to discuss those which are common to all. These are of two types: example [παράδειγμα] and enthymeme (since a maxim is a sort of enthymeme). Let us start with example; for example resembles induction [ἐπᾱγωγή], and induction is a principle of reasoning.
>
> There are two sorts of example—those which refer to things which have actually happened, and those which use made up cases. The latter are subdivided into parables [παραβολή] and fables [λόγοι], such as those of Aesop and the Libyan fables ... Parable is illustrated by the sayings of Socrates—e.g., saying that we ought not to choose our magistrates by lot, since this would be like choosing the athletes to represent us at the Olympic Games by lot rather than by their skill at athletics, or like sailors choosing their helmsman by lot, rather than one with the relevant knowledge.[55]

Although "induction" was introduced as a translation of Aristotle's term "ἐπᾱγωγή", his use of the word was broader than the modern use, covering any argument that established a universal truth by consideration of particular cases. This includes what William Kneale calls "intuitive induction",[56] in which the induction "exhibits the universal as implicit in the clearly known particular".[57] If by contemplating a particular case **A**, I can see that from the fact that **A** is **F**, it follows that **A** is **G**, then I am entitled to infer the universal truth that anything that is **F** is **G**.[58] One can put the induction here in the form: "When you see in the particular case why **A**'s being **F** implies that **A** is also **G**, you will recognize why anything that is **F** is **G**."

---

[54] See Reid, *Essays on the Intellectual Powers of Man*, Essay I, Chapter IV.

[55] *Rhet.*, II 1393a 23–1393b 7.

[56] *Cf.* the discussion in William Kneale, *Probability and Induction*, pp.30–37.

[57] *PostA*, 71a 8.

[58] One may think here of the way in which particular examples are typically used in academic debate to illustrate and establish general truths. Consider: "It is not from the benevolence of the butcher, the brewer, or the baker, that we expect our dinner, but from their regard to their self-interest. We address ourselves, not to their humanity, but to their self-love, and never talk to them of our own necessities, but of their advantages" (Adam Smith, *The Wealth of Nations*, I ii, pp.26–27). Here Smith is clearly using these particular cases to make a general point in economics. (So too, I am using this citation from Smith, to make a general point.)

If the "parables" of the *Rhetoric* "resemble induction" it is this intuitive induction that they resemble.

There are two reasons why Aristotle says that they only *resemble* induction. Firstly, the argument is not from the particular to the universal, but from one particular instance of a universal truth to another particular instance of that truth—short-circuiting the statement of the universal truth. Secondly, in the *Posterior Analytics* Aristotle was concerned with the use of induction to establish necessary truths, but here we cannot say that it is a necessary truth that we do not choose the athletes to represent us in the Games by lot, but only that it is highly intelligible that we do not. It is that intelligibility that is transferred to the case of the choice of magistrates.

If, however, this example "resembles" "*intuitive* induction", it also contrasts sharply with what we *now* call argument by induction. We can see the contrast if we consider Aristotle's characterization of parables as using made up or fictional cases. We may put Socrates' argument in the form: if you see why we do not choose the athletes for the Games by lot, you will realize why we ought not to choose the magistrates by lot. For that argument to work, however, it does not matter whether the person hearing the argument knows whether in fact athletes are chosen by lot: all that matters is that they should see why it would be a bad idea to do so. For that, a hypothetical case serves just as well as an actual case. In standard arguments by induction, as we now understand the phrase, it is essential that all the particular cases assembled to justify the inference to the universal conclusion should actually exist, but with an argument by analogy such as this fictional cases serve just as well as real ones.

One of the best ways to think of such arguments, whether in the form we encounter them in the *Posterior Analytics* or in the variant in the *Rhetoric*, is to think that we are being offered the particular case as a model. The particular case represents the universal, by being able to be used as a model for any other case of that universal. In the argument given in the *Rhetoric*, we are offered one situation—the choice of athletes for the Olympic Games—that can be used as a model of another—the choice of magistrates in the state. Such modelling is effected by setting up an open-ended series of analogical relations: the athlete is to the race as the magistrate is to the state; athletic prowess is to the athlete as wisdom is to the magistrate; winning is to the athlete as just decisions are to the magistrate and so on.

One point to stress about such modelling is that it is entirely informal and unsystematic. Whereas in the "scientific" use of analogy it is essential that an interpretation of the analogical formula is settled in advance and rigorously adhered to, here the speaker invites the audience to discover such analogical relations as seem to them appropriate and to follow analogical trains of thought as far as is fruitful, and to abandon such trains of thought if and when they go lame. Such lack of true systematicity is a characteristic mark of the use of analogy in metaphor and rhetoric.

Analogy and Metaphysics

One of the central problems in Aristotle's metaphysics is created by his doctrine of categories. On the one hand, he thinks of entities as belonging to different ontological categories—substances, qualities and relations, *etc.*—where entities are different in such a way that entities in two different categories cannot have any properties in common. If it makes sense to ascribe a property to a substance, the attempt to ascribe the same property to a quality will necessarily result in nonsense. On the other hand, if you engage in the kind of ontological enquiry that interests Aristotle—the study of being qua being—you will constantly find the need to use a vocabulary that is applicable in all the categories.

Let us suppose that your ontological enquiries lead you to posit different ontological categories: entities that are categorically different in such a way that it makes no sense to say of an entity belonging to one category the same thing as one says of an entity belonging to a different category. However, in a metaphysical enquiry you will constantly be led to talk of what is true of all the categories. The question is, then, "How are we to understand this use of language that apparently transcends the categories, when the mark of two entities belonging to distinct categories was apparently the impossibility of using the same language to talk of both simultaneously?"

In Aristotle's own case, he has in the first instance been concerned to analyse what it was for a *substance* to exist, and had presented a hylomorphic account, in which a substance is seen as informed matter. At least as far as the question what is it for things in different categories to exist is concerned, Aristotle's main proposed solution to this problem is outlined at the beginning of *Metaphysics*, Book IV, where he introduces the idea of what is now called, following G. E. L. Owen,[59] "focal meaning". Towards the end of the *Metaphysics*, however, Aristotle canvasses another possibility: that the concepts with which he conducts his enquiry, which have been developed primarily with the case of substances in mind, may be redeployed *by analogy* in other categories.[60]

What he experiments with in the following passages from the *Metaphysics* is the possibility of talking in the same way of entities in different categories such as colours and times. The proposal is that we use analogy to reinterpret the terms of the ontological analysis such as matter, form and privation. (This redness is to the surface that is red as Socrates is to the matter of which he is composed.)

---

[59]   Owen, "Logic and Metaphysics in Some Earlier Works of Aristotle".

[60]   The other significant passage in which Aristotle introduces analogy into his ontological investigations is at *Meta.*, VIII 1043a 5. That raises different issues from those that concern us here, and I shall return to this passage when I discuss Aquinas' account of analogy.

For there is analogy between all the categories of being—as straight is in length, so is flatness in breadth, perhaps odd in number, and white in colour.[61]

The truth is, as we said that in one way things have the same elements, in another, not. E.g., the elements of sensible bodies are, say, (1) as form, the hot, and, in another way, the cold as its privation; as matter, that which directly, and of its own nature, is potentially hot or cold. And not only are these substances, but so (2) are the compounds of which they are principles, and (3) any unity which is generated from hot and cold, e.g. flesh or bone: for the product of hot and cold must be different from them. These things, then, have the same elements and principles, although specifically different things have specifically different elements; but we cannot say that all things have the same elements in this way, but only by analogy: i.e. one might say that there are three principles, form, privation and matter. But each of these is different for each category of thing: e.g. in colour, they are white, black and surface, or, again in night and day, they are light, darkness and the air. And since it isn't only things that are inherent in an object which are its causes, but there are external causes as well, e.g. the moving cause, "principle" and "element" are not identical: but they are both causes. Principles are divided into these two kinds, and what moves or stops a thing is a kind of principle and substance. Thus, by analogy there are three elements and four causes or principles; but they are different in different cases, and the proximate moving cause is different in different cases. Health, disease, body, and the moving cause is the art of medicine. Form, a sort of disorder, bricks, and the moving cause is the art of building.[62]

These passages have a highly experimental feel, and many of the examples Aristotle offers are highly unconvincing. What is of interest, however, is the general strategy that Aristotle is proposing.

As Aristotle leaves the question, it stands in need of considerable clarification and development, but it is worth noticing the way that the same problem recurs in very different contexts and very different ontological enquiries. Thus when Russell set up his Theory of Types, the basic idea was that it was meaningless to predicate of a set belonging to one type what was predicated of a set belonging to another type. Hence Russell, when he wished to talk about different types simultaneously, was led to talk of the vocabulary being used as "systematically ambiguous", without saying what the systematicity consisted in. The spirit of Aristotle's proposal is that we appeal at this point to analogy: "this property is to type n as that property is to type (n + 1)".

But perhaps we can see the idea most clearly if we consider the case of Frege. For Frege, there were two radically different sorts of entities, objects on the one hand and functions (including concepts) on the other. The difference was such

---

[61] *Meta.*, XIV 1093b 18–21.
[62] *Meta.*, XII 1070b 11–29.

that it was strictly impossible to say anything about a concept that one says about an object and vice versa. Yet, at the same time, in expounding his theory, Frege constantly finds himself forced to use the same idioms to talk of concepts and functions as he used to talk of objects: that concepts were the references of predicates, just as objects were the references of names; that we could talk of the existence of both objects and concepts; and we could say when two concepts or functions were identical, when identity was for him a first level relation between objects.

Having construed identity as a relation between *objects*, Frege will nevertheless want to say whether two concepts are, or are not, the same. Given that he has completely ruled out the possibility of using the same language to talk about concepts that he uses to talk about objects, he is confronted by an apparent impasse. In attempting to resolve this apparently contradictory position, Frege writes:

> If we say "The meaning of the concept-phrase 'conic section' is the same as that of the concept-phrase 'curve of the second degree'" or "The concept conic section coincides with the concept curve of the second degree", the words "the meaning of the concept-phrase 'conic section'" are the name of an object, not of a concept; for their nature is not predicative, they are not unsaturated, they cannot be used with the indefinite article. The same goes for the phrase "the concept conic section". But although the relation of equality can only be thought of as holding for objects, there is an analogous relation for concepts. Since this is a relation between concepts I call it a second level relation, whereas the former relation I call a first level relation. We say that an object a is equal to an object b (in the sense of completely coinciding with it) if a falls under every concept under which b falls, and conversely. We obtain something corresponding to this if we switch the roles of concept and object. We could then say that the relation we had in mind above holds between the concept Φ and the concept X, if every object that falls under Φ also falls under X, and conversely.[63]

Here, he proposes that we get round it by constructing a relation that *can* be said to hold between concepts, but that at the same time has all the logical properties of identity. In this way, Frege proposes that we can use the properties and relations that are applicable to objects as a model for the properties and relations that are applicable to concepts, and then analogically extend the vocabulary we have introduced for objects to talk about concepts.

---

[63]   Frege, "Comments on Sense and Meaning", p.120.

Some Conclusions

From the foregoing discussion, the following points may be noted.

First, in Aristotle's appeals to analogy, the concept has been decisively extended beyond its mathematical confines. There are passages in the *Meteorologica*[64] where Aristotle shows a competent understanding of the mathematics of analogy, and also a number of insights in the *Organon* into the implications of the mathematical employment of analogy. However in none of the examples that I have discussed in this chapter can we interpret the analogical relationship in terms of mathematical ratios. What Aristotle does in these examples is extrapolate ideas derived from the mathematical theory of analogy to contexts where we need a more general notion of analogy.

For the most part he is surefooted in doing so, although there are occasional texts in which he seems to underestimate the difference between the mathematical and non-mathematical uses of analogy.[65] Throughout, Aristotle exploits the *continuities* between the mathematical and the non-mathematical case. When we come to look at Kant, we shall see, however, that Kant is equally concerned to stress the *discontinuities*. In this way, between them, Aristotle and Kant help us to see what the use of analogy outside of mathematics can, and cannot, do for us.

Second, this chapter makes clear how various are the uses to which Aristotle puts analogy. There is not just diversity of the topics in which he appeals to analogy: the ways in which analogy is put to work to illuminate the topics—questions in biology, in metaphysics, the nature of justice, and the way metaphor works—are remarkably different.

Aristotle starts out with a basically very simple idea, the idea that there are two different ways to compare things—a direct comparison where one notes common properties of the two things, and an indirect comparison where, whether or not the two objects have significant common properties, one effects the comparison by introducing a third and fourth term. He then shows in practice how that basic idea can be adapted in a wide variety of contexts in support of his claim that it is the indirect comparisons that can yield genuinely new insight; the direct comparisons are usually trivially obvious and the results obtained from such comparisons correspondingly trivial.

Third, there is one most obvious point that is of fundamental significance in the context of our present enquiry. One of the main things to interest Aristotle in the concept of analogy in all its varied applications is its capacity to establish comparisons between things that are too remote for direct comparison to be

---

[64] See, *e.g.*, *Mete.*, III. 375b 16–377a 12.

[65] In particular, unless I have missed something, *NE*, V 1131b 3–11 is virtually unintelligible. (H. Rackham gives the gloss: "It is shown that, if A:B::C:D, then A+C: B+D::A:B, i.e., if the shares are proportioned to the persons, their relative condition after receiving them will be the same as it was before." But that seems to involve a very free interpretation of the + sign, and, to put it bluntly, the resulting "mathematics" is bogus.)

possible. With analogy, we can compare things that are different in kind, no matter how strictly we interpret the idea of "different in kind", without violating the fact that they are different in kind. It is precisely because of this that we can find in Aristotle's use of analogy an initial indication of how it is that, when we move beyond Aristotle, analogy seems to offer a way of comparing God and humanity without violating the infinite difference between them.

Fourth, I have found it necessary on a number of occasions to appeal to the concept of a *model*. As we saw in Chapter 1, the idea of an analogical model is a natural development of the simple notion of analogy, where, instead of the single relationship "A is to B as C is to D", you set up a relationship between two domains. Here, one correlates elements in one domain with elements in the other, and establishes a whole series of analogical relationships between pairs of elements in one domain and pairs of elements in the other domain.

There is no text in Aristotle that shows he was explicitly aware of the idea of a model, or the way in which many of his examples of the use of analogy would, if fully worked out, involve an appeal to such models. However, as we have seen, the way in which he applies analogy frequently involves not just a single analogical comparison between two objects, but several analogical comparisons being made simultaneously between the objects in one domain and the objects of another domain. Such multiple analogical comparisons carried through systematically lead to setting up a mapping of one situation onto another, in such a way that the second situation is treated as a model of the first. This is a simple and natural extension of the idea of analogy, and one that I hope to show provides the basis for the application of analogy to the theological questions that primarily concern us.

At this stage I simply highlight these points, each of which will be important as the argument of this book progresses.

Chapter 3
Aristotle: Analogy and Language

An analogy is in the first instance not a linguistic phenomenon at all, but a relationship between objects in the world. However, given any set of things that are analogically related, we may straightforwardly find a linguistic application for analogy, in that we give a common name to the things that are analogically related. For instance, we use the word "wings" both for the organs of flight of birds and butterflies, since butterfly's wings: butterflies:: bird's wings: birds. This is basically a simple idea, which needs, however, further clarification. The purpose of this chapter is to spell out some of the implications of Chapter 2 for the linguistic application of analogy, including Aristotle's own discussions of those implications.

Analogy and Definition

Definition

We may begin by looking at the theory of definition, both as Aristotle received it and as he developed it.

1. The first point to note is that when Aristotle talks about definition he is for the most part talking about the definition of a thing, not, as would normally be the case nowadays, of a word. That is to say, if we were to ask, "What is the definition of a cow?", we would be asking "What is it about this cow that makes it to be the kind of thing it is?", "What is its bovine essence or nature?" In many contexts, the questions of the definition of a thing and of the definition of a word for that thing will simply transpose: it may seem that the questions "What is the bovine nature?" and "What justifies our applying the word 'cow' to something?" are simply equivalent. However, at least if we are concerned with defining "natural kinds", these two questions can come apart. If we want to define a cow in Aristotelian terms, we must study cows, to see what is essential to their continued existence. If we want to define the word "cow", we must look at the way people use the word. Even if the results of these two enquiries will overlap, they may well not coincide, particularly if the scientists studying cows include in their account facts not generally known about cows. The immediate relevance of this is that, in the cases that most interest us in our present enquiry, the question whether a term is used univocally or equivocally can frequently receive

two different answers. This is in cases where when we say both that A is F and that B is F, although it will be natural according to any reasonable criteria for sameness of sense to say that the word "F" is used with the same sense, the feature of A in virtue of which A is F is significantly different from the feature of B in virtue of which B is F.[1]

2. The standard account of definition within the Academy was definition by the method of division ("διαιρεσις"). This was initially propounded by Plato, particularly in the *Sophist* and the *Statesman*. In this you arrived at the definition of a term "F" by taking a larger class "A" that contained all the Fs, dividing it into two[2] smaller classes "B" and "C", where all the Fs were Bs, in turn subdivided the Bs and so on until eventually you arrived at a class that contained all and only the Fs. A typical definition arrived at in this way would be the supposed definition of "man" as a rational, sensitive, animate, material, substance. A natural way of representing such a definition is as a tree branching downwards ("A tree of Porphyry"), with the original largest class (substance) at the top, then we divide this, the highest genus, into the next two branches, subdividing into material and immaterial substances, and so on, until we arrive at the species to be defined at the bottom of the tree.

This theory of definition persisted as the main account of definition until the development of modern logic and the work of Frege in particular.[3] It is, however, extremely limited in its application and the vast majority of important definitions fall completely beyond its reach.[4]

Aristotle himself spends a great deal of time exploring the method of division in the *Posterior Analytics*. There are, however, places where he shows an awareness of the existence of scientifically significant concepts that cannot be defined by its means. For example, in Chapters 2 and 3 of Book I of the *Parts of Animals* he

---

[1] *Cf.* Aquinas, *Commentary on the Sentences* ..., I dist. 19, Q.5 a.2, ad 1: "For example, all bodies are considered equal in the intention of *corporeality*. Hence, the logician, who considers only intentions, says that the name *body* is predicated univocally of all bodies. However, the 'being' [*esse*] of this nature is not of the same character in corruptible and incorruptible bodies. Hence, for the metaphysician and the philosopher of nature, who consider things according to their 'being', neither the name *body* nor any other name is predicated univocally of corruptible and incorruptible bodies, as is clear from the Philosopher and the Commentator on *Metaphysics X*."

[2] It is unclear whether Plato himself insisted on a division into *two* classes, or would permit divisions into several classes. It is in the work of Speusippus that the insistence that each division should be into two classes ("the method of dichotomous division") becomes canonical.

[3] See, for example, Frege, "Boole's Logical Calculus and the Concept-script", pp.32–35.

[4] To give a simple example: the concept of an *aunt* can readily be defined in terms of the concepts of *parent* and *female*, but attempting to define it by the method of division leads nowhere.

presents a powerful series of arguments to show that the different species of animals cannot be defined by dichotomous division.[5] But the clearest cases of definitions recognized by Aristotle that lie beyond the scope of the method of division are definitions by analogy. We shall look into these in detail in the following section, but I shall lead into that section by considering the following passage:

> Yet a further method of selection is by analogy: for we cannot find a single word applicable to a squid's pounce, fish spine and bone, although these too possess common properties as if there were a single osseous nature.[6]

Let us suppose we have used the method of division to set up a Porphyry tree with the different species of animal at the bottom of the tree. We then cut across the tree, finding corresponding parts in different species, establishing such analogical relationships as cuttlebone: cuttlefish:: fishbone: fish:: monkey bone: monkey. Here we have completely different substances performing the same function for different species, and can use the analogical relationship we have established to introduce a new concept, *bone*, that is applicable across the whole spectrum of animal species. Although, as Aristotle says, in Greek there is no word corresponding to this concept, that is a pure accident, and indeed in English we do use the word "bone" to designate all these different substances. Because these different substances perform the same function for different animals, they have a number of common properties, such as texture and hardness, which are properties that any substance must have in order to fulfil the function of providing the skeletal structure of an animal. Thus although there is no natural kind (φύσις) *bone*, it is as if there were, and we may introduce a word to designate all the different bony structures.

What we have here is a familiar process in talking about the parts of animals— talking of the legs of wasps, cows and centipedes, or the eyes of fish, humans and flies. In this way, we have everyday examples of words used to group together a range of analogically related phenomena.

"The Kind of Definitions Archytas used to Accept"

Archytas of Tarentum was a philosopher, mathematician and the teacher of Eudoxus. Because only a few fragments of his writings survive, all discussion of him must be to a lesser or greater extent conjectural. Aristotle wrote three books on his work, now lost, and it has been conjectured that Plato based the figure of

---

[5] *PA*, 642b 5–644a 10. In these chapters, Aristotle is explicitly concerned to criticize not the method of division as such, but *dichotomous* division, and some of his arguments are specifically concerned with the impossibility of defining species by always dividing into two. Other arguments in these chapters, however, create difficulties for using the method of division as such to define animals.

[6] *PostA*, 98a 20.

Timaeus upon him. Although we cannot tell the precise nature of his influence upon either Plato or Aristotle, it could well be that Archytas was one of the first thinkers to explore the possibility of extending the concept of analogy beyond its mathematical confines, giving to it much the same significance that we now attach to the concept, and that it was under his inspiration that they both became concerned with the concept of analogy.[7]

Archytas' conception was of the universe as governed by number and analogy: what was primarily meant was that you could in principle give a description of the whole universe using only the resources provided by the mathematical theory of analogy.

The reason for introducing him into our discussion of Aristotle's use of analogy is that we may set the scene for our discussion of Aristotle by considering a set of quotations from Aristotle in which he sketches "the kind of definitions Archytas used to accept" since these quotations already encapsulate the major topics that are most relevant to our present enquiry and that we wish to throw light on in this chapter:

> the consideration of similarities is useful for forming definitions that cover widely differing subjects, e.g. "Wavelessness at sea and windlessness in the air are the same thing" (Since each is a state of rest), or "A point on a line and a unit in number are the same thing" (Since each is an origin [ἀρχή]). Thus, if we specify the genus to be that which is common to all the cases, the definition may be regarded as appropriate. This is how those who frame definitions usually proceed: they state that the point is the origin of the line, the unit the origin of number. It is clear that they are assigning them both to the genus of what is common to the two cases.[8]

> Likenesses must be studied between things in different genera, the formula for such likenesses being "As A is to B, so is C to D" (*e.g.* "As knowledge is to what is known, so is sensation to what is sensed"), and also "As A is in B, so is C in D" (*e.g.* "As sight is in the eye, so is reason in the soul", or, "As wavelessness is in the sea, so is windlessness in the air"). In particular, we must have practice in comparing genera which are remote; for in the other cases, the similarities will be more readily apparent.[9]

> As we said, just as in philosophy, metaphors should be transferred from things that are related, but not obviously so; it is a trait of a well-directed mind to perceive resemblances even between things that are remote. Thus, Archytas said that an arbiter and an altar were the same, for both are a refuge for someone who has been wronged. Or, if you were to say that an anchor and a rope hung from a hook were the same, but one hung from above, the other from below. And to say

---

[7] One specific conjecture that is sometimes made is that Aristotle's account of justice as analogy in the *Nicomachean Ethics* was derived from Archytas.

[8] *Top.*, I 108b 23ff.

[9] *Top.*, I 108a 6ff.

that the cities have been "levelled" is to use the same term for widely differing things: the land surface, and the powers of the citizens.[10]

That is why some who define a house say that it is stones, bricks and timber, and so cite what is potentially a house, *i.e.* the matter; some say that it is a container for sheltering people and property, or something of that sort, giving the actuality; and some combine the two, giving the substance compounded out of these. (It would seem that the definition by differentia is that of form and actuality, while that by constituent parts is, rather, that of matter.) The last of these also holds for the kind of definitions Archytas used to accept; for they are definitions combining matter and form. For example, "What is windlessness?" "Stillness in a large extent of air—the air is the matter, the stillness is the actuality and substance". "What is wavelessness?" "Levelness of sea—the sea is the material substrate, the levelness, the actuality or form".[11]

The difficulty in interpreting this last passage is deciding what Aristotle is referring to in talking of "the kind of definitions Archytas used to accept". Carl Huffman assumes that the definitions referred to are those of "windlessness" (νηνεμία) and "wavelessness" (γαλήνη).[12] Although this seems a straightforward reading, it is hard to make sense of the whole passage on this assumption: why would Archytas have given a definition of "windlessness"? What is special about such a definition that makes it worth singling out by Aristotle as an example of "the kind of definitions Archytas used to accept"? This banal and obvious definition does not seem to warrant being mentioned as a special kind of definition.[13]

We make sense of this passage if we suppose that when Aristotle talks of "the kind of definitions that Archytas used to accept" he was referring to a type of definition with which his audience would be familiar, and furthermore that this

---

[10]   *Rhet.*, III 1412a 9–17.

[11]   *Meta.*, VIII 1043a 14–25.

[12]   Huffman, *Archytas of Tarentum*, p.494: "The four things of which we can be sure Archytas offered definitions ('windlessness,' and 'calm-on-the-ocean' in A22 and 'arbitrator' and 'altar' in A12) are striking, precisely because they are not in themselves important concepts." On my account, Archytas is not defining any of these four terms. As Huffman says, they are not important concepts, and it is difficult to see why Archytas should have defined them. This is a difficulty that nothing in Huffman's subsequent discussion does anything to alleviate. On my reading, what Archytas is defining is not these four terms, but, rather, what windlessness and wavelessness, or what an arbiter and an altar, have in common, the point of these examples being to illustrate the power of analogy in the definition of new concepts. Aristotle is then suggesting that the general form of such definitions can be explained by appealing to his concepts of matter and form: "this form is to this matter as that form is to that matter".

[13]   Andrew Barker in his criticism of Huffman ("Archytas Unbound", pp.315–318) shares with Huffman the assumption that the definitions at stake are that of "windlessness" and "wavelessness" and concludes that it is wrong to suppose on the basis of this text that Archytas had anything very interesting to say about definition.

type of definition is illustrated in the two passages I have quoted from the *Topics*, where the pair of terms "windlessness" and "wavelessness" do indeed occur, but not as separate items to be defined but as components used in constructing the definition of a further term, "a calm" (ἡσῦχία). In that case, we can see Archytas as making a genuinely innovative proposal in the theory of definition that would have interested Aristotle directly. Archytas is proposing that we can define a concept not, as is the case with the method of division, by specifying a common property possessed by all the objects that fall under the concept, but by specifying an analogical relationship such that all the objects falling under the concept are related by analogy, so that since windlessness is to the air as wavelessness is to the sea, we may see them as both falling under the concept of a calm.[14]

We may now paraphrase the passage I have quoted from the *Metaphysics* along the following lines: some people define something such as a house by citing the constituents of which it is composed; others define it by citing its form or what it is for; yet a third group offer definitions that combine matter and form ("a house is bricks and mortar arranged so as to create a space for people to live in"). We may also include in this third group those who put forward the kind of definitions Archytas advocated (this form is to this matter as that form is to that matter).

1. Although the word is not used in the passages quoted, it is clear that they provide examples of what I am calling, and what Aristotle himself elsewhere calls, "analogy" ("ἀναλογία"). However, with these examples we see that the concept has been transformed from the concept as we originally encountered it within mathematics. It would be nonsense to talk here of the *ratio* of windlessness to air or of a point to a line. Here, the formula "A is to B as C is to D" has been generalized from simply meaning "the ratio of A to B is the same as the ratio of C to D" ("$A/B = C/D$") to mean "A stands in the same relation R to B as C does to D" ("$R(A, B) = R(C, D)$"). This transformation has a number of significant implications.

   The first and most obvious implication is that the restriction placed upon the concept of a ratio in Euclid V, Definition 3: "Ratio is a mutual relation of two magnitudes *of the same kind* to one another in respect of quantity"

---

[14]   Jamie Dow has drawn my attention to the following passage in the *Gorgias* (465b 6–c 4), where Plato is trying to explain what he means by "flattery" when he talks of rhetoric as a kind of flattery (κολᾰκεία): "Well, to avoid long-windedness, I shall put it to you like a geometer … as cosmetics is to gymnastics, so is sophistry to law-giving, and as cookery is to medicine, so is rhetoric to justice." This is a beautiful example of the kind of definition that is at stake here, showing its full potential. The examples cited here do not obviously have anything in common, and Plato's concept of "flattery" clearly cannot be defined by the method of division, so he here resorts to a definition that shows the ways in which the different instances of flattery are analogically related. It is interesting to find an example such as this already in Plato showing an awareness of a style of definition that does not use the method of division, whether or not he is influenced by Archytas.

need no longer apply. In fact in the main example Aristotle cites from Archytas, it would be absurd to talk of the absence of waves as being "of the same kind" as the sea.

The second implication is one that will move into the foreground when we come to look at Kant's discussion of analogy and its application to the problem of religious language, with his contrast between the "constitutive" use of analogy within mathematics and the "regulative" use of analogy outside of mathematics.[15] In the mathematical application of analogy, when we consider the formula "A/B = C/D", if we are given three terms, B, C and D, the value of A is determined a priori and it will be possible to calculate what that value will be. When, however, we move from the formula "A/B = C/D" to the more general "R(A, B) = R(C, D)", such an a priori determination will typically be lacking, with the result that even if in some particular context we establish that in a certain respect A is the analogue of C, that is of itself not sufficient to determine what A is, or even its further properties over and above the holding of the analogical relationship. As Kant says, in such cases, analogy is "only regulative": "The relation yields, however, a rule for seeking the fourth term in experience, and a mark whereby it can be detected."[16]

The third implication is that once we replace the formula "A/B = C/D" by the more general "R(A, B) = R(C, D)", the claim that A is an analogue of C has to be regarded as elliptical: A is an analogue of C, with respect to a given B, D and relation R. The claim that A is an analogue of C is thus an incomplete claim, and the onus is on anyone making such a claim to be able to specify the missing terms of the analogical relation. Aristotle himself rarely does specify the relation R he has in mind, but it is almost invariably the case that it is clear from the context how he would fill out the claim that something was analogous to something else.[17] The important point here is that there is an onus on anyone who claims there to be an analogy between A and C to be able to specify, if challenged, what the missing relation R actually is in virtue of which this is true. Theologians, in particular, are frequently prone to neglecting to discharge this obligation.

2.   "A point on a line and a unit in number are the same thing (Since each is an origin [ἀρχή])." The example given in the first of these three quotations provides an excellent illustration of something that can equally be illustrated by the related English notions of an origin, beginning or starting point. *Analogy enables us to group together, as falling under a single concept,*

---

[15]   *CPR*, B222–223.

[16]   Ibid.

[17]   The nearest to an exception to this is in his treatment of metaphors by analogy in the *Rhetoric*, where, as we saw in the last chapter, the reader has to do a great deal of work to discover the analogical relation at stake in his claim that a certain metaphor is a metaphor by analogy.

completely heterogeneous entities. We can create concepts such that the objects falling under those concepts can belong to completely different categories, whether we are thinking of Aristotle's set of categories or some other categorial scheme. In Aristotle's own example, if we ask "what properties does a point share with the unit of number?", we may be hard put to it to come up with a sensible answer. Nevertheless, if we say "the point is to the line as the unit is to the number series", we may form a concept under which both the point and the unit fall, namely the concept of *being a starting point.*

Consider a related example in English—that of being an "opening", as in a chess opening, the opening chapter of a book, the opening shots in a battle, the opening batsmen in cricket, the opening night of a play. Here we have an extremely heterogeneous set of applications of the word "opening" in highly diverse contexts, where what makes an opening to be an opening looks very different as we move from case to case. For instance, in many of the cases, the word carries with it the temporal connotations of being the earliest in a series, but in others, references to time are completely out of place. But what justifies this use of the same word in these various contexts is an underlying analogical scheme: the opening chapter is to the rest of the book as the opening moves of a chess game are to the rest of the game, as the opening shots are to the rest of the battle, etc.

In this way, we can see how analogy can make possible "transcendentals", concepts that are applicable in all the categories, and also, in our present context, how it is possible that analogy can permit us to form concepts that are applicable to both God and human beings, while still respecting the scholastic maxim that "God is not in a genus."

3. The final point is the most obvious, but for our purposes the most important. What we see in these quotations for the first time is the possibility of the *linguistic* application of the concept of analogy. The possibility of using analogy to define concepts automatically gives us the possibility of introducing words for those concepts—predicates that are such that the objects to which those predicates are truly applicable do not possess a common property to justify the application of that predicate, but where what justifies the application is the fact that these objects are all analogically related to each other.

Thus, if we consider Archytas' somewhat artificial example, which was presumably constructed to illustrate the idea of a new kind of definition, rather than for its practical importance, the word "calm" can be applied to a wide variety of situations. We have a calm sea, a calm sky, a calm temperament, or a period of calm following a riot. What justifies these different uses of the same word is not a common property possessed by these different "calms", but the underlying analogical pattern identified by Aristotle.

The *Oxford English Dictionary* lists the word "calm" as one that is used "literally of the weather, air, or sea" and figuratively in all its other uses. There is, however, no good reason to describe any of these uses as "figurative": they all fall within the scope of the standard literal meaning of the word. The interesting point to note is that in a case like this there is no principled answer to the question "is the word 'calm' used in only one sense or in many?" That is to say, on the one hand, we could begin with a sense of the word "calm" that was restricted in its application to the weather, and then think of the word as acquiring other senses by analogical extension, but, on the other hand, we could think of the word "calm" as having only one sense, namely a sense in virtue of which it is applicable to any phenomena that satisfy the underlying analogical pattern. What this example shows is something that will recur throughout our enquiry, namely, that the question "does a word used analogically have more than one *sense*?" is an unhelpful question: our criteria for sameness or difference of sense are not sufficiently refined to answer such a question.[18] Instead we should replace that question with other, more tractable, questions, such as "is it the case that someone who had learnt what it meant to describe the weather as 'calm' *ipso facto* learnt what it would mean to describe the sea as 'calm'?" I shall return to this point at the end of this chapter.

---

[18] One can see the kind of difficulties that arise with this question if one considers a proposal made by James Ross in *Portraying Analogy*. Taking his lead from a passage in Aristotle's *Topics* (I, 106a 1–107b 37), Ross proposes a series of criteria for sameness of sense (pp.37–47), including such items as that if "F" in context A has the same sense as "F" in context B, then an antonym of "F" in context A will also be an antonym of "F" in context B. For instance, if we ask whether the word "lose" has the same sense when talking about losing an election as it does when talking about losing a pencil, we note that we win, but do not find, an election, and find, but do not win, a pencil. The trouble with this is that such criteria leave us in the lurch in precisely the cases that interest us in discussing the analogy of names. Consider for example the word "narrow", as used (1) to speak of a narrow alley; and (2) to speak of a narrow mind. In both cases the antonym of "narrow" is "broad" ("a broad street", "broad-minded"). However, the fact that "narrow" has the same antonym in both contexts can be equally well explained by saying that this is because the word "narrow" has the same sense in both contexts and by saying that as applied to a mind it has an analogically extended sense and that the word "broad" undergoes the same analogical shift in sense, with the word "narrow" and its antonym changing their meanings in precisely the same way simultaneously. In fact, Aristotle himself notes this possibility with respect to the pair "λευκός"/"μέλας" as applied to sounds and to colours (*Top.*, I 106a 22–29), and in this case goes beyond the tests he is outlining, by claiming that in this case the difference is obvious, since sounds and colours belong to different categories. (It may be remarked that, as I read Aristotle, in the *Topics* he is not proposing in any strict sense *criteria* for sameness of sense or meaning, but simply rules of thumb for detecting ambiguity.)

Analogy and Ambiguity

Two questions that seem to arise from what I have just said: "are we to think of naming things by analogy as a species of ambiguity (or, in Aristotle's terms, homonymy)?" and "what does Aristotle mean by '*chance*' (τύχη) when he contrasts naming things by analogy with cases of chance homonymy?" One of the main points to make is to emphasize a point that I made about definition. When Aristotle talks of homonymy,[19] his way of talking does not map straightforwardly onto modern ways of talking of ambiguity, or sameness or difference of sense.

Homonyms and Synonyms

> When things have only a name in common and the explanation (λόγος) of being corresponding to the name is different, they are called homonymous. Thus, for example, both a man and a picture is an "animal" (ζῷον). These have only a name in common and the explanation of being corresponding to the name is different; for if one is to say what being an animal is for each of them, one will give two distinct explanations.

When things have the name in common and the explanation of being corresponding to the name is the same, they are called synonymous. Thus, for example, both a man and an ox are animals: each of these is called by a common name, "animal", and the explanation of being is also the same; for if one is to give the explanation of each, what being an animal is in each case, one will give the same explanation.[20]

Here I have deliberately translated "λόγος" as "explanation", rather than "definition",[21] since it seems to me that talking of "the same definition" or using words "in the same sense" can easily beg questions or be misleading, at least to modern ears. Asking whether words are used with the same meaning or in the same sense is too blunt an instrument in our present enquiry.

---

[19]   This equally applies to mediaeval writers asking whether a word is used "univocally" or "equivocally". *Cf.* Richard Cross, "Idolatry and Religious Language".

[20]   *Cat.*, 1a 1–11. One point to note about this passage that is a minor obstacle to translation is that the word "ζῷον" is in Greek genuinely ambiguous, being the word both for an animal and a picture. This has sometimes confused people who have thought Aristotle was contrasting calling a bull an animal and calling the bull in a picture an animal. Aristotle's example is actually, however, a far simpler and more clear-cut case of ambiguity.

[21]   J. L. Ackrill, for example, uses the translation "definition" and Jonathan Barnes in "Homonymy in Aristotle and Speusippus" (p.66) proposes the following account: "x_1, x_2, …, x_n are homonymous if and only if there is some term A such that (i) x_1 is A and x_2 is A and … and x_n is A; and the meaning of A is different in each of the sentences 'x_1 is A', 'x_2 is A', … 'x_n is A'." One reason for not following either of them is that, at least in the cases that most interest us here, questions as to whether a word is, or is not, used with the same meaning tend to leave us in the lurch.

Something that has frequently been noted about this passage is something that I believe is not without significance in the present context. For Aristotle, it is not, as we normally think, words that are synonymous or homonymous but the things named by those words: it is the man and the picture themselves that are the homonyms, not the word "ζῷον". The significance that I believe this may have is that if you ask whether the "λόγος" for applying a name in two cases is the same or different that can be understood in two different ways. If you are thinking of the words, you will naturally interpret that as asking whether the word has the same, or different, meaning. If, however, you are thinking of the things, it is more natural to interpret that as asking whether the property of the one thing that makes it appropriate to apply the word (that in virtue of which a man is a ζῷον) is the same or different from the property that makes it appropriate to apply the same word to the other (that in virtue of which a portrait is a ζῷον). For the simple case of ambiguity that he is concerned with in the *Categories* there may seem little difference between these two questions. The question "is what makes an *F* to be an *F* in the two cases the same or different?" will in this case receive the same answer whether we regard it as a question about the meanings of the word "*F*" in the two cases, or about the natures of the two *F*s.

However, with the far more complex cases that concern Aristotle in his later writings, these two questions, particularly in cases of analogous names, can receive different answers.[22] Thus, if we take a case that would be for Aristotle a clear case of analogous naming, the word "long" as applied to *War and Peace* and to the Canadian Pacific Railway, it is natural to say that the word does not change its meaning, and is used in precisely the same sense when we say "*War and Peace* is a long novel" and "the Canadian Pacific Railway is a long railway", but we may very well think that the properties of the novel and the railway in virtue of which these sentences are both true are very different.

In fact, when we probe the question whether, in the cases that now interest us, we are concerned with a case of a word having the same or a different meaning, and equally whether the properties of the objects that make it appropriate to apply the one word are the same or different, we find that our criteria for sameness and difference of meanings and properties are not sufficiently robust to give any unequivocal answer. Consider, for example, Aristotle's repeated claim that an amputated hand, or the hand of a corpse, is a hand "in name only", and that calling the hand of a living person and that of a corpse both "hands" is a case of homonymy. For instance:

---

[22]   Although I shall postpone discussion of this case until Chapter 4, when Aristotle says in *Metaphysics* IV that "being is said in many ways", Aristotle might mean *either* (1) that the word "exists" has many senses and is multiply ambiguous; *or* (2) that, for example, it is a very different matter for a substance to exist and for a quality to exist. And (1) and (2) look to be very different claims, with the second having far greater plausibility than the first.

> Thus it is only too clear that a corpse is a man homonymously. So is the hand of a dead man a hand in name only, just as a sculptured flute might still be called a flute, for it also is some kind of instrument.[23]

Despite this being a somewhat idiosyncratic contention, Aristotle's reason for saying this is clear enough. For him, the parts of animals such as hands were identified by their function, and it was only in virtue of their being able to perform their functions that they were the parts they were. In this way, the detached hand, which, in the nature of the case, could not grasp or perform any of the other functions of a hand, was properly speaking not a hand at all, and it was only by homonymy that we continue to call it a hand.

Even if, however, we grant Aristotle's conception that a hand is not identified just by its shape or material composition, but primarily as an organ, by its function for a living human being, it is still not clear that we should say either that in calling an amputated hand "a hand" we were using the word "hand" in a different sense or that the amputated hand lacked one of the essential properties for being a hand. What is, however, clear is that even if we were to follow Aristotle in describing this as a case of homonymy, these two different uses of the word "hand" belong together, and anyone who learns the word at all will automatically use it in both senses.

"'Chance' Homonymy"

There is a phrase in the passage in the *Nicomachean Ethics* in which Aristotle introduces the idea of things being called by the same name by analogy that is worth commenting on explicitly. This is the phrase "by *chance* homonymy" (ἀπὸ τύχης ὁμωνύμοις):

> But in what way are different things called "good"? For they do not seem to be called by the same word by chance homonymy. Possibly they are all called "good" because they derive from one good, or all contribute to one good. Or perhaps they are called "good" by analogy: for as sight is good in the body, so is reason in the soul, and similarly another thing in something else.[24]

It is clear that there are many instances in which we use the same word with two entirely different meanings. For instance, we use the word "bull" both for the animal and for a papal edict. There is no connection whatever between these two uses, not even an etymological connection, let alone a connection in meaning. It is in this case pure chance that we use the same word for these two different things and we would, for instance, have no grounds for believing that, in languages other than English, we would find that the same word was used for the animal and for the edict.

---

[23]	*Mete.*, 389b 31–390a 2.
[24]	*NE*, I 1096b 28.

Let us, however, consider a different case, the case of the use of the word "milk" both for cow's milk and for the milk of a coconut. Here it seems equally obvious that, although it is natural to describe this as a case of a word having two different senses, it is entirely intelligible that the same word should be used for these two different phenomena. We would expect any speaker of the language to be able to explain why the same word is used in these two cases. However, although this double use of the word "milk" is comprehensible and so in that sense we are not confronted by a case of "chance homonymy", it still remains an accidental feature of the English language that there should be this double use. We would not be surprized to discover other languages in which this double use was not replicated. Equally, someone who had learnt the word "milk" only as the word for cow's milk would be in no position to predict that coconut milk would also be called "milk".

It seems that later writers like Porphyry would have regarded this example as indeed a case of homonymy that was not by chance. I believe, however, that Aristotle was after a stronger idea than that illustrated by the case of "milk". If we consider the example of the word "good" (ἀγαθός) that Aristotle gives us as an example of a word used in many ways, but not by chance homonymy, then if someone learns to use the word "good" at all, they thereby learn to use it in all the various ways indicated by Aristotle. If someone understands the sentence "This is a good time to do it", we would find it incomprehensible if they did not also understand the sentence "This is a good place to do it". For Aristotle a word like good is used homonymously because it is predicable in all the categories, and things that are in different categories cannot have anything univocally in common.

But even if we grant him that, when someone can use the word "good" at all, they are thereby able to use it in all the categories. If we say that a word like "good" "is said in many ways", it is still the case that those different ways form a system of interrelated ways, in such a manner that when we acquire the meaning of the word "good" we simultaneously learn to use it in all these ways. In fact, what we learn is not a set of isolated, if related, ways of using the word, but a system of uses. If we say that "the meaning of the word is its use in the language", then the different uses of "good" constitute a single use. We cannot say that about the two uses of the word "milk".

Potentiality (Δύναμις)

There is one case that deserves special mention, in which Aristotle's text indicates a different possibility of the linguistic use of analogy. This is in his treatment of "δύναμις" ("potentiality") in Book IX of the *Metaphysics*. Not only is his discussion of great intrinsic interest, it indicates a use of analogy that has relevance far beyond this particular case.

Book IX presents us with a model of the analysis of a complex concept, in which Aristotle traces the intricacies of the different ways of speaking about potentiality, and the interrelationships between the different uses of the word "δύναμις". What concerns us here is not the full complexities of that analysis, but the following passage:

> In fact, "Actuality" means the presence of the thing, but not in the way we call "potentially" e.g. when we talk of "a [statue of] Hermes in the wood", and "the half-line in the whole", i.e. it could be separated out; in the same way we call a man "a student" even while he is not studying, if he is capable of studying. That which is present in the opposite sense to this is present actually. What we mean is clear in each case from an induction of cases, and we must not seek a definition of everything but must grasp the analogy, that it is as (1) the man who is building is to the builder who is not building at present, and (2) what is awake is to what is asleep, and (3) what is seeing to what has its eyes shut but has sight, and (4) what has been separated out of the matter to the matter, and (5) the finished article to the raw material worked. Let actuality be set down as one side of this division and let potentiality be the other.
>
> But things are not all said to exist actually in the same way, but by analogy— "as this is in that (or to that), so this is in that (or to that)" for the relation is either that of movement to potentiality, or of substance to some particular matter.[25]

Here Aristotle first draws attention to the extraordinary variety in the cases in which we can say that A is potentially B, stressing that in the different cases the relation between A and B is surprisingly different: there is a very different relation between the block of wood and the statue that can be made out of it, on the one hand, and that between the man who knows how to build and the man when he is actually building. But despite these differences, these are all clearly cases that everyone will recognize as cases of one overarching concept, which we call "potentiality".

---

[25]   *Meta.*, IX 1048a 39–1048b. If I understand him correctly, I believe that Erich Przywara's understanding of Aristotle's account of analogy goes badly astray through his misinterpretation of what Aristotle is claiming in this passage. On p.115 of *Analogia Entis*, he interprets Aristotle as claiming in the second paragraph of this quotation that there is an analogy between a potentiality and the corresponding actuality. It is, however, clear that what Aristotle is saying is that you can see an analogy between different cases of the relation of potentiality to actuality. In so far as I can understand Przywara's way of reading the passage at all, he is seeking authority in Aristotle for treating the kind of "focal meaning" that I shall examine in the next chapter as an instance of analogy. In a way, Przywara's mistake here is understandable, since the relation between potentiality and actuality does form the basis for very interesting cases of focal meaning, where words that have their primary application to describe an actuality have a secondary application to describe that which has the potentiality for that actuality. (For instance, by a "tennis player" we can either mean someone who is now actually playing tennis, or someone who knows how to play tennis.)

How then do we arrive at such a concept? Aristotle first warns us against seeking a definition. Most plausibly, this is because it is too primitive a concept to be analysed in terms of anything simpler.[26] Instead, he proposes that we survey a range of cases in which we say that A is potentially B:

1. This block of marble is potentially a statue.
2. This acorn is potentially an oak tree.
3. This builder is potentially someone actually building a house.
4. This man looking the wrong way is potentially someone seeing the Eiffel Tower.
5. This kitten is potentially sighted.

As we move from case to case, the relation of potentiality to actuality is surprisingly different ("things are not all said to exist actually in the same way"): the marble can be made into a statue, the acorn will naturally grow into an oak tree, the builder has acquired the skills necessary for building, and so on. Yet Aristotle is inviting us to see an analogy between all these different cases, and to abstract from them a more general relation, which we may express by "A is potentially B".

We have here a different kind of linguistic application of analogy from that which we have looked at so far. Hitherto, we have been concerned with introducing a word that is applicable to a range of analogically related objects (the legs of a dog, an insect, a centipede, a bird …). Here, however, we are concerned with introducing a word for the analogical relation itself. We first directly recognize that, despite the great individual differences between them, these cases are analogous. It is that recognition, and that recognition alone, that is used to identify and name the analogical relation itself, the "R" in "ARB = CRD". It is natural to think that to establish the existence of an analogy one must first settle how to interpret the formula "A is to B as C is to D"—the value of "R" in "ARB = CRD", and only then will one be in a position to state that A is analogous to B. Indeed, in many of the cases we have looked at so far, this is the case. Here, however, the reverse happens. We only succeed in identifying the relation that underpins the analogy by a direct perception of the analogy itself.

This example introduces something that turns out to be one of the deepest and most puzzling features of analogy, particularly of those analogies that most concern us —analogy across categories or between things that are remote. If we say "A is to B as C is to D", we are committed to saying that the relation of A to B

---

[26] As so often with fundamental concepts in philosophy, you rapidly discover that any attempt to define the concept results in circularity. For instance, if we say that A is potentially B if and only if A can be transformed into B, the only way to explain the relevant sense of "can" involved will be in terms of potentiality. Clearly, when we say that a builder *can* build a house we are making a stronger claim than that it is logically possible that he should do so. It is, however, impossible to specify that stronger claim without appeal to the concept of potentiality.

is the *same* as the relation of C to D, and yet we frequently encounter cases where A and C are different in kind, in such a way that it seems just as difficult to say that A and C can stand in the same relation as to say that A and C have the same property as each other. This problem is often unnoticed and I shall return to this problem in the final chapter. For now, I shall just mention two places where the problem is tackled in two very different ways.

Talking about the relation of God to the world, Kant says:

> In the way that a watch, a ship, and a regiment are related to an artisan, a builder, and a commander, the sensible world (or everything that makes up the bases of this sum total of appearances) is related to the unknown.[27]

He then goes on to say that analogy "signifies ... *a perfect similarity* [*eine vollkomme Ähnlichkeit*] between two relations in wholly dissimilar things".[28] The question inevitably arises, "Can we really say that the relation of God to the world is the *same* relation as the relation of an artisan to a watch?" Kant's answer, which I shall return to in Chapter 5, is to appeal to his distinction between schematized and unschematized categories. Although the schematized (temporal) relation of cause and effect that holds between the artisan and the watch could not hold between God and the world, the *same* unschematized relation of cause and effect (that of ground to consequent) could, and it is the latter relation that can be used to interpret the analogy.

In his book, *The World of Imagery*, Stephen Brown, discussing the metaphor "You are the light of the world",[29] writes:

> The apostles as preachers cause enlightenment, light causes enlightenment. But two different species of enlightenment, the one physical, the other intellectual or spiritual; and two correspondingly different kinds of causality (physical and moral) are involved. This may be expressed in the form of two proportions, thus:—
>
> (1) The Apostles as preachers of Christianity (a): the "enlightenment" of men's minds and hearts (b) :: cause (c): effect (e)
> (2) Light (x): the lighting up of surrounding objects (y) :: cause (c^1): effect (e^1)
>   ...
> Accordingly it brings together, equates, the two proportions, and we get a proportion of proportions.
>
> $(a/x)/(c/c^1) = (b/y)/(e/ e^1)$.[30]

---

[27]   *Prolegomena*, p.146 (Ak. 4:357).

[28]   *Prolegomena*, pp.146–147 (Ak. 4:357); my italics.

[29]   Matt. v, 14.

[30]   *The World of Imagery*, p.72. (On p.71, Father Brown cited Suarez as making a similar proposal.)

Where Kant had interpreted the analogy by finding a more abstract relation that could hold between the disparate terms, Brown piles analogy upon analogy. Despite the extraordinary difficulty in interpreting what his final formula actually means, he is in effect saying that although there is not the same relation between the apostles and the world as that between a light and its environment, there are analogous relations.

I shall return in the final chapter to look again at these two alternative approaches to the problem we encounter here.

Final Comments, Metaphor and the Analogy of Names

We may bring together the ideas of this chapter by returning to the question that I raised above (p.61): does the word "calm" as applied to weather and to states of mind have one sense or several? Or, is it perhaps used metaphorically when we talk of a calm mind?

As we have seen, Aristotle claims both that successful metaphors are based on analogy and that analogy can be used to explain one of the ways in which words can "be said in many ways". There is a strong case for both claims. However, the fact that analogy underlies *both* these uses of language has led a number of authors to assimilate the two cases, and treat the word "analogy", at least in its linguistic application, as a synonym for "metaphor". Aristotle himself, however, clearly regards these as two different phenomena.

Differentiating the two cases is, however, quite a subtle business. Cajetan, for example, struggles to clarify the distinction, calling the metaphorical case, "the analogy of improper proportionality" and the other case, "the analogy of proper proportionality". However, his account seems to be circular, explaining what is meant by "improper" in terms of metaphor, and vice versa.[31] In modern times, the work of George Lakoff is marked by a failure to draw any distinction, with the result that metaphor is discovered in the most unlikely places, as when we are said to be using metaphor when we talk of winning or losing arguments.[32]

The best way to throw light on the distinctions that are to be made here is to see what is at stake in making one decision rather than another in the concrete case. We saw above that in the case of the word "calm", as used to talk of a calm sea and a calm mind, there seemed to be three possible ways of regarding this use of the same word in very different contexts. We might say (1), following Archytas'

---

[31] See *The Analogy of Names*, §§.25, 75–76. In fairness to Cajetan, his remark that "[metaphorically] analogous terms ... resemble terms that are analogous by analogy of attribution" (§76) is a suggestive insight. The point is that, just as there would be no point in describing the climate as healthy were it not for its relation to healthy animals, so there is no point in describing a meadow as smiling (Aquinas' example) were it not for its relation to a smiling face.

[32] See, for instance, Lakoff and Johnson, *Metaphors We Live by.*

lead, that there was a single sense of the word "calm" that was applicable to a wide range of analogically related phenomena, or (2) that the word "calm" had two senses, the second of which was an analogical extension of the first, or, finally (3) that in talking of a calm mind we were talking figuratively (which presumably means metaphorically here). At that stage, however, I gave no indication how one would decide between these different possibilities. It looked in fact a matter of arbitrary choice, which of these three possibilities we adopted.

To see what is really at issue here, we need to engage in the exegesis of a text where these three possibilities confront us, and see what differences emerge between them. We may take here Darwin's use of the word "select" as he uses it in the *Origin of Species*, in talking both of artificial (human) selection and natural selection. It is clear that, *somehow*, Darwin is using such words as "select" and "struggle" in an innovative way. How are we to understand such innovation?[33] We may look in turn at the three ways of interpreting his text.

1. Darwin is speaking metaphorically when he talks of nature selecting.

    In favour of this: if we regard the talk of selection as metaphorical, we keep alive the comparison with farmers selecting; we can explore such comparisons ever further: metaphor is a readily extensible phenomenon, and we can instantly produce such sentences as "It may be said that natural selection is daily and hourly scrutinizing, throughout the world, every variation, even the slightest; rejecting that which is bad, preserving and adding up all that is good."[34] We do not have to suppose that in addition to "select" acquiring a special meaning, so too does "scrutinize". We talk of nature as though we were talking of a farmer, and then continue to do so.

    Against this: it is tricky to handle arguments involving metaphor. An argument's validity depends on the words having a single sense throughout, and it is difficult to see what is going on in an argument whose premise has the word "select" applied literally to Man, and a conclusion in which the word is applied metaphorically to Nature.

2. Darwin is introducing a new concept of selection that is applicable to both Nature and Man. The word "select" is used throughout the *Origin* to refer to that concept, whether speaking of Nature or Man. This would follow Archytas' proposal that we could use analogy to define new concepts,

---

[33]   There is no need to suppose that Darwin himself would have been able to give a worked out answer to such a question. We may, however, note that in Chapter 3 of the *Origin*, talking about the word "struggle", Darwin says: "I should premise that I use this term in a large and *metaphorical* sense including dependence of one being on another, and including (which is more important) not only the life of the individual, but success in leaving progeny" (my italics). There is, of course, no reason to ascribe to Darwin a fully considered theory of metaphor here, or to treat his claim that "struggle" is used metaphorically as authoritative.

[34]   *Origin*, Chapter 4.

grouping together as falling under a single concept a range of analogically related phenomena. The advantages and disadvantages of regarding the word "select" in this way are the converse of those for metaphor.

In favour of this: this way of regarding the word "select" is required for many of the central arguments of the *Origin*, specifically for those arguments that have premises concerning what happens when humans select to conclusions about what will happen when Nature selects. There are also passages in which Nature and Man are talked of as selecting in the same sentence: what sense could we make of the claim that Nature was a more efficient selector than Man, if the word "select" had a different sense when talking of Nature selecting from that which it has in a human context?

Against this: the comparison with human selection moves into the background when talking of Nature selecting, and it is ill suited to making the kind of explorations of that comparison that Darwin undertakes.

3. The word "select" as applied to Nature is used in a special, technical, sense for use in biology, this sense being an analogical extension of its sense in human applications.

In favour of this: biologists can go about their work in talking about evolution by natural selection, without worrying whether what they say when they talk about selection would be equally applicable to everyday cases of human selection.

Against this: this is only possible once the theory of evolution by Natural Selection is well established and understood. It cannot be used in first introducing the theory. It would therefore be anachronistic to read such a use back into the text of the *Origin* itself. One also clearly loses the advantages of (1) and (2). (This last point is essentially the same point as had been made by Duns Scotus in his objection to regarding "being" as applied to God being used in a special, analogically extended, sense. And we may generalize the point at issue: what could we make of a passage such as Mark 10:18: "Jesus said to him, "Why do you call me good? No one is good except one—God", unless the word "good" has a single sense that is equally applicable (truly or falsely) to God and human beings?).

A detailed reading of the text of the *Origin* shows Darwin oscillating between the first and the second of these three possibilities. Interestingly, this never creates any difficulty, except when it confuses people into thinking that Darwin is committed to regarding Nature literally as Demeter, as some kind of supervisory goddess.

What reflection on this example shows is that the question we looked at earlier, "Does a word such as 'calm', when we talk both of a calm sea and a calm mind, have one sense, or two senses—an original sense and an analogically extended sense—or is it perhaps only metaphorically that we talk of a mind as calm?", seemed intractable because we were looking at it independently of a particular context in which the word was being used. Each of the possible answers to that question is a genuine possibility, and it depends upon the particular occasion on which it is being used, which answer is the most appropriate.

We cannot, that is to say, give a *general* answer to the question, "When Darwin uses the word 'select' does it have one or more than one sense, or is Darwin speaking metaphorically?" In some contexts it is appropriate to give one answer to that question, in another context, another. The question only gains real purchase if we leave on one side the general question, and instead turn to the question how the word is functioning in each specific context in which it is used.

Chapter 4
Thomas Aquinas

The "Analogy of Attribution"

In order to understand Thomas Aquinas' account of analogy and religious language, we depart temporarily from the understanding of the word "analogy" that we have been following so far. Among mediaeval theologians "*analogia*" became a generic term, covering all cases where a word was used in many different ways, but where it was not by chance that the same word was used. For this, we must return to Aristotle.

Aristotle, Metaphysics *IV, 1003a 33–1003b 18*

First let us look again at this passage from the *Nicomachean Ethics*:

> But in what way are different things called "good"? For they do not seem to be called by the same word by chance homonymy. Possibly they are all called "good" because they derive from one good, or all contribute to one good. Or perhaps they are called "good" by analogy: for as sight is good in the body, so is reason in the soul, and similarly another thing in something else.[1]

Aristotle offers us here two different patterns for a word being used in different ways but not "by chance homonymy". Authors such as Aquinas will call both these different ways cases of "*analogia*". Since the two cases function very differently I believe this broad use of the term to be unhelpful and liable to lead to unclarity as to the precise force to be attached to the term in interpreting particular passages, and I prefer Aristotle's usage. Both in this chapter and in subsequent discussions, however, there is little alternative but to go along with mediaeval usage.

In the last two chapters, we have seen that throughout Aristotle's writings he devotes great attention to what he calls "analogy". By comparison, his other pattern is only occasionally mentioned. There is, however, one discussion of it that is of major importance, and which is indeed crucial for understanding both Aristotle's own conception of metaphysics and the mediaeval discussions of analogy:

> A thing may be said to "be" in many ways, [Τὸ δὲ ὂν λέγεται μὲν πολλαχῶς] but all with reference to one thing, one particular kind of thing, and is not said to "be" by mere homonomy. Just as everything which is "healthy" has reference to

---

[1] *NE*, I 1096b 28.

health, one thing in that it preserves health, another in that it produces it, another in that it is a symptom of health, another because it is capable of it. And that which is "medical" has reference to the art of medicine, one thing being called medical because it possesses it, another because it is naturally adapted to it, another because it is a function of the medical art. And we shall find other words used similarly to these. So, too, there are many ways in which a thing is said to be, but all refer to one starting-point; some things are said to be because they are substances, others because they are affections of substance, others because they are a process towards substance, or destructions or privations or qualities of substance, or productive or generative of substance, or of things which are relative to substance, or negations of one of substance itself. It is for this reason that we say even of non-being that it *is* non-being. As, then, there is one science which deals with everything that we call healthy, the same applies in the other cases also. For it is not only in the case of things which share one common nature that the investigation belongs to one science, but also in the case of things which are related to one common nature; for in a sense even these have one common notion. It is clear then that it is the work of one science also to study being, *qua* being.–But in all cases a science deals chiefly with that which is primary, and on which the other things depend, and in virtue of which they are called what they are. If, then, this is substance, it will be of substances that the philosopher must grasp the principles and the causes.[2]

G. E. L. Owen[3] traces the development in Aristotle's thought up to this passage from a text in the *Eudemian Ethics* where Aristotle argues, against Plato, that there cannot be a science of being in general in view of the extraordinary variety amongst the different things that we wish to say exist: we would, for instance, have to give a completely different account of what it was for a man to be from that which we would give of his grin's being. Because of this, we could only work at the level of abstractness and generality required for a science of being qua being by using all our key terms in such a way that they only applied ambiguously to different things, so that we only create the illusion of a single, unified, science. But by the time that he comes to write the passage just quoted from the *Metaphysics*, Aristotle has concluded that there can nevertheless be a science of being qua being, despite the great diversity of things that we wish to say are. Although things may be said to be in many different ways, it is not a matter of chance ambiguity when we say of all of them that they are. In this way, although there cannot be the sort of homogeneous science of being qua being that he had attacked in the *Eudemian Ethics*, there could be such a science that studied the relationships between the different things that we say are.

The pattern that Aristotle is proposing in the *Metaphysics* for this case of "words being used in many ways" is that we have a primary or basic use of the word,

---

[2]   *Meta.*, IV 1003a 33–1003b 18.

[3]   In "Logic and Metaphysics in Some Earlier Works of Aristotle".

together with a range of secondary uses, where the secondary uses are explained by their relation to the primary use, but not vice versa. Thus, to take his example, we may talk of "healthy cows", a "healthy climate", a "healthy complexion", "healthy urine", "healthy teeth" and so on. Here the primary application of the word "healthy" is to plants and animals—they are what are "really" healthy, and the other things in the list are called "healthy" because they are all in one way or another related to the health of plants or animals. The healthy climate is such as to foster health in animals; a healthy complexion is a sign of health in its host and so on. What is characteristic of this case is a definite ordering of priority and posteriority, which is clear enough in the case of health. Unless we talked of the health of plants and animals, there would be no point or sense in using the word "healthy" to describe the other things mentioned. This phenomenon illustrated by the word "healthy" has been called by various names such as the analogy of attribution, *per prius et posterius*, and, by G. E. L. Owen, "focal meaning".

There is no generally agreed terminology here. In particular, the phrase "analogy of attribution" is sometimes restricted to cases such as "healthy" where calling a climate "healthy" does not imply anything about the *intrinsic* properties of the climate. For my purposes, however, in what follows I shall use the term "analogy of attribution" as a generic term, covering all cases where we have a primary use of a word, and secondary uses that are explained in terms of that primary use.

Some Examples

Aristotle's example of healthy (ὑγιεινός) provides us with an excellent introduction to the idea he is after here. This example is, however, so extensively appealed to in later discussions that it is treated as *the* paradigm case of an analogy of attribution. This is potentially misleading, since there are a number of features of the case of "healthy" that may be taken to be essential to the idea of the analogy of attribution but that are in fact only features of this particular case and by no means essential to the general idea of the analogy of attribution. It is worth mentioning three characteristics of the case of "healthy" in particular that are by no means characteristic of analogy of attribution in general.

1. It is natural to spell out the case of healthy in *causal* terms: a healthy climate causes health in animals, a healthy complexion is caused by the health of the person with that complexion, and so on. In a large number of cases, however, the relation between the primary application of the word and the secondary applications cannot be seen in causal terms at all—no matter how broadly we construe the notion of causality. I believe the insistence on the part of Thomist theologians on interpreting the analogy of attribution in causal terms seriously distorts the discussion here.[4] As we shall see,

---

[4]   Consider, for instance, Cajetan's division of the analogy of attribution: "This type of analogy can come about in four ways, according to the four genera of causes (we will for

Aquinas does spell out his account of analogical naming of God in such causal terms, but it is not the only way in which the analogy of attribution could be made to account for religious language, and it is not even the most promising way.

2. "Healthy" presents us with a very clear case of "extrinsic denomination". That is to say, the *only* reason for describing a climate as healthy is its relation to the health of animals. Considered purely in itself there is nothing healthy about the climate, and it neither shares any obvious properties with, nor has the slightest resemblance to, a healthy animal. (A criminal lawyer is not necessarily a criminal, and a Foreign Secretary will not be foreign.) It is precisely for this reason that the analogy of attribution can look an unpromising basis for religious language.[5]

3. Although it is entirely natural and comprehensible that we should use the word "healthy" in this range of different ways, it appears a relatively superficial and dispensable feature of our language. It is easy to imagine a language in which there was no word corresponding to healthy with all these different uses, but, say, a word corresponding to "healthy" for describing animals and a phrase that transliterated as "health giving" for climates. In the cases that are of potential philosophical or theological interest, it is characteristically not obvious whether or how we could avoid using the same word in different ways.

The aim of this chapter is to explore the way that Aquinas will make use of this form of analogy in his account of the way in which we can use human language to ascribe perfections to God. As a preliminary to that, it is worthwhile to free ourselves from the misleading aspects of the case of "healthy" and to obtain a feel for the diversity of the ways in which such an analogy can work, by briefly surveying a range of examples of the analogy of attribution, many of them much closer to the cases that ultimately interest us than is "healthy".

1. *"Railway track", "railway ticket", "railway guard", and so on*: this example may be used to indicate how the phenomenon Aristotle draws attention to is widespread in our everyday use of language. We have a

---

the moment call the exemplary cause the formal cause)" (*NA*, p.15).

[5]   This was one of the principal reasons for Cajetan's preference for the "analogy of proper proportionality" in his account of religious language. In fact, having insisted that the analogy of attribution is "according to extrinsic denomination", he seems to tie himself in knots trying to undo the damage that that would do to his account: "It should be carefully noted that this first condition of this mode of analogy, namely, that it is not according to the genus of inherent formal causality, but always according to something extrinsic, must be understood formally and not materially" (*NA*, p.17). As Cajetan was well aware, it was precisely at this point that Aquinas had carefully differentiated the case of "healthy" from the cases that interested him (*On the Sentences* ... I, dist. 19 q. 5a . 2 *ad* 1).

primary use of the word "railway" to describe the track, and an open-ended list of other uses to describe things that are, in one way or another, related to the railway track. (A railway ticket grants one access to the railway track, and so on). The second point of this example is to show that, despite Cajetan's "division of the analogy of attribution" quoted in footnote 4, few, if any, of the relations between the primary application of the word "railway" and its secondary applications can be explained in causal terms, no matter how broadly we construe the notion of cause.

It is also important to note that even with an everyday example such as this, all the different things for which we use the word "railway" belong together. Just as Aristotle notes that all the various things that we call "healthy" are treated by a single science, so too, it would be appropriate for a history of the railways to mention all the different things that we call "railway".

2. *Tokens and types*: let us consider the most familiar example of the type/token distinction. We say both that an article was 6,000 words long, and that the author used 250 different words in the article. In the first instance, we are counting words as tokens, in the second, words as types. Of these two different ways of using the word "word", it is the word as type that is the primary application, and the word as token that is the secondary application: what makes the particular sound that we make when we utter a word a token of that word is the fact that it is produced *as* a token of that type of word.

3. *Geometrical terms*: geometrical terms such as straight, circle and square have a perfectly straightforward empirical employment and are also used by geometers themselves. It is quite correct to describe a cushion as circular, buildings as rectangular or to say that village A is twice as far from village B as village C. At the same time, we readily concede that the cushion isn't perfectly circular, and indeed, given any empirical exemplar, that it falls short of the ideal represented by the concept used. On the other hand, when the geometer talks of a straight line, it makes no sense to say that perhaps the line is not perfectly straight. In this way, we have two uses of these terms. Of these it is the geometer's use which is the primary application, and the empirical employment secondary, since we explain the empirical use of these terms as approximations to the standards set by the geometrical use. This case is particularly important for our present enquiry for two reasons. Firstly, because this is a case where it is plausible to assume that people will master and learn to use the terms in their secondary application and it will only be by a subsequent act of reflection upon that secondary application that they arrive at their primary application: as we shall see, this initially paradoxical idea is crucial for what follows. Secondly, because this case is explored by Plato in the *Phaedo*[6] and represents a train of thought

---

[6] *Phaedo*, 74–76.

in Plato that will, even if by a circuitous route, lead to Aquinas' doctrine of analogous names.

4. *Representations*: this is one of the clearest and most straightforward cases of the analogy of attribution. We use the same vocabulary to talk about sculptures, paintings and other representations as we do to talk about the subjects of those representations. It is a case where we have no alternative but to do so. We cannot describe the lions in Trafalgar Square without using the word "lion", or describe a naturalistic painting save by describing what is represented. The other point to note about this case is that although it is clearly a case of what Cajetan called "extrinsic denomination"—we call the lion in Trafalgar Square a lion solely in virtue of its relation to real lions—this does not rule out there being a resemblance between the analogates, or its being essential to the analogy that there should be such resemblance.

5. *Visual imagery*: we ascribe the same colour words both to our visual sensations and to objects in the world, talking of a "red afterimage" and "a red pillar box". It is interesting in this case that deciding which of these two ways of speaking is the primary application of the word "red" and which the secondary raises difficult philosophical issues. Is a red visual sensation explained as one that is such as would be caused by a red object, or a red object, one such as to cause red sensations? For our purposes, a significant question to raise about this case is "Can we talk of a *resemblance* between something and our idea of it?" On the one hand, it seems nonsense to say that a red afterimage resembles a red flower,[7] but on the other hand, in the case of complex imagery, it seems appropriate to talk of at least a structural resemblance between the image and what it is an image of. We have here an instance of a phenomenon that will be important later—that of what is called by Aquinas "exemplary causation".

6. *"Being"?*: given its central status in Aristotle's discussion, this case should be included, but it is not altogether clear how it is meant to work. Obviously Aristotle is giving *ontological* priority to substance: Socrates' grin is dependent on Socrates for its existence and for Socrates' grin to exist is for Socrates to be grinning. We are, however, here concerned with a linguistic thesis concerning "*words* being used in many ways".[8] How this thesis is supposed to run is certainly not as straightforward as was the case for "healthy", or any of the other cases we have listed. Perhaps the thought is that a claim that Socrates' grin exists is more properly expressed as the claim that Socrates exists in a certain way, or that any claim about Socrates' grin can be reduced to a claim in which Socrates is the subject.

---

7 *Cf.* Berkeley, Treatise §9: "an idea can be like nothing but another idea".

8 Ontological pluralism—the claim that there exist radically different kinds of entity—is clearly distinguishable from the claim that the word "exist" is used with a different meaning when talking about such different entities.

7. *A possible red herring*: there are cases where we select one object as a paradigm case of being F, and explain what it is for other objects to be F by their relation to that paradigm: we may think of the use of type specimens in biological taxonomy, or the metre rule in Paris. A stick is one-metre long if it is the same length as the metre rule. Here we *appear* to have an ordering of priority and posteriority. However, the metre rule is a metre long in precisely the same sense as the stick. (It is as long as itself.) In this way, the mere fact that we explain what it is for B to be F by citing the relation of B to A is insufficient to establish that we have a case of the analogy of attribution.

Priority and Posteriority

The key idea here is that of one thing being prior to another, but this idea needs careful handling. Partly this is because in the cases that will interest us it requires difficult reflection to determine which of two things is prior and partly because there are many different senses in which one thing may be said to be prior to another. These two reasons are not independent: one reason it can require subtle reasoning to determine which of two things is prior is that it is frequently tempting to infer fallaciously that because a thing is prior in one sense it must also be prior in other senses also.

We can see something of the complexity involved in deciding which of two uses of a word is primary and which is secondary if we return to the case of word tokens and word types. Suppose, as I argued, that the primary application of the word "word" was to refer to word types rather than word tokens. When, however, we turn from the word "word" itself to the vocabulary we use to talk about words, we use the same basic vocabulary to describe both words-as-tokens and words-as-types. We can say of the word "heard" that it rhymes with "bird", whether we are thinking of the word types or two particular tokens of those types. Here we are talking about the sounds of the words, and the only sense we can give to ascribing a sound to a word type is to say that this is how tokens of that type will sound, the primary application of the word "rhyme" is in the description of word tokens, and the secondary in the description of types. On the other hand, if we say that the word "type" comes from the Greek "τύπος", that is naturally taken as referring in the first instance to the word type and only secondarily to its tokens. In this way, what counts as a primary and what a secondary use of these words alternates, depending on whether we are principally thinking of the word as an abstract object or of its physical characteristics.

Let us next consider Aristotle's surveys of the complex network of senses of the terms "prior" (πρότερος) and "posterior" (ὕστερος) at *Categories*, 14a 26–14b 9 and *Metaphysics* V 1018b 9–1019a 14. At *Metaphysics* 1018b 10–13, he first gives a generic account:

> Since in each genus something is primary and the origin, something may be
> prior from being nearer a certain origin, defined either baldly and by its nature or
> with reference to a certain thing or somewhere or by certain people.[9]

He then goes on to show the wide variety of ways in which we may talk of one
thing being prior to another. There are, however, four senses of priority that
Aristotle emphasizes and that recur in his writings. These are also the ones that
we may take as the most basic senses, and that are most important for our present
enquiry.[10] A may be prior to B (1) temporally, (2) in definition, (3) in knowledge
and (4) ontologically:

1. A is temporally prior to B, if B occurs after A, or, possibly, B *cannot* occur
   until A has occurred.
2. A is prior in definition to B, if to give an account of what B is you must
   mention A, but not vice versa.
3. A is prior in knowledge to B, if you cannot learn about B unless you already
   know about A, but not vice versa.
4. A is ontologically prior to B, if B cannot exist unless A exists, but not vice
   versa, or if B is dependent for its existence on A, but not vice versa.

Thus, there cannot be railway tickets until there are railway tracks; you explain
what a railway ticket is in terms of its relation to a railway track, but need not
mention railway tickets in explaining what a railway track is; and you cannot
know that this is a railway ticket without knowing how it relates to a railway track;
and so on. In a large number of cases, as here, these different sorts of priority fit
naturally together, with what is prior in one sense also being prior in others.[11]
However, apart from the fact that if A is ontologically prior to B, B clearly cannot

---

9   Rather ironically, this general definition does not seem to fit what at *Cat.* 14a 27
Aristotle describes as "'prior' in its proper and primary sense"—that of earlier in time, since
for Aristotle time had no beginning, there was no origin to be close to or distant from, and
at *Meta.* V 1018b 14–19 he is forced to give an account that is back to front: the prior time
is that which is *furthest* from a designated point, *i.e.* the present.

10   I should also mention as possibly in the background in the present discussion
the use that Aristotle mentions at *Cat.* 14b 3–9 as the strangest use of all: "Besides the
three senses we have mentioned, whatever is better or more highly esteemed is said to be
naturally prior."

11   *Cf. Meta.*, VII 1028a 31–b1: "Now there are several senses in which a thing is said
to be prior; yet substance is prior in every sense—(1) in order of definition, (2) in order of
knowledge, (3) in order of time. For none of the other categories can exist independently,
but only substance. And this is first in definition too, for in the definition of each term the
definition of its substance must be present. And we think we know each thing most fully,
when we know what it is, e.g. what man is or what fire is, rather than when we know its
quality, its quantity, or its place; since we know each of these predicates also, only when we
know what the quantity or the quality is."

be temporally prior to A, these are logically distinct notions, and it is in general impossible simply to infer that because something is prior to something else in one sense, it must also be prior in other senses. It is, in particular, important in this whole discussion to keep distinct the claim that something is ontologically or metaphysically prior and the claim that it is prior in definition. Whether we are talking about metaphysical priority or linguistic priority, however, is what frequently turns out to be one of the most difficult issues to resolve, both in itself and in the interpretation of Aquinas.

Equally tricky is distinguishing "prior in knowledge or acquaintance" and "prior in definition". At first sight, these two seem to collapse into one another: how can B be defined in terms of A, and yet it be possible to know about B before knowing about A? In some important cases, however, the relation between the two priorities can be much more complicated than that would suggest.

These cases include one of Aquinas' most interesting and significant claims. As we shall see, he makes the apparently paradoxical claim that although it is inevitable that, when we master our language, our first use of that language is in the description of terrestrial phenomena, the primary application of the words for the divine perfections—just, wise, merciful and so on—is in talking about God and not His creatures. Thus the order of primacy in knowledge and of primacy in definition is here reversed.

As a preliminary to looking at that, we may consider an analogous case in Aristotle:

> Things are prior and better known in two ways; for it is not the same to be prior
> by nature and prior in relation to us, nor to be better known and better known
> by us. I call prior and better known by us what is nearer to perception, prior and
> better known *simpliciter* what is further away. What is most universal is furthest
> away, and the particulars are nearest; and these are opposite to each other.[12]

This is a somewhat obscure passage, but I may illustrate what I take to be Aristotle's meaning by considering the related case of word tokens and word types, where I have argued that the primary application of the word "word" was to refer to word types not word tokens. However, when a child learns a language, its initial encounter is with word tokens, not word types. It is these that it hears and uses, and it is only by hearing and using word tokens that it can eventually acquire the idea of a word type. There is no direct route to the idea of a word type that bypasses the initial handling of word tokens. A child grasps the idea of a word type by subsequent reflection upon its use of word tokens. So that even if we insist that the notion of a word type is prior in definition to that of a word token, arriving at the concept of a word type necessarily requires a prior acquaintance with word tokens.

---

[12] *PostA*, 71b 35–72a 5. (Here I have substituted "better known" for his "more familiar" throughout in what is otherwise Jonathan Barnes' translation.)

Some Developments in Aquinas' Thought on Analogy and Divine Names

*Initial Explorations (*Quaestiones disputatae de Veritate *and the* Commentary on Boethius' "de Trinitate"*)*

As George Klubertanz has brought out,[13] there is considerable progression in Aquinas' thought on analogy and it is important to pay attention to the chronology of his works in interpreting him.[14] The most dramatic change between the *Quaestiones disputatae de Veritate* and his later work is that in the earlier work, he weighs the merits of two different kinds of analogical predication—on the one hand, what I am calling the "analogy of attribution":

> There is a certain agreement between things having a proportion [*proportio*] to each other from the fact that they have a determinate distance between each other or some other relation to each other, like the proportion which the number two has to unity in so far as it is the double of unity.[15]

and on the other hand, what Aristotle meant by analogy, and what Aquinas calls proportionality (*proportionalitas*):

> The agreement is occasionally noted not between two things which have a proportion between them, but rather between two related proportions—for example, six has something in common with four because six is two times three, just as four is two times two.[16]

Aquinas then finds that if we are concerned with predicating something analogously of God and creatures, the analogy of attribution is wanting, and that only proportionality will serve:

> In those terms predicated analogously of two realities according to the first type of analogy, there must be some definite relation between the things having something in common analogously. Consequently, nothing can be predicated analogously of God and creature according to this type of analogy; for no creature has such a relation to God that it could determine the divine perfection.[17]

---

[13]   See G. Klubertanz, *St. Thomas Aquinas on Analogy*.

[14]   If Cajetan is an unreliable interpreter of Aquinas on analogy, it looks very much as if the main reason for this is that he is treating the early work, *dV*, as normative for his understanding of Aquinas.

[15]   *dV*, p.113.

[16]   Ibid.

[17]   Ibid.

Clearly everything hangs on the interpretation of this passage, and in particular the first sentence.[18] Whatever can be said for or against the use of the analogy of attribution in this context, this is a bad argument, as Aquinas was himself soon to come to see. In his *Commentary on Boethius' "de Trinitate"*, he writes:

> Things can be understood to agree in two ways: first from the fact they belong to the same genus of quantity or quality, like the relation of surface to surface or of number to number, insofar as one is greater than the other or equal to it, or the relation of one heat to another. In this sense there can be no proportion between God and creatures because they do not share a common genus. Second, things can be said to agree from the fact that they fit into some order. In this sense we understand the proportion between matter and form, maker and thing made, and other things of this sort. This kind of proportion is needed between the knower and the knowable object, because the knowable object is a sort of actuality of the knowing power. And in this sense there is also a proportion of creatures to God, as the effect to its cause, and the knower to the knowable object. However, owing to the infinite transcendence of the Creator over the creature, there is no proportion of the creature to the Creator such that the creature receives the full power of His influence or knows Him perfectly, as He perfectly knows Himself.[19]

Aquinas had been misled in *de Veritate* by thinking in terms of the mathematical notions of *proportio* and *proportionalitas*. If you translate "*proportio*" as "ratio" and "*proportionalitas*" as "analogy" (used in its original mathematical sense), what Aquinas had said would make perfect sense. If we return to the explanations from Euclid that I looked at in Chapter 1, a ratio was there defined as a certain relation between magnitudes *of the same kind*, and one of the reasons for advancing beyond the simple notion of ratio to the more complicated notion of analogy was that the latter, unlike the former, did permit trans-categorial comparisons—between magnitudes that were different in kind. Since there is no genus common to God and man, it would make no sense to talk of the *ratio* of God to a creature—of the infinite to the finite—but it might make sense to compare the ratio between two infinite beings to that between two finite beings.

But, of course, if we are concerned with the language we use to talk about God, the notion of a ratio in any strict sense is misplaced, and we have to interpret "*proportio*" in such a way as to cover a range of other relations, and there is no good reason to suppose that the restrictions upon what could be related introduced by the notion of ratio would still apply.

As Aquinas' thought progresses, proportionality will move more and more into the background, and "proportion", or the analogy of attribution, will become the

---

[18] "Quia ergo in his quae primo modo analogice dicuntur, oportet esse aliquam determinatam habitudinem inter ea quibus est aliquid per analogiam commune."

[19] *BT*, p.23.

dominant idea. We can gain an initial idea of the way in which Aquinas' thought will develop if we consider another passage, also from his commentary on Boethius' *de Trinitate*, where he gives an account of our knowledge of God.

> Now we can consider from three points of view the relation in an effect that falls short of equality with its cause: with respect to the coming forth of the effect from the cause, with respect to the effect acquiring a likeness to its cause, and with respect to its falling short of perfectly acquiring it. So the human mind advances in three ways in knowing God, though it does not reach a knowledge of what He is, but only that He is: first, by knowing more perfectly His power in producing things, second, by knowing Him as the cause of the more lofty effects which, because they bear some resemblance to Him, give more praise to His greatness, and third, by an ever-growing knowledge of Him as distant from everything that appears in His effects. Thus Dionysius says that we know God as the cause of all things, by transcendence, and by negation.[20]

We have here an epistemological theory of our knowledge of God based upon a metaphysical theory of God and His relation to the world. We posit God as the transcendent cause of the world we know; we next claim that since an effect resembles its cause, we may posit in God the excellent original of the good properties we find in the world; and finally we recognize that the effects fall short of and are but pale reflexions of their divine cause. For Aquinas, it is grasping this metaphysical theory that makes it possible for us to have such knowledge of God as we have, and also to recognize how severely limited that knowledge is.

It is this theory of our knowledge of God that will in its turn eventually underpin a linguistic theory: how it is possible for our human words to be applied by analogy to God: when we ascribe a perfection to God, we are taking some good feature of the world and regarding the divine perfection as the pre-eminent cause of that good feature, recognizing that the good feature will resemble its divine original, even while falling infinitely short of it.

Analogical Predication *(the* Summa contra Gentiles *and* Quaestiones Disputatae de Potentia Dei*)*

It is in these middle period works that Aquinas' mature theory of analogical predication is worked out. At this stage, I shall attempt simply to expound it, leaving discussion of it until later. There are two main components of the theory to consider: the idea of "causal participation", and the contrast between "univocal causation" and "equivocal causation".

> Effects that fall short of their causes do not agree with them in name and nature. Yet, some likeness must be found between them, since it belongs to the nature

---

   20   *BT*, p.22.

of action that an agent produce its like, since each thing acts according as it is in act. The form of an effect, therefore, is certainly found in some measure in a transcending cause, but according to another mode and another way. For this reason the cause is called an *equivocal* cause. Thus, the Sun causes heat among those sublunary bodies by acting according as it is in act. Hence, the heat generated by the Sun must bear some likeness to the active power of the Sun, through which heat is caused in this sublunary world, and because of this effect the Sun is said to be hot, even though not in one and the same way. And so the Sun is said to be somewhat like those things in which it produces its effects as an efficient cause. Yet the Sun is also unlike all these things in so far as such effects do not possess heat and the like in the same way as they are found in the Sun. So, too, God gave things all their perfections and thereby is both like and unlike all of them.[21]

I shall examine the claim that an effect must resemble its cause in detail later. For now, I shall just sketch what I think is the underlying idea. Consider an entity *A* that is such that it will, under appropriate circumstances, naturally cause an effect *B*. (A fire will normally heat its surroundings.) It will then lie in the nature of *A* to cause *B*, so that an investigation of *A* would reveal something about *A* that makes it prone to cause *B*, and which would be such that an omniscient investigator could predict the occurrence of *B* from the study of *A*. The argument is that this is only possible if *A* resembles *B* in some way, or at the very least, contains within itself something that resembles *B*.

Causation here is seen as a sort of contagion, and indeed a contagious disease provides a simple illustration of the idea. In the case of one person infecting another with a disease, the patient acquires precisely the same disease as was possessed by the person who had the disease originally. This gives us the idea of "univocal" causation. There are, however, a range of cases in which the causal process involves a diminution of the feature that is transmitted from the agent to the patient: the room heated by a fire will be cooler than the fire itself. In particular, there will be cases where the agent is qualitatively different from and in important respects superior to the effect, in such a way that for Aquinas, it is impossible for the agent and the patient to have any properties univocally in common. This brings us to the example of the Sun heating a stone.

To make sense of this example, think of a cosmology in which the heavenly bodies, including the Sun, were seen as immutable and incorruptible, and therefore not having any properties implying mutability or corruptibility in their bearers. The heat that we are familiar with is then seen as a property of sublunary bodies and, as such, could not be a property of the Sun, even though the Sun had the power to generate heat in the bodies we find around us. But in line with the theory of causal participation, the Sun must possess some property which, although not sublunary heat, bore some sort of resemblance to it—a superior version of heat. It would

---

[21]   *SCG* I, Chapter 29, p.138.

be impossible for the Sun to transmit *its* heat to a stone, since the causal process would be restricted by the stone's capacity to receive heat. Because the stone could not tolerate the Sun's heat, the most that it can receive from the Sun is the inferior version of heat with which we are familiar. (Obviously, we ought not to object to the obsolete cosmology involved in this example, which is simply being set up as a model for what Aquinas wants to say about divine causation.)

When we then say that the Sun is hot, we are not ascribing to it the same property as that which we ascribe to the stone. We are ascribing to it that superior property that resembles heat, which enables it to heat the stone. Thus we have here a form of analogy of attribution. The important point to note here, however, is that the case is quite different from that of the healthy climate. When we talk of the climate as healthy, *all* we mean is that the climate is such as to promote health in animals. But in the example that Aquinas offers, we do not mean only that the Sun causes heat in terrestrial bodies, but that it has that pre-eminent heat that enables it to cause the everyday heat with which we are familiar.[22] Whereas, as Cajetan stressed,[23] calling the climate "healthy" is a case of extrinsic denomination and tells us nothing about the intrinsic properties of the climate, when, on Aquinas' account, we call the Sun hot, we are talking of its intrinsic properties. If the Sun, then, has an intrinsic property that resembles the heat of the stone, why not say that we use the word "hot" as a generic term that can be applied univocally to both the Sun and the stone? We can gather Aquinas' answer from what he says of the corresponding case of terms applied both to God and creatures.

> I answer that it is impossible for anything to be predicated univocally of God and a creature: this is made plain as follows. Every effect of a univocal agent is adequate to the agent's power: and no creature, being finite, can be adequate to the power of the first agent which is infinite. Wherefore it is impossible for a creature to receive a likeness to God univocally. Again it is clear that although the form in the agent and the form in the effect have a common ratio, the fact that they have different modes of existence precludes their univocal predication: thus although the material house is of the same type as the house in the mind of the architect, since the one is the type of the other; nevertheless *house* cannot be univocally predicated of both, because the form of the material house has its being in matter, whereas in the architect's mind it has immaterial being. Hence, granted the impossibility that goodness in God and in the creature be of the same kind, nevertheless good would not be predicated of God univocally:

---

22   *Cf.* a passage I shall return to: *ST*, 1a 13, 2: "Nevertheless these words are not used to *mean* His causal acts. 'Living' in 'God is living' does not mean the same as 'causes life'; the sentence is used to say that life does pre-exist in the source of all things, though in a higher way than we can understand or signify."

23   *NA*, pp.16–17, 27.

since that which in God is immaterial and simple, is in the creature material and manifold.[24]

Finally, we may note the following passage:

> Thus, therefore, because we come to a knowledge of God from other things, the reality in the names said of God and other things belongs by priority in God according to His mode of being, but the meaning of the name belongs to God by posteriority. And so He is said to be named from His effects.[25]

The position outlined in this passage seems not only natural, but inevitable. Aquinas had argued that God's perfections have an *ontological* priority over against their human counterparts, but now argues that *linguistically* this priority is reversed. When we master a language, we use it in the first instance to talk about human beings and their empirical environment, and only subsequently come to think and talk about God, redeploying the vocabulary we have learnt in their human context to refer to God and his attributes. Hence, we must explain the use of language to talk about God in terms of the use of that language to talk about His creatures.

What we have here is one of the most significant differences between the *Summa contra Gentiles* and the *Summa Theologiae*. The position I have outlined from the *Summa contra Gentiles* may be described as the "common sense" conception, which we may contrast with the deeper position adopted in the *Summa Theologiae* that I shall turn to next.

The Final Position (the *Summa Theologiae*)

For the most part, the account of analogy that we find in the *Summa Theologiae* follows the account that we have just been looking at in the *Summa contra Gentiles*. I shall therefore concentrate here on one idea that seems the most interesting and significant development in his thought. He now claims *linguistic* priority for the application of words to God.

At the end of the last section, we saw that in the *Summa contra Gentiles* Aquinas put forward an apparently straightforward argument that the primary application of the words we predicate of God was the application of those words to creatures. In the *Summa Theologiae*, his position is altogether more subtle:

> we read in *Ephesians*, "I bow my knees to the Father of our Lord Jesus Christ, from whom all fatherhood in heaven and on earth is named"; and the same seems

---

[24] *dP*, q.7 art.7.
[25] *SCG* I, Chapter 34, p.148.

to apply to other words used of God and creatures. These words are, then, used primarily of God.[26]

The scriptural basis that Aquinas indicates here for his position is strong, and I shall return to it when I come to consider the more radical version of Aquinas' claim presented by Karl Barth. For now, there are two things to consider: how Aquinas meets the obvious objections to his position, and how in detail he conceives this primacy.

I begin by looking at his more nuanced understanding of the idea that was crucial in the *Summa contra Gentiles* presentation: that "God is named from His effects."

> Sometimes that from which a name is derived is different from what it means. Thus, the word "stone" (*lapis*) is derived from the fact that it hurts the foot (*laedit pedem*), but it does not mean something that hurts the foot, but instead to signify a certain kind of body; otherwise everything that hurts the foot would be a stone. In the same way, we may say that these kinds of divine names are derived from His causal activity; for the perfections of creatures are the representations of God, although in an imperfect manner, following various sorts of His causal activity, and that is how our intellect knows and names God according to each kind of causal activity. Nevertheless these words are not used to *mean* His causal acts. "Living" in "God is living" does not mean the same as "causes life"; the sentence is used to say that life does pre-exist in the source of all things, though in a higher way than we can understand or signify.[27]

The question he is addressing here is whether it is possible to use words to characterize God as He is in Himself (*substantialiter*) or only to characterize His relation to the world. Aquinas' discussion is marred only by his unfortunate example of the alleged etymology of the word "*lapis*". The trouble with the example is not that the etymology is bogus, but that it suggests that when Aquinas talks about "that from which a name is derived" he is talking about etymology and not about the meanings of words.

For a better example, I believe, and one that fits the surrounding text, consider the way in which we name diseases. Characteristically, diseases initially at least are identified by a syndrome of symptoms that the disease produces. For a long time the underlying pathological process that gives rise to those symptoms may remain completely unknown. In that way, "we name the disease from its effects". However, and this is Aquinas' point, the name that we introduce is introduced as the name of the disease itself, and not of that syndrome of symptoms. Equally, the

---

[26] *ST*, 1a 13, 6. I believe that what Aquinas is arguing for in this passage is a form of what is now called "semantic externalism". I will discuss this in detail when I look at Barth, who makes a similar move to Aquinas at this point.

[27] *ST*, 1a 13, 2.

name cannot be treated as meaning "that which causes these symptoms", since different diseases may produce the same symptoms. In this way, even if our only evidence for the existence of the disease is its symptoms, we still use the name of the disease to name the (possibly unknown) pathological process that produces the symptoms and not the symptoms. So, Aquinas argues, when we talk of God's "justice" or "mercy", we are naming his intrinsic attributes and not merely talking about the effects of His justice and mercy, even if "in a higher way than we can understand or signify".

He has still to deal with the obvious objection, which he presents as follows:

> It seems that words we use of God apply primarily to creatures. For we speak of things as we know them since, as Aristotle says, words are signs for things as understood. But we know creatures before we know God, hence our words apply to creatures before they apply to God.[28]

To which he replies:

> Whenever a word is used analogically of many things, it is used because of some order or relation to some central thing. In order to explain an extended or analogical use of a word it is necessary to mention this central thing. The primary application of the word is to the central thing that has to be understood first; other applications will be more or less secondary in so far as they approximate to this use. ...
>
> When we say He is good or wise we do not simply mean that he causes wisdom or goodness, but that he possesses these perfections transcendently. We conclude, therefore, that from the point of view of what the word means it is used primarily of God and derivatively of creatures, for what the word means— the perfection it signifies—flows from God to the creature.[29]

This is highly compressed to the point where at first sight it does not look as though Aquinas is offering a reply to the objection. But I believe we can spell out his idea by returning to Plato's discussion in the *Phaedo* of geometrical terms. Plato's basic point is that if we take a geometrical term such as "equal in length", we never find it to be perfectly exemplified in experience—at least in the sense that, given any two sticks that we judge to be equal in length, we can always make sense of the idea that on closer inspection one will turn out to be shorter than the other. The geometer describes an ideal, or standard, to which empirical phenomena approach to a greater or lesser extent. When, however, we first learn the meanings of these geometrical terms, we inevitably start with their empirical employment, talking of square buildings or round cushions. But part of what we learn, when we learn to apply those words empirically, is that we can make sense

---

28   *ST*, 1a 13, 6.
29   *ST*, 1a 13, 6.

of the idea that to a greater or lesser extent they fall short of perfect squareness or roundness, and that what we mean in calling things square or round is that they approximate to an ideal of squareness or roundness. Even though it is only by subsequent reflection on our everyday practice of classifying everyday objects as square and round that we arrive at the geometer's conception of squareness and roundness, it is the geometer's conception that explains our everyday practice and not vice versa.

In the same way, although it is inevitable that the first use we make of words such as "good", "wise" or "just" is in the description of sublunary phenomena, and that we only subsequently learn to apply them to God, as the perfect instantiation of goodness, wisdom and justice, this is no barrier to saying that the primary application of such words is to God, as setting the standard by which all earthly goodnesses, wisdoms and justices are to be measured and judged.

An Alternative Account: "Exemplarism"

Aquinas' main account is the one we have been looking at: an account in terms of causal participation that is based on the model of the Sun heating a stone. There is, however, a second, and possibly third, strand in Aquinas' thought about the nature of the resemblance between the Creator and the creature that recurs throughout his writings, in terms of "exemplarism"—God's creation of the world according to the divine Ideas in His mind. I shall conclude my survey of Aquinas' account by looking briefly at this.

> with the exception of what is generated by chance, the form must be the end in view in every kind of generation. Moreover for the agent to act for the sake of the form, the likeness of the form must be in the agent. This can happen in two ways. In some agents, e.g., those which act by nature, the likeness of the thing to be produced already exists as a natural object: thus a man produces a man and fire produces fire. In other agents, namely those which act through intellect, the form of the thing to be produced already exists in its intelligible condition: thus the form of the house already exists in the mind of the architect. This can be called the idea of the house, because the architect intends to make the house to the pattern of the form which he has conceived in his mind. Now since the world is not made by chance, but is made by God acting as an intellectual agent, as will be shown below, there must be in the divine mind a form, to the likeness of which the world is made. And that is what we mean by an idea.[30]

Whereas the main account that Aquinas offers us is in terms of a general doctrine of efficient causation, whereby an efficient cause always produces its likeness in its effect, there are several passages such as the one just quoted that introduce

---

[30]   *ST*, Ia 15, 1.

another different account of the likeness of an effect to its cause. This is based not on the idea of causation in itself, but on the specific form of causation involved in deliberate causation, illustrated by the case of an architect with some sort of blueprint in his mind of the house that is being built.

This second account is much less fully developed by Aquinas than the first, and it is difficult to see how the two accounts are meant to be reconciled. Even if they are not strictly incompatible, they give quite different explanations for there being a resemblance between God and His creation. It is also difficult to see whether, or how, such an account could be developed into an explanation of the required resemblance.

1. The resemblance posited here is not in the first instance between God and His creation, but between God's idea of the created world and that created world. It is by no means obvious that one can infer anything about God's own nature from the nature of His ideas. What Aquinas requires at this point is what Emil Brunner writes in his controversy with Karl Barth: "The world is the creation of God. In every creation the spirit of the creator is in some way recognizable. The artist is known by all his works."[31] But in the human case at least that seems simply false. What can we really infer about the properties of Schubert from *Winterreise*? There certainly do not seem to be any obvious properties shared by the composer and his music. So the comparison with the architect leaves us in the lurch. We therefore need to enter into the obscurities of the discussion of the divine ideas in *ST* 1a, 15. There Aquinas seeks to hold together two apparently incompatible positions: that "an idea in God is simply the divine essence"[32] and that "There are many Ideas in God".[33] Both of these positions are certainly needed to support the claim that there being a resemblance between God and His creation follows from the fact that in order to create it, God must have had an Idea of that creation. Aquinas' own "solution" is to say: "'Idea' is not the name for the divine essence as such, but in so far as it is the likeness or intelligible nature of this or that thing. Hence there are said to be many Ideas in so far as the one essence provides the intelligibility of many natures."[34]

   This yields the startling doctrine, "God in his essence is the likeness of all things".[35] It is unclear how this is to be understood or whether this solves the problems confronting exemplarism.

2. The resemblance posited between God's Idea of His creation and that creation must be, in the first instance, a resemblance between the Idea and

---

[31] *Nature and Grace*, p.24.

[32] *ST*, Ia 15, 1.

[33] *ST*, Ia 15, 2.

[34] *ST*, 1a 15, 2 ad1.

[35] *ST*, Ia 15, 1.

the *whole* creation.[36] If He has Ideas of particular things within creation that is a consequence of the fact that He cannot have an Idea of the whole without having Ideas of its parts. What is required, however, is a resemblance between God and particular excellences *within* the creation— that there could not be particular just acts within the world unless God were Himself supremely just. These particular excellences might, however, be by-products of a creative process directed to wholly different ends.

The other possible strand in Aquinas' thinking is introduced by his citation of Genesis i, 26 in contexts in which he discusses the resemblance between God and creatures: "Then God said, 'Let us make man in our image, after our likeness'."[37] Although this is characteristically presented as a support for Aquinas' usual account, the text points in a quite different direction. Whereas in the case of the architect and the house, we were concerned with a resemblance between the architect's idea and the house as a supposed necessary prerequisite of his creating anything whatsoever, in the text from Genesis we are concerned with a resemblance consequent upon a deliberate intention that there should be such a resemblance. The difference between the two cases is the difference between, on the one hand, the resemblance between Rembrandt's idea of "The Night Watch" and the painting itself and, on the other hand, the resemblance between Rembrandt himself and one of his self-portraits. Genesis certainly provides a far more secure basis for positing a resemblance between God and His creation than does the rest of Aquinas' presentation of exemplarist ideas.

However, Aquinas simply quotes the Genesis text and does not elaborate on its significance, not even differentiating it from the case of the architect and the house. Also, whereas it looks as if he wishes to develop his whole account of religious language on the basis of an underlying metaphysical theory, the doctrine that human beings are created in the image of God belongs to revealed theology.

Discussion

"An Agent Produces its Like"[38]

The Achilles heel, or less tendentiously, the linchpin, of Aquinas' account as we have been examining it is his doctrine of causal participation claiming some sort of resemblance between a causal agent and its effect. This is repeated several times

---

[36] *Cf. ST*, 1a 15, 2: "the order of the universe as a whole is the special object of God's intention".

[37] *E.g., SCG* I, Chapter 29, p.138.

[38] *SCG* I, Chapter 8, p.76.

throughout his mature writings, and forms there the basis for his doctrine of the analogy between God and creatures.

If we grant him that, we may say, the rest follows. However, it is precisely this claim that looks to most modern readers as counterintuitive and unsubstantiated. One initial point to make about this claim is that it must be regarded as a *general* claim about causality, which can be illustrated by the Sun's heating a stone, and not, say, a specifically theological claim concerning divine causation. If it were to be regarded as a specifically theological claim then it could not be appealed to in natural theology as a basis for the way we are to think about God: specifically theological claims can only be made *after* we have established God's existence and established a way of talking about God.

There are two claims here: that there is a resemblance between the cause and its effect, and that in some cases we have "equivocal" or "analogical" causation where the cause is qualitatively superior to its effect. Aquinas' argument for these claims is, however, presented in an extraordinarily compressed form, and difficult to interpret in such a way as to yield the desired conclusion. I shall consider two versions that Aquinas offers.

> Effects that fall short of their causes do not agree with them in name and nature. Yet, some likeness must be found between them, since it belongs to the nature of action that an agent produces its like, since each thing acts according as it is in act.[39]

> whatever perfection exists in an effect must be found in the effective cause: either in the same formality, if it is a univocal agent—as when man reproduces man; or in a more eminent degree, if it is an equivocal agent—thus in the Sun is the likeness of whatever is generated by the Sun's power. Now it is plain that the effect pre-exists virtually in the efficient cause: and although to pre-exist in the potentiality of a material cause is to pre-exist in a more imperfect way, since matter as such is imperfect, and an agent as such is perfect; still to pre-exist virtually in the efficient cause is to pre-exist not in a more imperfect, but in a more perfect way.[40]

Perhaps the most plausible explanation for the widespread belief in the mediaeval period that the effect of an efficient cause must resemble the cause seems to be that there are several striking cases of causation where features of the cause are replicated in the effect: the fire heats the room, the father resembles his son, the billiard cue moves in a certain direction in order to move the ball in the same direction, and the architect has a plan that resembles the building.[41] It is surely not

---

[39]   *SCG* I, Chapter 29, p.138.

[40]   *ST* I, 4, Art. 2.

[41]   Cf. *dV*, 21, 4: "omne agens invenitur sibi simile agere" ("Every agent *is found to* effect something like itself", my italics).

chance that Aquinas reverts to the Sun heating the stone and a man fathering a son as his examples of causal agency. At a time when the underlying physics and biology were scarcely understood, it may well have appeared to be the best explanation of all these cases that they were manifestations of a general metaphysical principle of causation.

However, with the growth of modern physics and biology there has developed a much better understanding of why in these particular cases features of the cause should be replicated in the effect, without the need to appeal to a general metaphysical principle guaranteeing such replication. Also, the explanation for the similarity of the effect and the cause is very different for the different examples: since the reason that a son resembles his father has nothing in common with the reason that a fire heats a room, it no longer looks as if these examples were all manifestations of a single principle of causation. With this, the apparent *empirical* support for the claim that an efficient cause must resemble its effect crumbles.

In Aquinas' presentation, however, it looks as if he intends the claim as an a priori claim that can be arrived at by analysis of the notion of cause—or, rather, efficient cause or agent. In attempting to come to terms with his argument, I shall first consider two more modern attempts to defend his conception.

> Since all the effect has comes from its cause and is the gift of the cause, and since the cause cannot give what it does not possess, at least in some higher equivalent way, then under pain of unintelligibility there must be *some* resemblance between the effect and its cause, at least in the most fundamental order of existence and the latter's satellite properties, such as unity.[42]

Unless it is just a play on the word "give", this argument seems to me to be question-begging. The sense in which it is obviously true that you cannot give what you don't possess—giving someone a present, or, in general, giving something *away*[43]—is clearly irrelevant, and in some other senses of "give" this can sound preposterous: it would be absurd to say that a sculptor cannot give a shape to a block of marble unless he himself possessed that shape.

What Clarke is getting at may however be what Garrigou-Lagrange argues in the following passage, which is to my mind clearer than the explanations Aquinas himself gives.

---

[42]   W. Norris Clarke, *The Philosophical Approach to God*, p.54.

[43]   *Cf. SCG*, Bk. III, lxix: "Now this is a ridiculous proof to assign of a body not acting, to point to the fact that no accident passes from subject to subject. When it is said that one body heats another, it is not meant that numerically the same heat, which is in the heating body, passes to the body heated; but that by virtue of the heat, which is in the heating body, numerically another heat comes to be in the heated body actually, which was in it before potentially. For a natural agent does not transfer its own form to another subject, but reduces the subject upon which it acts from potentiality to actuality."

If every agent produces, not an indifferent effect whatsoever, but a determined effect which belongs to it by right, *though it does not tend towards this effect,* and is not *ordained* for it; if, *e.g.*, the acorn produces the oak rather than the poplar, though it is not ordained for the one rather than the other; if the eye sees rather than hears, though it is not naturally predisposed for the former act rather than the latter–it follows that there is no way of explaining by the *principle of sufficient reason* how it is that the effect is definitely established and essentially refers to a definite cause. Unless these qualities were somehow present in the efficient cause, they could not be produced in the effect. Now, they are there merely in a *virtual* manner, inasmuch as the efficient cause *tended* to produce this particular effect rather than any other, and inasmuch as it was ordained for this effect.[44]

This is an altogether more subtle, and, initially at least, more persuasive, argument. If agent A is *such as* to produce effect *F* in B, then its nature must be such that one could see from the study of A alone that it will produce such an effect. This, however, could only be the case if B's becoming *F* were somehow prefigured in A. We can only make sense of that being so if there is some feature of A that resembles its characteristic effect.

This argument is, however, flawed. Even if we restrict our attention to causal *agency*, as this argument demands, an agent only produces its characteristic effect *under certain circumstances*, and the agent is only one element in a complex causal process. In this way, although we blame the agent for the effect, it is only the agent in interaction with its surroundings—the other elements in the causal process—that actually produces the effect. Because of that, we have no reason whatever to suppose that "the effect pre-exists virtually" in the agent, *considered in isolation.*

It may be replied to this objection that although that may hold for agency in general, in the special case that really interests us, that of *divine* causation, at least in the case of *God* acting, He cannot possibly be thought of as just one element in a causal process. In this unique case, He alone is wholly responsible for the effect. However, even if we were to grant that in this special case there must be *some* sort of resemblance between God and His creation, the real difficulty would remain. That idea—that there is "some sort of resemblance"—falls far short of what is required: that only a perfectly just God could create a world that contained instances of justice.

---

[44] R. Garrigou-Lagrange, *God: His Existence and Nature*, I, p.201. (There is an oddity in the example given of the acorn and the oak: the acorn *becomes* the oak and does not cause it.) Perhaps this can be considered as a gloss on the obscure explanations in Aquinas himself (*SCG* I, Chapter 29, p.138): "Effects that fall short of their causes do not agree with them in name and nature. Yet, some likeness must be found between them, since it belongs to the nature of action that an agent produces its like, since each thing acts according as it is in act." And (*ST* I, 4, 2): "It is plain that the effect pre-exists virtually in the efficient cause."

Aquinas, Plato and Aristotle

Although this book is not intended as an historical study, Aquinas is clearly working in a context of ideas whose ultimate roots go back on the one hand to Aristotle and on the other to Plato. It is therefore appropriate and instructive to compare and contrast the account that Aquinas has offered with ideas that can be found in Plato and Aristotle. This is particularly true of the critical idea of the resemblance of cause and effect.

Aristotle

The authority of Aristotle is frequently claimed for the idea that in a causal transaction the patient would come to be like the agent. In particular, the following two passages appear to give warrant for such an idea:

> It is, then, now reasonable to hold both that fire heats and that what is cold cools and, in general that an agent makes the patient like itself; for the agent and the patient are contraries, and coming to be is a process into the contrary, so that the patient must change into the agent, since only in that way will coming to be be a process into the contrary.[45]

And:

> It follows that in one sense what is acted upon is acted upon by what is like it, in another sense by what is unlike it as we have explained. That is to say, while being acted upon it is unlike, after it has been acted upon it is like the agent.[46]

However, despite the fact that the passage from *de Anima* in particular has sometimes been cited as an Aristotelian source for the idea of causal resemblance, I believe that it is only by reading these passages out of context that they can be seen as giving any support for the *general* principle of causal resemblance required for Aquinas' argument.

The fullest discussion in Aristotle is in *de Generatione et Corruptione*, and it is there that we can best discover his meaning in these passages. The context is one in which Aristotle is developing what could be called his fundamental physics. This theory has three features that we need to take into account.

Firstly, it is presented as an empirically based theory:

> The reason why we have not the power to comprehend the admitted facts is our lack of experience. Hence those who have lived in a more intimate communion with the phenomena of nature are better able to lay down such principles as can be connected together and cover a wide field; those, on the other hand, who

---

[45]   *G&C*, I 324a 10–14.

[46]   *dAn.*, 417a 18–20.

engage in long discussion without taking the facts into account are more easily detected as men of narrow views.[47]

Secondly, it is a theory based on the four elements (στοιχεῖα), earth, air, fire and water. Thirdly it is primarily concerned with the "last agent" (ἔσχατον ποιοῦν) in a causal chain. (We can say both of the doctor that he cures the patient and of the wine that it cures the patient, but it is the wine that is the last link in the causal chain and that is in immediate physical interaction with the patient.[48])

The theory then outlined in the passage from *de Generatione et Corruptione* is that the basic form of causal interaction in the physical world is that in which an active element such as fire comes into contact with its opposite (something cold) it moves that thing towards itself, making it more like itself. But whatever can said for or against this (and of course, no one now accepts the idea of the four elements), it seems very unlike Aquinas' position and, in itself, to lend little support to it:

1. The argument in terms of contraries that Aristotle offers for the idea that an agent will make its patient like itself is completely different from Aquinas' argument.

2. Aristotle's discussion here only concerns immediate causal interactions between the elements, where the agent comes into actual contact with the patient: although he will cite examples such as wine curing a patient, such causal transactions are to be seen as capable of being broken down into a set of causal interactions between the elements that combine to form the wine and the elements that combine to form the patient's body. Aquinas, by contrast is making a metaphysical claim about the nature of causality in general.

3. The causal transactions that Aristotle is talking about involve the transference of *qualities* from one body to another and not structural properties or the transference of form, whereas many of Aquinas' applications of his principle require the transference of complex formal features from the agent to the patient.

Plato

Although Aristotle is frequently appealed to as the source of the idea that an effect resembles its cause, it is more instructive to compare the account we have been looking at with ideas to be found in Plato, and in particular to the "Allegory of the Cave".[49] This comparison is immediately suggested by Aquinas' continual

---

[47]   *G&C*, I 316a 5–11.

[48]   *G&C*, I 324a 25–30. For excellent discussions of this whole passage, see Dorothea Frede "*On Generation and Corruption* I.10: On Mixture and Mixables", especially pp.299–302, and Marie Louise Gill, *Aristotle on Substance*, pp.198–200.

[49]   *Republic* 514a–520a.

illustration of his conception with the example of the Sun. I am not concerned here with the question of the influence of Plato, either direct or indirect, upon Aquinas, but with the parallelism between Aquinas' doctrine and the allegory.[50]

The Allegory of the Cave is deeply suggestive, however difficult it may be to interpret in detail. Its main outlines are familiar. We are chained up in a cave only able to see shadows of puppets cast by a fire. If someone were to free himself and ascend from the cave and see the Sun itself, he would initially be dazzled and if he were to return to the cave he would be regarded by his companions as ridiculous, but as he became accustomed to seeing the Sun, he would eventually appreciate that the Sun "controls everything in the visible world and moreover is in a way the cause of all [τρόπον τινά πάντων αἴτιος] that he and his companions used to see".

Unencumbered by metaphysics, the picture Plato is painting is one in which, because we do not know the Form of the Good—the standard or criterion for judging what is and what is not good—we are imprisoned in a world of appearances so that we count as good, not what is good, but what appears to us good.[51] If someone were to discover the Form of the Good—the standard for judging what really was, and did not merely appear, good, they would make judgments that seemed to everyone to be ridiculous.

Plato will subsequently place a metaphysical interpretation upon this by hypostasising the forms, and in particular seeking to explain the goodness of everyday things and acts by seeing them as imitating the form of the Good. However this account is to be worked out, it does not seem to be part of Plato's conception that the Form of the Good is an *efficient* cause of particular goods. (I take it that is why, in the Allegory of the Cave he adds the qualification "in a way" to his reference to the Sun as "the cause of all that he and his companions used to see".)

To convert this into the account that we have been looking at from Aquinas, you need only take two steps. Firstly, rejecting the idea of the separate existence of the Forms, one replaces such an idea by making God the Form of the Good ("God is goodness itself").[52] And, secondly, one explains the resemblance between God and creatures by substituting straightforward efficient causation for Plato's "*in a way* the cause", supplementing this with the doctrine "that an agent produce its like".

"Are Words Predicated Primarily of God or Creatures?"[53]

Despite the prominence given by Aquinas to his doctrine of causal participation, it is arguable that his most important contribution to the theory of religious language is his argument for the idea that the words we use for divine perfections have their

---

[50]   Aquinas discusses the relation of his position to that of Plato in *ST* I, 6, Art. 4.

[51]   One may think here of the frequency with which philosophers discussing ethics are driven back on appealing to their "intuitions".

[52]   *SCG* I, Chapter 38.

[53]   *ST*, 1a 13, 6.

primary use in their application to God and that their everyday use in talking about creatures is a secondary use. I looked above at his arguments for this paradoxical sounding claim. Here I want to comment on its significance, and in particular on the way in which it is this claim that allows Aquinas to steer a narrow path between agnosticism and anthropomorphism.

If we give *linguistic* primacy to the everyday use of the words that we then go on to use in talking about the divine perfections, it is virtually impossible to avoid either agnosticism or anthropomorphism. That is to say, if, on the one hand, we base our account of religious language on purely causal terms, after the model of the healthy climate and the healthy cow, our claim that God is just reduces to seeing God as the unknown something that causes there to be just things in the world. If, on the other hand, we seek to explain our claim that God is just by exploiting a supposed resemblance between God and a just man, no matter how much we refine our concepts and add superlatives, in one way or another we are reducing God to a superior human being.

By way of contrast, Aquinas will insist that we do not measure God by the human, but that God is the measure of the human. He frequently stresses that "is an image of" is an antisymmetric relation, so that we may not convert the claim that man is made in the image of God into making God in man's image. For instance:

> it is more fitting to say that a creature is like God rather than the converse. For that which is called *like* something possesses a quality or form of that thing. Since, then, that which is found in God perfectly is found in other things according to a certain diminished participation, the basis on which the likeness is observed belongs to God absolutely, but not to the creature. Thus, the creature has what belongs to God and, consequently, is rightly said to be like God. But we cannot in the same way say that God has what belongs to the creature. Neither, then, can we appropriately say that God is like a creature, just as we do not say that man is like his image, although the image is rightly said to be like him.
>
> All the less proper, moreover, is the expression that God is likened to a creature. For likening expresses a motion towards likeness and thus belongs to the being that receives from another that which makes it like. But a creature receives from God that which makes it like Him. The converse, however, does not hold. God, then, is not likened to a creature; rather, the converse is true.[54]

When, then, we say that God is just ("is justice itself"), we are saying that He perfectly realizes the standard of justice of which the people and acts that we in this world call just are ambiguous, fragile and warped copies. God is the measure according to which all that we call just is to be measured, even though, since in this life we do not know God in Himself, we can form no positive conception of what

---

[54]   *SCG* I, Chapter 29, p.139.

such perfect justice actually looks like, and even though there is no safe inference from the nature of the things we regard as just to the true nature of divine justice.

If this reversal of priorities, whereby we explain human justice in terms of divine justice and not vice versa, avoids anthropomorphism, and regards with suspicion any attempt to import human conceptions of justice into the divine, does not Aquinas' account become indistinguishable from agnosticism?—God is certainly just, but we do not know what that amounts to. To be sure, part of Aquinas' purpose in appealing to analogy is to stress how limited in this life our knowledge of God is. As we already saw, when we looked at his *Commentary on Boethius' de Trinitate*, Aquinas sees as an integral part of our knowledge of God "an ever-growing knowledge of Him as distant from everything that appears in His effects".[55] Although the account may avoid agnosticism, it does so only by a hair's breadth, and the point of the appeal to analogy is just as much to stress how little we know or understand God's nature as to claim a resemblance of the creature to the Creator.[56]

Aquinas and Cajetan

For a long time, Cajetan's *de Nominum Analogia* was regarded as a trustworthy vademecum to the thought of Aquinas on analogy.[57] Latterly, through the work of Aquinas scholars such as Hampus Lyttkens,[58] George Klubertanz[59] and Ralph McInerny,[60] its status has been radically challenged. Klubertanz argued that there was considerable development and change in Aquinas' thinking about analogy, and that if, like Cajetan, you approached the texts of Aquinas on the assumption that they were all equally authoritative for an interpretation of his doctrine of analogy, you would go badly astray. The ideas of an early work such as *de Veritate*—in particular the rejection of the analogy of attribution in favour of the analogy of proportionality—had been superseded by the time of the *Summa Theologica*. Hence, if you treated the account of analogy given in *de Veritate* as normative for your understanding of Aquinas' mature thought you would inevitably distort the theory of analogy developed in the two *Summas*.

It seems to me that this case has been made out definitively. But I do not believe that it was only for this reason that Cajetan went astray. *De Nominum Analogia* is, after all, not presented simply as an interpretation of Aquinas, but as Cajetan's

---

[55] *BT*, p.22.

[56] I return in the final chapter to look again at the question whether Aquinas really does avoid agnosticism.

[57] To give just one example, in Garrigou-Lagrange's treatment of analogy (*God: His Existence and Nature*, II 206–221), he treats Cajetan as having almost equal authority to Aquinas, and, like Cajetan, makes *de Veritate* a key text for the interpretation of Aquinas.

[58] *The Analogy between God and the World*.

[59] *St. Thomas Aquinas on Analogy*.

[60] *The Logic of Analogy*.

own attempt to develop a doctrine of analogy, even if one in which Aquinas is treated as the key authority. It might in fact be fruitful to look at Cajetan not just as an interpreter of Aquinas, but also as (unconsciously) trying to correct him. It was not just on the authority of *de Veritate* that Cajetan insisted that the analogy of proportionality was the only form of analogy that could provide the solution to the problem of divine names: he has his own arguments for this position, arguments that are not to be found in Aquinas:

> This analogy [the analogy of proportionality] excels above the others mentioned above both by dignity and name. By *dignity* because it arises from the genus of inherent formal causality, for it predicates perfections that are inherent in each analogate, whereas the other analogy arises from extrinsic denomination.[61]

His thought here seems to run along the following lines: the mark of the analogy of attribution is that we have a primary use of the word "F" when we call As F, and a secondary use when we call Bs F because of the relation of the Bs to As that are F. Only the As are really F, the Bs are merely related to things that are F. Of itself the use of the analogy of attribution does not even imply a resemblance between the Bs and the As. However:

> It should be carefully noted that this first condition of this mode of analogy, namely, that it is not according to the genus of inherent formal causality, but always according to something extrinsic, must be understood formally and not materially.[62]

The thought in this somewhat convoluted passage seems to be that although the analogy of attribution is only used in such a way that in calling the Sun hot we mean that it causes heat in stones, this does not rule out the possibility that there *is* an intrinsic property of the Sun that resembles the heat of the stone and that enables it to heat the stone. If, however, the analogy of attribution only permits us to express the extrinsic properties of the Sun—its being the cause of heat in the stone—to express the intrinsic property of the Sun that resembles heat in the stone, we need to go beyond the analogy of attribution, and instead say that when we talk of the heat of the Sun, we mean that property which is to the Sun as heat is to the stone. That is to say, it is only the analogy of proportionality that will enable us to designate the intrinsic properties of the Sun: the causal relation between the Sun and the stone may give us the grounds for believing that that there are such intrinsic properties, but linguistically (formally), as Aquinas stressed, when we talk of the Sun as hot, we do not *mean* that the Sun causes the stone to be hot; what we mean, rather, is that the Sun has that intrinsic property that enables it to heat the stone.

---

[61] *NA*, p.5.
[62] *NA*, p.17.

[handwritten marginalia: theory of proportional]

There may also be a second, deeper, train of thought in Cajetan: there are two fundamental elements in Aquinas' thought: on the one hand, God "is not in a genus"[63]—God cannot be thought of as one good thing alongside other good things—and on the other hand, there is a resemblance between God and creatures: how can we assert a resemblance between two things without discovering a genus to which they both belong? Here we may appeal to Aristotle who saw the "analogy of proportionality" as a way of comparing things that were too remote to be compared directly.

Whatever may be said for or against these trains of thought, they are certainly not Aquinas', who appears to allow for the analogy of proportionality only in the explanation of what it is to speak metaphorically about God. This may be because the analogy of proportionality appears not to give him what he most wants: the analogy of proportionality is a symmetric relation, and cannot obviously be used to give an ordering of priority and posteriority. In the last resort, where Cajetan, considered as an interpreter of Aquinas, seems to have gone wrong is his initial assumption that the analogy of attribution is always to be explained in causal terms *[handwritten marginalia: Cajetan]* (if A is called "F" in the primary sense, B is called "F" in the secondary sense if it is the cause of A's being F). Once you make that assumption, the reading Cajetan gives of Aquinas can appear compelling. But it is precisely that assumption that makes him an unreliable guide to Aquinas.

Conclusion

In the account we have been looking at, Aquinas has given us a highly integrated natural theology, in which his metaphysics, epistemology and theory of religious language fit together perfectly. The central theme that runs through this account, the idea that links the different elements together, is the idea of "causal participation"— a conception of causality according to which both "an agent produces its like" and also there is "*analogical*" causation, in which a cause is superior to its effect. However, this idea is also the most dubious. Even if more can be said in favour of this conception of causality than I have suggested, it is impossible to see how it could be developed to yield the desired result: that only a perfectly wise, just and living being could create a world that contained instances of wisdom, justice and life. It is clear that without the doctrine of causal participation, Aquinas' natural theology is in jeopardy. The "Five Ways" on their own would only succeed in establishing something extremely thin, falling far short of the idea that the world was created by a living intelligence.

However, from the point of view of the present study, the important point to notice is that his doctrine of religious language is statable and discussable quite apart from this doctrine. Even from a purely Thomist perspective, Norris Clarke is simply wrong when he writes:

---

[63]   *SCG* I, Chapter 25.

There is only one bridge that enables us to pass over the cognitive abyss between ourselves and God and talk meaningfully about Him in our terms: the bridge of causal participation, or more simply of efficient causality, taken with all its implications. If God were not the ultimate causal Source of all the perfections we find in our world, we would have no way of talking meaningfully about Him at all. It is the causal bond which grounds all analogous predication about God.[64]

As Aquinas insists, when we say that God is good or wise, we do not mean that God is the cause or source of goodness or wisdom. On the contrary, we are talking about God's intrinsic properties. When Aquinas claims that the words that we use in talking about God are predicated primarily of God rather than creatures, the priority at stake has nothing to do with causal priority, or a relationship of ontological dependence. Instead, the priority claimed for our words when they are used to talk about God rather than creatures resides in the fact that God is essentially good, wise and just—is goodness, wisdom, justice itself, setting the standard for all creaturely perfections. Creatures are called good, wise or just to the extent that they measure up to divine goodness, wisdom and justice.

I shall eventually compare Aquinas' position here with that of Karl Barth, who makes apparently the same claim at *CD* II/1, pp.228–231. Whether they are really saying the same thing must at this stage be left as an open question.

---

[64] *The Philosophical Approach to God*, p.54.

Chapter 5
Immanuel Kant

Kant's idiosyncratic account of religion is unlikely to find many adherents, either among orthodox believers or unbelievers. For most readers, despite the central significance that Kant himself attached to it, and despite the fact that his religious concern was one of the driving interests of the whole critical philosophy, it is the least convincing element in his whole philosophy. However, from the point of view of the present study, his account has great importance. Arguing from his premises, he offers a complete and fully coherent theory of analogy and religious language that is fully adequate for his purposes, but perhaps *only* for his purposes. For, part of the significance of Kant's discussion—a significance that goes far beyond his own account of religion—is that it shows how attenuated an account of religious language may be offered by analogy. At least, it shows that this is so if one follows a very natural interpretation of the role of analogy in one's account of talking about God, and if one remains "within the limits of reason alone", whether that means Kant's moral theology or natural theology more generally. Donald MacKinnon talks of Kant's "style of '*theologia negativa*'"[1]: the question is: if Kant is right in his account of the way analogy can be used to make sense of religious language, does analogy, as might appear, offer us a more positive account of such language than a pure *theologia negativa*, or does it inevitably lead back to such a purely negative account?

Kant's Philosophy of Religion

To understand Kant's account properly, it must be set in the context of his overall conception of religion and faith in God, and so we must first give a sketch of that, taking our bearings from two famous quotations: "I therefore had to deny *knowledge* in order to make room for *faith*",[2] and "religion is (subjectively speaking) the recognition of all our duties as divine commands".[3] But although both these quotations are famous, interpreting them is far from straightforward.

---

[1] "Kant's Philosophy of Religion", p.144.

[2] *CPR*, Bxxx.

[3] *Religion within* ... p.177 (Ak. 6:154).

Knowledge and Certainty

One of the central aims of the *Critique of Pure Reason* is to restrict all *knowledge* to the world of experience, the phenomenal realm, and to expose as illusory any claim to knowledge of what transcends any possible experience, the noumenal realm. In particular, in the *Dialectic* he will seek to expose as illusory any attempt to prove the existence of God. From a theoretical point of view, Kant's position must be characterized as one of complete agnosticism. By the same token, he believes he has shown atheism to be impossible: by placing God purely in the noumenal realm, reason is equally impotent to establish His existence or non-existence. In all that follows, I believe, if we are to understand Kant's position correctly we have to take this agnosticism with full seriousness, and interpret his claim to be (subjectively) certain that God exists in a way that is compatible with it.

> No one, indeed, will be able to boast that he *knows* that there is a God and a future life: if he knows this, he is the very man for whom I have long and vainly sought.[4]

Yet alongside this he will claim practical, moral, certainty that there is a God, and that this certainty is just as great as "ever could be had by mathematical propositions originating in the nature of things".[5] So it is being claimed that we can be certain of claims that we could have no theoretical grounds for believing whatsoever.[6] To understand this paradoxical position, we have to discover what the nature of the certainty being claimed is. In the first *Critique*, after giving a preliminary sketch of the kind of argument for the need to postulate the existence of God that we shall be looking at later, he gives the following explanation of "moral belief":

> Since, therefore, the moral law is at the same time my maxim (reason prescribing that it should be so), I inevitably believe in the existence of God and a future life, and I am certain that nothing can shake this belief, since my moral principles would thereby be overthrown, and I cannot disclaim them without becoming abhorrent in my own eyes.[7]
>
> ... No, my conviction is not *logical*, but *moral* certainty, and since it rests on subjective grounds, I must not even say "*It is* certain that there is a God *etc.*", but "*I am* morally certain *etc.*"[8]

---

4   *CPR*, B857.

5   Pölitz, p.415 (Ak. 28:1083).

6   In the Pölitz lectures, he also insists that we can make no sense of the claim that the existence of God is *probable*, since he argues we can only talk of probability with respect to the phenomenal world. See p.414 (Ak. 28:1082).

7   *CPR*, B856.

8   *CPR*, B857. *Cf.* the footnote on *CJ*, p.365 (Ak. 5:471): "Faith is a confidence in the promise of the moral law; but the moral law does not contain this promise: it is I who put it

We can understand Kant's position here best by considering initially not the case of God or a future life but the other postulate of practical reason—freedom. Here at least Kant's argument for the need for such a postulate is much more straightforward than in the case of the other two postulates,[9] and with that it perhaps becomes clearer what "moral certainty" amounts to.

To take myself seriously as a moral agent is to regard myself as morally responsible for what I have done, and, in any situation in which there is choice between doing what is morally demanded of me and the wrong thing, to regard it as always open to me to do the right thing, no matter in what way my upbringing and circumstances seem to constrain me. For Kant, this means seeing myself as the ultimate originator of my action. So that on the one hand, he will argue that *everything* in the phenomenal world, including human actions, are fully causally determined in such a way that whatever I do would in principle be predictable from the past background of my action, but on the other hand I must simultaneously adopt another standpoint and regard myself as a *homo noumenon*, who is completely free to act purely in accordance with the dictates of morality. The difficulties that Kant's "positive use of the concept of a noumenon" runs into are well known, but do not concern us here: in the present context what we are interested in is simply the train of thought that leads him to speak the way he does. In so far as I am thinking morally I shall never regard myself as exonerated when I behave immorally by saying, "Given who I am and my background it was inevitable that I should act as I did." I will treat it as unquestionable that I *could* have done the right thing, and that I am guilty if I do the wrong thing.

In this way, although I have no theoretical grounds whatever for believing that I was free to act otherwise than I did, and in fact have every reason to suppose that in principle a full causal explanation of my choices and actions was possible, nevertheless as long as I regard myself as a moral agent I shall treat it as certain that I was free in doing what I did, so that what he said about belief in God and immortality can be applied to belief in freedom: "I am certain that nothing can shake this belief, since my moral principles would thereby be overthrown, and I cannot disclaim them without becoming abhorrent in my own eyes."[10] It seems

---

there, and on a morally sufficient basis."

[9] For present purposes, I leave on one side the postulate of immortality, where the case for the need for the postulate is even more difficult to make out than the postulate of God.

[10] *CPR*, B856. *Cf.* Pölitz p.357 (Ak. 28:1012): "[the moral theist] thereby renders superfluous everything that the sceptical atheist attacks. For he needs no speculative proofs of the existence of God; he is convinced of it with certainty, because otherwise he would have to reject the necessary laws of morality which are grounded in the nature of his being".

that when Kant talks of practical or moral certainty in such a case, it comes close to saying that I am morally obliged to believe that I am free.[11]

This account seems clear and intelligible, and I believe explains what Kant means by "practical" or "moral" certainty in circumstances where all theoretical certainty is in the nature of the case necessarily impossible. What we must turn to is something where the argument seems much less straightforward: the claim that Kant is in the same sense morally certain that there is a God. What we are after is an account that runs along the same lines for the postulate of God as that which we have just seen for the postulate of freedom.

The Summum Bonum *"Proof"*

Whatever the difficulties that confront Kant's conception of human beings as phenomenally determined, but noumenally free, it is clear why he insisted on the postulate of freedom, and why he thought our conception of ourselves as moral agents was in jeopardy without such a postulate. By contrast, the postulate of God appears, initially at least, contrived. Kant presents proofs of the need for such a postulate in a number of different works, and many of these proofs seem deeply unconvincing, and frequently difficult to reconcile with Kant's own central moral concerns. These different accounts are also difficult to reconcile with one another. I believe that there is a genuine concern here, and these different accounts are witnesses, not to Kant's wish to gerrymander a proof of the need for this postulate, but to the fact that he found it difficult to hit the nail on the head. At least for present purposes, I shall offer a reconstruction of what I believe that concern to be: a concern that he comes closest to bringing into focus at the end of *The Critique of Judgment*. Let us first consider two other passages that are in different ways unsatisfactory, and which point in very different directions from one another:

> *Happiness* is the state of a rational being in the world in the whole of whose existence *everything goes according to his wish and will*, and rests, therefore, on the harmony of nature with his whole end as well as with the essential determining ground of his will. Now, the moral law as a law of freedom commands through determining grounds that are to be quite independent of nature and of its harmony with our faculty of desire (as incentives); the acting rational being in the world is, however, not also the cause of the world and of nature itself. Consequently, there is not the least ground in the moral law for a necessary connection between the morality and the proportionate happiness of a being belonging to the world as part of it and hence dependent on it … Nevertheless, in the practical task of pure

---

[11]   *Cf. CJ*, p.365 (Ak. 5:471): "[Faith] is the mind's steadfast purpose to assume as true what we must necessarily presuppose as a condition for the possibility of achieving the highest moral final purpose, and to assume this because of obligation to this final purpose, and despite the fact that we have no insight into whether achieving this purpose is possible, or for that matter whether this is impossible."

reason, that is, in the necessary pursuit of the highest good, such a connection is postulated as necessary: we *ought* to strive to promote the highest good, (which must therefore be possible). Accordingly, the existence of a cause of all nature, distinct from nature, which contains the ground of this connection, namely of the exact correspondence of happiness with morality, is also *postulated* ... That is, it is morally necessary to assume the existence of God.[12]

... there must exist a being *who rules the world according to reason and moral laws*, and who has established in the course of things to come a state where the creature who has remained true to his nature and who has made himself worthy of happiness through morality will actually participate in this happiness; *for otherwise all subjectively necessary duties which I as a rational being am responsible for performing will lose their objective reality.* Why should I make myself worthy of happiness through morality if there is no being who can give me this happiness? Hence without *God* I would have to be either a visionary or a scoundrel. I would have to deny my own nature and its eternal moral laws; I would have to cease to be a rational being ... the ungroundedness of Hume's proposition, when he wants to derive all morality from particular moral feelings, is sufficiently demonstrated by morality; and *this* proposition: that here virtue is already sufficiently rewarded, has experience against it. Hence the duties of morality are apodictically certain, since they are set before me by my own reason; but there would be no incentives to act in accord with these duties as a rational human being if there were no God and no future world.[13]

Whatever could be said in favour of either of these passages, they are clearly offering completely different justifications of the need to postulate God, and both passages seem deeply flawed, even if in opposite ways.

The quotation from the *Critique of Practical Reason* looks to be simply a fallacious argument. The justification for the claim that we "ought to endeavour to promote the *summum bonum*" in addition to simply obeying the moral law is highly dubious. However, even if we grant Kant that we ought so to do, the argument to show that it follows that there is a need to postulate the possibility of the *summum bonum* is fallacious. This is a misapplication of the idea that "'Ought' implies 'Can'". From the fact that I ought to endeavour to bring it about that p, it

---

[12]   *CPrR*, pp.240–241 (Ak 5:124–125).

[13]   Pölitz, p.407 (Ak. 28:1072–1073). Earlier, on p.356 (Ak. 28:1011–1012), he had said: "[The human being] tries to act according to the duties he finds grounded in his own nature; but he also has senses which present the opposite to him with a blinding bedazzlement, and if he had no further incentives and powers to resist it, then he would in the end be blinded by their dazzle. Hence in order that he may not act against his own powers, he is set by his own reason to think of a being whose will is those very commands which he recognizes to be given by themselves *a priori* with apodictic certainty." This perhaps comes closer to what Kant is after than the passage quoted from p.407.

doesn't follow that it is possible that I should bring it about that *p*, but only that it is possible that I endeavour to bring it about. A defence lawyer whose client does not plead guilty has a clear duty to endeavour to persuade the jury that his client is innocent, even in cases where it will not be possible to succeed and even in cases where the lawyer himself does not believe it will be possible to succeed. Certainly in such a case it would be absurd to say that there was a duty to *succeed* in persuading the jury of the innocence of the client. Kant is assuming in the present case that from the fact that it is possible for me to try to *Φ* we may infer that it is possible for me to *Φ*, and it simply doesn't follow.

Given the general context of Kant's ethics, the passage from p.407 of the Pölitz *Lectures* seems extraordinary. (It is so extraordinary that one wonders whether Kant's lectures have been faithfully transcribed at this point.) Here he seems to be arguing that I must have an incentive to act morally, and that that incentive can only be that it is to my ultimate advantage so to do, "for otherwise all subjectively necessary duties which I as a rational being am responsible for performing will lose their objective reality." Basic to Kant's whole position is, however, that, when I act morally, I am only truly doing my duty if I do what I do for no other reason than that it is my duty. It looks simply impossible to hold that position together with what we are being told here. What he is saying seems to amount to: "I am doing my duty for no other reason than that it is my duty, and I am doing this because it is to my ultimate advantage so to do" and that doesn't seem to describe any coherent human attitude whatever.

It is possible to conclude from all this that Kant is simply fabricating a way of integrating his religious belief and his ethical theory, and many have followed Hegel in so concluding. I believe, however, that these different purported "proofs" are evidence of Kant's groping after a genuine concern, which, given his general framework, makes sense of his need to postulate God.

The Need to Postulate God

The two accounts I have just looked at miss that concern on opposite sides. Kant is trying to hold in balance two ideas that initially can look incompatible: on the one hand, one ought to do one's duty and follow the dictates that reason laid upon one, simply because it was one's duty, regardless of the consequences of so doing. This means that one does what one ought to even when the foreseeable consequences of one's action are bad, and one does not do what one ought not to do, no matter how great the foreseeable good consequences of acting wrongly may be.[14] On the other

---

[14]   This leads notoriously to Kant writing in the way he does in the 1797 essay "On a Supposed Right to Lie from Philanthropy". Here Kant may be seen as taking his principle to its logical extreme: if his position here seems highly implausible, it may be more because he is assuming an over simple account of what one's duty is in such a situation than because the principle itself is at fault. *Cf.* Rom. iii, 8: "And why not do evil that good may come?— as some people slanderously charge us with saying. Their condemnation is just."

hand, morality must make sense. Even though the demands of morality are laid upon us by reason itself, unless there were some point to acting morally, unless I could conceive there to be some human interest that was served by my abiding by the principle of doing my duty simply because it was my duty, the moral stance that Kant is advocating would appear curiously futile, and morality itself would be undermined. Kant is seeking to reconcile these two ideas, to each of which he is committed, by postulating that there must be in the end some harmony between the world of morality and the world of nature, such that the person who acts with moral integrity is at the same time acting in accordance with the way the world is. The postulate of God is at bottom the postulate of a guarantor of such a harmony.

Perhaps also Kant failed to bring his idea into true focus because of a misguided attempt to provide a rigorous proof of the need for the postulate. In any case, it is possible to come closer to what I think was his real concern if we consider a passage where he proceeds far more informally and does not strive to cast his idea in the form of such a proof: this is the passage towards the end of the *Critique of Judgment* where Kant considers the plight of "a righteous man (Spinoza, for example), who actively reveres the moral law but who remains firmly persuaded that there is no God, and (since as far as achieving the object of morality is concerned, the consequence is the same) that there is also no future life".[15] Such a man is portrayed as acting without requiring "that complying with that law should bring him an advantage, either in this world or in another: rather, he is unselfish and wants only to bring about the good to which the sacred law directs all his forces".[16] He will, however, find himself completely at odds with the world around him. Kant shocked many of his contemporaries when he introduced the idea of radical evil into his account of humanity in *Religion within the Boundaries of Mere Reason*, but there is a refreshing realism in Kant's discussion that contrasts sharply with the somewhat preposterous optimism about human nature of many of the early Enlightenment thinkers. It is against that background that he writes:

> Deceit, violence, and envy will always be rife around him, even though he himself is honest, peaceable, and benevolent. Moreover, as concerns the other righteous people he meets: no matter how worthy of happiness they may be, nature, which pays no attention to that, will still subject them to all the evils of deprivation, disease, and untimely death, just like all the other animals on the earth. And they will stay subjected to these evils always, until one vast tomb engulfs them one and all (honest or not, that makes no difference here) and hurls them, who managed to believe they were the final purpose of creation, back into the abyss of the purposeless chaos of matter from which they were taken.[17]

---

[15] *CJ*, pp.341–342 (Ak. 5:452).

[16] Ibid.

[17] *CJ*, p.342 (Ak. 5:452).

"Spinoza" is portrayed as scrupulously and disinterestedly obeying the moral law that his reason lays upon him, but at the same time confronted by a world in which his doing so apparently serves no human interest whatever—neither his own interest nor that of those around him. The concern here echoes that of Plato in Book II of the *Republic* where Glaucon contrasts the perfectly just man and the perfectly unjust man, and argues that, given the way the world is, it is the perfectly unjust man who makes a success of his life, and even that it is he, rather than the perfectly just man, who benefits his fellow men.[18] In this way, the central question of the *Republic* is raised: "Why is it better to be just than unjust?" In the same way, Kant sees his righteous atheist as confronted by the question: "What is the purpose of morality? Even if my reason demands of me that I live according to these moral dictates, I am apparently condemned thereby to a life of pointless misery."[19] So that although he acts morally with complete disinterest, Kant sees his position humanly speaking as undermined, unless he can in some way think that there is a purpose to morality, and that it is at least possible that that purpose should be achieved. Hence there is a need to postulate a goal for moral activity, but a goal that cannot be achieved by any single individual. The individual is commanded to "act in accordance with the maxims of a member giving universal laws for a *merely possible* [*bloß möglichen*] kingdom of ends".[20]

This command, however, makes full sense if we can at least hope that thereby an actual kingdom of ends might ultimately arise. In this way, if the stance of acting morally purely because this is the way reason dictates we should act is not to be undermined, we must at least entertain the realistic hope that some good will thereby come about: that the world is progressing towards an ideal state, where that ideal state is primarily characterized as a "*summum bonum*", a highest good in which happiness is proportioned to virtue, but which will involve a number of related ideas, such as a kingdom of ends, an ethical commonwealth[21] and a state of perpetual peace.[22] The empirical world, however, does not appear to be oriented towards such a goal: it is a world where human wickedness prevails. The hope, therefore, is a hope despite appearances. It is a hope that, nevertheless, by the grace of God, the goal of morality is attainable. Precisely by postulating a God shaping the ultimate destiny of humanity, the moral agent can refuse to compromise his

---

[18]   *Cf.* Luke xxii, 25–26: "And he said to them, The kings of the Gentiles exercise lordship over them; and those in authority over them are called benefactors. But not so with you."

[19]   *Cf.* I Cor. xv, 19: "If for this life only we have hoped in Christ, we are of all men most to be pitied."

[20]   *Groundwork*, p.88 (Ak. 4:439) (my italics).

[21]   *Religion within ...* p.132 (Ak. 6:97).

[22]   *Metaphysic of Morals*, pp.490–492 (Ak. 6:354–355); *Toward Perpetual Peace* (Ak. 8:343–386).

moral principles, sustained by the hope that "We know that in everything God works for good with those who love him".[23]

Curiously, it is precisely because of Kant's insistence that we do what is right regardless of the consequences that the need for a goal for morality becomes urgent. This perhaps becomes clearest in the first appendix to *Toward Perpetual Peace*: "On the Disagreement between Morals and Politics with a View to Perpetual Peace"[24], with its basic theme, "the tutelary god of morals does not yield to Jupiter (the tutelary god of power)".[25] Here he sees an inevitable conflict with the practical politician, who insists on compromising moral principles in the name of *Realpolitik*.

> But now the practical man (for whom morals is mere theory), bases his despairing denial of our benign hope (even while granting *ought* and *can*) strictly on this: that he pretends to see in advance, from the nature of the human being, that *he* is never *going to will* what is required in order to realize that end leading toward perpetual peace.[26]

Kant's basic position in *Toward Perpetual Peace* had already been stated at the end of the discussion of the right to war in *The Metaphysic of Morals*:

> Now morally practical reason pronounces in us its irresistible *veto*: *there is to be no war*, neither war between you and me in the state of nature nor war between us as states, which, although they are internally in a lawful condition, are still externally (in relation to one another) in a lawless condition; for war is not the way in which everyone should seek his rights. So the question is no longer whether perpetual peace is something real or a fiction, and whether we are not deceiving ourselves in our theoretical judgment when we assume that it is real. Instead we must act as if it is something real, though perhaps it is not ... And even if the complete realization of this objective remains a pious wish, still we are certainly not deceiving ourselves in adopting the maxim of working incessantly toward it. For this is our duty, and to admit that the moral law within us is itself deceptive would call forth in us the wish, which arouses our abhorrence, rather to be rid of all reason and to regard ourselves as thrown by one's principles into the same mechanism of nature as all the other species of animals.[27]

Despite a strong pacifist tendency in his thinking, Kant was not a pacifist, and in the sections preceding this section has made clear the circumstances in which

[23] Rom. viii, 28.
[24] *Toward Perpetual Peace*, pp.338–347 (Ak. 8:370–380).
[25] Ibid., p.339 (Ak. 8:370).
[26] Ibid.
[27] *Metaphysic of Morals*, p.491 (Ak. 6:354–355).

for him it is legitimate for a country to go to war. The question prompted by
this quotation is: why was he not? Given his moral rigorism and his talk of an
"irresistible *veto: there is to be no war*", how can he possibly regard there to be
circumstances in which waging war is legitimate? The answer lies in one of the
most difficult dimensions of Kant's ethical thinking, a dimension that is easy to
overlook if one approaches Kant's ethics primarily through the *Groundwork of the
Metaphysic of Morals*, say,[28] but which emerges clearly in his religious writings:
that is to say the idea of a moral command that is issued not to individuals but to
the whole of humanity, giving a *political* thrust to his ethical concerns. Thus in
Religion within... we read:

> Just as the juridical state of nature is a state of war of every human being against
> every other, so too is the ethical state of nature one in which the good principle,
> which resides in every human being, is incessantly attacked by the evil which is
> found in him and in every other as well ... just as the state of a lawless external
> (brutish) freedom and independence from coercive laws is a state of injustice and
> of war, each against each, which a human being ought to leave behind in order to
> enter into a politico-civil state, so is the ethical state of nature a *public* feuding
> between the principles of virtue and a state of inner immorality which the natural
> human being ought to endeavour to leave behind as soon as possible. Now, here
> we have a duty *sui generis*, not of human beings toward human beings but of the
> human race toward itself. For every species of rational beings is objectively—in
> the idea of reason—destined to a common end, namely the promotion of the
> highest good as a good common to all. But, since this highest moral good will
> not be brought about solely through the striving of one individual person for his
> own moral perfection but rather requires a union of such persons into a whole
> toward that very end, [*i.e.*] toward a system of well-disposed human beings in
> which, and through the unity of which alone, the highest moral good can come
> to pass, yet the idea of such a whole, as a universal republic based on the laws
> of virtue, differs entirely from all moral laws (which concern what we know
> to reside within our power), for it is the idea of working toward a whole of
> which we cannot know whether as a whole it is also in our power: so the duty in
> question differs from all others in kind and in principle.[29]

Although, at the individual level, Kant's ethics is entirely governed by the principle
"'Ought' implies 'Can'", the goal of morality—that which makes sense of human
morality—is the establishment of an ethical commonwealth embracing the whole
of mankind, which is a goal entirely beyond the power of any individual on their
own to bring about. Were such a commonwealth to come about, there would be

---

[28] Even in the *Groundwork*, however, towards the end of Section II in the discussion
of the "kingdom of ends" the ideas that we shall be discussing here and that move into the
foreground in later writings are indicated. See pp.87–88 (Ak. 4:438–439).
[29] *Religion within ...*, pp.132–133 (Ak. 6:97–98).

perpetual peace—a state in which going to war would be simply unthinkable. In such a commonwealth there would be harmony between virtue and happiness, and there would never be a conflict between doing the morally right thing and the consequences of so doing.

In the world as it actually is, however, it is easy to think of circumstances in which doing the "right" thing—what reason dictates we should do—can have terrible consequences and circumstances in which doing the "wrong" thing seems the only way to bring order out of chaos. We may consider here a clear case: the dropping of the atomic bombs on Hiroshima and Nagasaki. It has frequently been argued that this was the only way to prevent a long continuation of the war against Japan, which would have cost many more lives, including the lives of innocent Japanese, than were lost in the two cities. We are not concerned here with whether that claim is true or not. What we are concerned with is that the act involved the deliberate killing of innocent human beings—as clear a violation of the categorical imperative as could be imagined and an extreme case of treating human beings as means, not ends. For Kant (and not only for Kant) the dropping of the bomb was simply an act of murder that ought never to have been contemplated, and even to engage in the kind of computation aimed to show that more lives would thereby be saved is a sign of moral corruption.

Kant's stance would seem to leave him vulnerable to the accusation that his insistence on a *rigorous* adherence to the moral law puts him out of touch with the world as it really is, and can even be regarded as a form of self-indulgence. If that is so, Kant's moral stance might seem to be undermined if he has no reply to the person who urges him to accommodate himself to the world as it in fact is—a world in which as he freely concedes:

> Hobbes's statement, *homo hominum naturalis est bellum omnium in omnes*, has no other fault apart from this: it should say, *est status belli ...etc.* For, even though one may not concede that *actual* hostilities are the rule between human beings who do not stand under external and public laws, their condition (*status iuridicus*), *i.e.* the relationship in and through which they are capable of rights (of their acquisition and maintenance) is nonetheless one in which each of them wants to be himself the judge of what is his right *vis-à-vis* others, without either having any security from others with respect to this right or offering them any: and this is a condition of war, wherein every man must be constantly armed against everybody else.[30]

The basic form of his reply is that this "condition of war" is a state "which the natural human being ought to endeavour to leave as soon as possible".[31] If we achieve an ethical commonwealth, a state of perpetual peace—a situation in which *everyone* automatically obeys the moral law, and treats every human being as an

---

30   *Religion within ...*, p.132 (Ak. 6:97).
31   Ibid.

end and not a means—then the kind of conflicts just envisaged would no longer arise. We ought therefore to strive to devote all our energies to establishing such a commonwealth, such a state of perpetual peace, a necessary condition of which is our being prepared ourselves rigorously to follow the moral law and behave *as if* we were already members of such a commonwealth.[32]

In *Toward Perpetual Peace*, he then presents his position as a running battle with "the practical politician" who "takes the stance of looking down with great satisfaction on the theoretical politician as an academic who, with his ineffectual ideas, poses no danger to a state".[33] To repeat the quotation I gave earlier:

> But now the practical man (for whom morals is mere theory) bases his despairing denial of our benign hope (even while granting *ought* and *can*) strictly on this: that he pretends to see in advance, from the nature of the human being that *he is* never *going to will* what is required in order to realize that end leading to perpetual peace.[34]

If Kant is to have a reply to this "practical man", he must be able to present it as a real possibility that the state of perpetual peace will at some time in the future arise. He must be able to *hope* for this as the final goal for humanity, and hope for it as a real possibility and not merely a logical possibility. Only then can he refuse to reconcile himself to the world as it now is.[35]

It is here that I believe we find the real locus for Kant's insistence on the need to postulate God, as the basis for a reply to the question "What may I hope for?":

> We can already anticipate that this duty [the duty laid upon the human race to become members of an ethical community] will need the presupposition of another idea, namely, of a higher moral being through whose universal organization the forces of single individuals, insufficient on their own, are united for a common effect.[36]

---

[32] *Cf. Groundwork*, p.87 (Ak. 4:438): "Consequently, every rational being must act *as if* he were by his maxims at all times a lawgiving member of the universal kingdom of ends" (my italics).

[33] *Perpetual Peace*, p.317 (Ak. 8:343).

[34] *Perpetual Peace*, p.339 (Ak. 8:371). *Cf.* Mary McCarthy: "If someone tells you he is going to make a 'realistic decision,' you immediately understand that he has resolved to do something bad ... if you hear someone say that it is time for a government to follow a realistic line, you can interpret this as meaning that it is time for principles to be abandoned" ("American Realist Playwrights", p.296).

[35] Heb. xiii, 14: "For here we have no lasting city, but we seek the city which is to come."

[36] *Religion within ...*, p.133 (Ak. 6:98).

Recognizing all our Duties as Divine Commands

We are now in a position to suggest an interpretation of Kant's enigmatic claim that to believe in God is to recognize all our duties as divine commands. What is enigmatic about this claim is that on either of two natural interpretations it is completely at odds with virtually everything else Kant says, either about morality or about religion.

According to the first interpretation, Kant is simply *reducing* religion to morality: talking about God's Commandments is simply a mythological way of talking about the moral law. (At one point in the Pölitz lectures, he is indeed prepared to refer to God as "a personification of the moral law".) Taken in isolation this quotation may be susceptible of such a reading and Kant's writings insisting on the intimate connection between morality and religion undoubtedly inspired many later anti-realist accounts of religious language in which God became nothing more than a logical construction out of the moral or religious life. However, this was certainly not Kant's own intention, even though in the *Metaphysic of Morals* he comes close to interpreting the formula in precisely this way.[37] This reading cannot, however, be Kant's ultimate intention. It is impossible to square such an interpretation with *any* of Kant's writings that are explicitly devoted to religion, and it would be impossible to square either with what we have already seen Kant to mean by faith or the need to postulate God.

The second interpretation, however natural, is even more clearly at odds with Kant's whole ethical theory. According to this, the believer in God is the person who acts morally because the duties of morality are commanded by God. Such an interpretation would completely undermine Kant's insistence on the autonomy of the moral agent, and on the fact that it is reason alone that lays the demand to act morally upon us. In fact there are several passages where he is careful to guard against such an interpretation. For example:

> if he believed [in the existence of God] and complied with his duty sincerely and unselfishly according to his conscience, and yet immediately considered himself free from all moral obligation every time he experimentally posited that he might some day become convinced that there is no God, his inner moral attitude would indeed have to be in bad shape.[38]

In the light of all that I have outlined so far of Kant's philosophy of religion, we must take "believing in God as recognizing all our duties as divine commands" instead as combining in epigrammatic form two basic ideas: firstly, we may read it metaphorically as giving expression to Kant's "rigorism" in ethics, as stressing

---

[37]   See p.564 (Ak. 6:443–444). The final sentence of §18 of *The Doctrine of Virtue* in particular has a "reductionist" sound: "In this (*practical*) sense it can therefore be said that to have religion is a duty of the human being to himself."

[38]   *CJ*, p.341 (Ak. 5:452).

the ultimate authority of our moral duties: if it is our moral duty to do something, we ought to do it no matter what else may be the case, and regardless of the possible consequences of our action. We ought not to allow any consideration— even considerations such as pity for those who may be hurt by our action—to stand in our way. And secondly, the idea that in so acting we may have confidence ("certainty") that we are acting in accordance with the will of God, who, as "Holy Legislator", will guarantee an ultimate harmony between the world of nature and the world of morality, so that our strict adherence to moral principles is not pointless and in vain.

Kant on Religious Language and Analogy

We thus postulate God as a "holy legislator" of this world, but as located entirely in a supersensible realm. Kant has "removed knowledge to make room for faith", but that requires that faith should be possible. At the very least, that is to say that the religious claims we make must have a content that is intelligible to us. For that, they must be expressible in human language. Human language is, however, structured and dedicated to the description of the phenomenal world, whereas faith is directed towards a noumenal reality for which our everyday concepts are completely inappropriate.

The "Boundary of Pure Reason"

How then are we able to think about a being that transcends all possible experience?

> Our principles, which limit the use of reason to possible experience alone, could accordingly themselves become *transcendent* and could pass off the limits of our reason for limits of possibilities of things themselves … if a painstaking critique did not guard both the boundaries of our reason even with respect to its empirical use, and set a limit to its pretensions.[39]
>
> It is true: we cannot provide, beyond all possible experience, any determinate concept of what things in themselves may be. But we are nevertheless not free to hold back entirely in the face of inquiries about those things; for experience never fully satisfies reason; it directs us ever further back in answering questions and leaves us unsatisfied as regards their full elucidation.[40]

Within the context of such a conception of the transcendent and this conception of religion, the problem of religious *language* clearly arises in a particularly acute

---

[39] *Prolegomena*, p.141 (Ak. 4:352). It should be noted that Kant later acknowledges that this use of the concept of a boundary is metaphorical: see §59 (p.149 [Ak. 4:360]).
[40] Ibid.

form. Kant will at the outset stress that the pure *unschematized* categories—*substance*, *cause* and so on—since these contain in their unschematized form no admixture of empirical content, can be straightforwardly and univocally applied to God without compromising the absolute transcendence of God that marks Kant's whole approach to religion.

> Every reality is either given to me through pure reason, independently of any experience, or encountered by me in the world of sense. I may ascribe the first kind of reality to God without hesitation, for realities of this kind apply to things in general and determine them through pure understanding. Here no experience is involved and the realities are not even affected by sensibility. Hence if I predicate them of God I need not fear that I am confusing him with an object of sense. For in this case I am not ascribing anything to Him but what is true of Him as a thing in general.[41]

But although this is important, it is in an important sense empty:

> But these concepts determine only *the concept of a thing* in general. They are only predicates *in abstracto* which the deist ascribes to God. It is impossible for us to be satisfied with them alone, for such a God would be of no help to us; he would indeed be a thing, but one wholly isolated and by itself, standing in no relationship to us.[42]

But to go beyond this and flesh out our concept of God, we have no alternative but to "take materials for the concept of God from empirical principles and empirical knowledge",[43] and specifically borrow language from the human sphere, and talk of God as if we were talking of a human being. Hence it appears that we cannot talk of God without becoming involved in more or less gross anthropomorphism. This is the charge that Kant sees Hume as having made against any form of theism:

> His dangerous arguments relate wholly to anthropomorphism, of which he holds that it is inseparable from theism and makes theism self-contradictory, but that if it is eliminated, theism falls with it and nothing but deism remains—from which nothing can be made, which can be of no use to us, and can in no way serve as a foundation for religion and morals.[44]

Kant's task then is to develop an account of religious language that will meet Hume's challenge.

---

[41] Pölitz, p.364 (Ak. 28:1020).
[42] Ibid.
[43] Ibid.
[44] *Prolegomena*, §57, pp.145–146 (Ak. 4:356).

> If we combine the injunction to avoid all transcendent judgments of pure reason with the apparently conflicting command to proceed to concepts that lie beyond the field of immanent (empirical) use, we become aware that both can subsist together, but only directly on the *boundary* of all permitted use of reason—for this boundary belongs just as much to the field of experience as to that of beings of thought.[45]

As Kant acknowledges, this talk of a boundary must be taken metaphorically:[46] whatever we make of Kant's "positive use of the concept of noumenon", it would clearly be an absurd caricature of his position to think of the phenomenal and noumenal realm as two regions abutting one another. As he goes on to say, what he means is that we interpret all our talk about anything, such as God, that transcends any possible experience not as saying anything about God as He is in Himself, but solely as talking about the *relation* of God to the world of experience. In this way our language will reach right up to the limits of experience without ever transgressing those limits.

For we then do not attribute to the Supreme Being any of the properties *in themselves* by which we think the objects of experience, and we thereby avoid *dogmatic* anthropomorphism; but we attribute those properties, nonetheless, to the relation of this being to the world, and allow ourselves a *symbolic* anthropomorphism, which in fact concerns only language and not the object itself.[47]

He will then begin the next section of the *Prolegomena*[48] by saying "This type of cognition is cognition *according to analogy*", so that our next task is to understand his conception of analogy and the way that conception fits with the account of religious language that I have just outlined.

Mathematical and "Philosophical" Analogy

The main account of the application of analogy to the problem of religious language is to be found outside his writings on the philosophy of religion, in the continuation of the passages we have just been looking at in the *Prolegomena*, paragraphs 58–59.[49] But before looking at that account we must first set the scene

---

   [45]   *Prolegomena*, p.146 (Ak. 4:356).

   [46]   *Cf.* the beginning of §59 of the *Prolegomena* (p.149 [Ak. 4:360]).

   [47]   *Prolegomena*, p.146 (Ak. 4:357).

   [48]   *Prolegomena*, §58 (pp.146–149 [Ak. 4:357–360]).

   [49]   The brief discussion of "the noble way of analogy" in the *Lectures on the Philosophical Doctrine of Religion* pp.366–367 (Ak. 28:1023–1024) simply summarizes points that Kant spells out elsewhere. The footnotes on p.107 of *Religion within the Boundaries of Mere Reason* (Ak. 6:65) and on pp. 356–357 of *CJ* (Ak. 5:464) give somewhat shorter versions of the account to be found in the *Prolegomena* but with significant minor variations that serve to amplify the account I am treating as his main account.

for it by interspersing another discussion of analogy also to be found outside his writings on religion, in the first *Critique*. Although he is not concerned in that context with the case of religious language, the point he is making there forms a necessary background for a full appreciation of the way he develops his doctrine of analogy when he does turn to the analogy between God and the world. The idea at stake in the first *Critique* has profound implications, not only for Kant's own philosophy of religion but for the use of analogy in natural theology in general, even for forms of natural theology that have little in common with Kant's own approach to religion.

> In philosophy analogies signify something very different from what they represent in mathematics. In the latter they are formulae which express the equality of two quantitative magnitudes, and are always *constitutive*, so that, if three terms of the proportion are given, the fourth is thereby given, that is, can be constructed. But in philosophy the analogy is not the equality of two quantitative but of two qualitative relationships, and from three terms we can acquire a priori knowledge only of the relation to a fourth, not of the fourth term itself. The relation yields, however, a rule for seeking the fourth term in experience, and a mark whereby it can be detected. An analogy of experience is, therefore, only a rule according to which a unity of experience may arise from perception. It does not tell us how mere perception or empirical intuition in general itself comes about. It is not a principle *constitutive* of the objects, that is, of the appearances, but only *regulative*.[50]

Where Aristotle had explored and exploited the continuities between the mathematical and non-mathematical uses of analogy, Kant highlights a major difference that will become crucial when he turns to the question of religious language. The context of this passage from the first *Critique* is the preamble to the "Analogies of Experience", where Kant is to argue for the necessity of a thoroughgoing analogical structure to the world of experience, so that, *e.g.*, his doctrine of causality will be based on a regular succession that can be expressed in the form: "event A is to event B as event C is to event D", and he is insisting that although we can know a priori that such a structure can be found, so that we can know that every event has a cause, what the causal laws are and what the cause of any particular event is can only be discovered by empirical investigation—an empirical investigation that is, however, guided by the knowledge that there is such an analogical structure to experience.

We can illustrate Kant's point with a far simpler example, which is not bound up with his particular way of construing the causal relation in the first *Critique*. We may consider, on the one hand, a simple case of mathematical analogy: $x/34 = 3/2$. Here it is a straightforward matter of arithmetical computation to work out that x

---

[50]   *CPR*, B222–223.

= 51. In this case there is an a priori guarantee that it is precisely this number that satisfies this equation: in Kant's terminology, the analogy is "constitutive".

Let us, on the other hand, consider a use of analogy outside mathematics, such as Aristotle's use of analogy in his biological writings. As we saw, central to Aristotle's method in biology was exploring analogies between parts of animals, where analogues were functionally equivalent parts (scales are to fishes as feathers are to birds). To take one of his examples, the trunk is to an elephant as a hand is to a human being.[51] What we know at the outset is that in so far as an elephant can do the same thing as a human being—grasp and pick things up—there will be a part of the elephant that corresponds to the hand. But from that fact alone it will be impossible to predict that it is the trunk that carries out this function, and it will be impossible to predict the characteristics of the trunk that enable it to discharge this task. All we know at the outset is that there is a part of the elephant that enables it to pick things up. The establishment of the analogy is a prelude to a detailed empirical investigation, such as that which Aristotle will go on to undertake. The analogy on its own is simply "a rule for seeking the fourth term in experience, and a mark whereby it can be detected"—that is to say, is "regulative".

If, in this way, analogy outside mathematics is, as in this example from Aristotle's practice, a prelude to empirical enquiry, this has profound implications for the use of analogy in theology. If our understanding of religious language is based simply upon the positing of analogies between terrestrial phenomena and God, then this implies that the significance of what we say in talking about God is far more restricted than might initially appear. For in this case, the positing of an analogy cannot function as a prelude to a further empirical enquiry, since God's transcendence rules out the possibility of such enquiry.[52]

---

[51]   Aristotle, *PA*, 658b 27ff.

[52]   It is perhaps worth emphasizing that, even though Kant does not absolutely rule out the possibility of divine revelation (see, for example, Pölitz, p.445: "But reason can *neither deny nor prove* the possibility of such things" [Ak. 28:1119]), there runs through all his writings on religion an extreme scepticism about the possibility of appealing to religious experience or divine revelation in this connection: his grounds being the lack of any criteria for testing the validity of such appeals. For instance, in *Religion within ...* he writes: "The persuasion that we can distinguish the effects of grace from those of nature (virtue), or even to produce these effects in us is *enthusiasm* [*Schwärmerei*]; for nowhere in experience can we recognize a supersensible object, let alone exercise influence upon it to bring it down to us, though there do occur from time to time in the mind movements that work toward morality but which we cannot explain, and about which we are forced to admit our ignorance: 'The wind bloweth where it listeth ... but canst not tell whence it cometh, *etc.*' To want to *perceive* heavenly influences is a kind of madness in which, no doubt, there can also be method (since those alleged inner revelations must always attach themselves to moral, and hence rational, ideas), but which nonetheless always remain a self-deception detrimental to religion" (p.193 [Ak. 6:174]). And in *Conflict*, p.283 (Ak. 7:63): "For if God should really speak to a human being, the latter could never *know* that it was God speaking."

The contrast between the two cases becomes fully apparent if we consider the following passage from Aristotle:

> Yet a further method of classification is by analogy: for we cannot find a single word applicable to a squid's pounce, fish spine and bone, although these too possess common properties as if there were a single osseous nature.[53]

Here Aristotle is interested in the possibility of classifying things not on the standard basis of belonging to species of some genus, but because the things grouped together were analogically related. In English, unlike Greek, we do indeed have the single word "bone" for the case that he cites ("cuttlebone", "fishbone" and "animal bone"). As he indicates, a major part of his interest lies in the fact that in an instance such as this, although we group the substances together initially because of the analogical relationship (cuttlebone is to the squid as fishbone is to the fish as monkey bone is to the monkey), and although they are completely different substances, we discover that they possess a range of common properties, "as if there were a single natural kind". The properties that Aristotle has in mind are properties that they have in common *because* they are analogically related. That is to say, given the analogical relationship—that each provides its host with a skeletal structure—it is to be expected that there will be such common properties—hardness, texture *etc.*—namely properties that enable the substances to perform the function of providing a skeletal structure.

But although in such cases there may well be such common properties, the nature and extent of such properties cannot be inferred simply from the existence of the analogical relationship: it requires further empirical investigation to establish what they are. Without such further empirical investigation—which in the nature of the case there cannot be in the case of God—we cannot infer from the existence of the analogical relationship alone any specific common properties of the analogues.[54]

---

[53] Aristotle, *PostA*, II. 98a 20–23.

[54] It may clarify matters to compare what I have been saying here with Peter Byrne's account in *Kant on God*. It may be that my disagreement with Byrne is terminological rather than real. Byrne sees Kant as rejecting both the "analogy of attribution" and the "analogy of proper proportionality". I believe that Kant used the word "analogy" in a purely Aristotelian way—that is only to mean what came to be known as the "analogy of proper proportionality". Byrne writes (p. 69), and so far I am in agreement with him: "According to proper proportionality, we can ascribe intelligence to God in so far as we presume there must be a property in God that plays the same role in his nature and activities that intelligence plays in human nature and its activities." Byrne, however, continues: "Analogy of proper proportionality is out because Kant's drastic agnosticism about the divine nature forbids us giving an account of it such that we could then understand the role alleged properties like intelligence play in it." I see nothing wrong with saying that on Kant's understanding of analogy, there is *some* property in God that plays the same role in His activities that intelligence plays in human activities. Kant's austere understanding of

Analogy in the Prolegomena

We may now return to the discussion of analogy in the *Prolegomena*. As we saw, Kant has begun that discussion of analogy in the *Prolegomena* by freely conceding to Hume that if we wish to advance beyond deism to theism—that is to say beyond a merely metaphysical hypothesis with a conception of God with only "ontological properties" to a conception in which we ascribe properties that give to our belief in God a genuine religious interest, all our language for talking about God is inevitably anthropomorphic. Kant will indeed contend that this is so, even in cases such as the words "understanding" or "just" where it is not immediately obvious that this is so:

> If, however, I separate understanding from sensibility, in order to have a pure understanding, then nothing but the mere form of thinking, without intuition, is left; through which, by itself, I cannot cognize anything determinate, hence cannot cognize any object. To that end I would have to think to myself a different understanding, which intuits its objects, of which, however, I do not have the least concept, since the human understanding is discursive and can cognize only by means of universal concepts.[55]

And in *Religion within the Boundaries of Mere Reason* he writes:[56]

> It is plainly a limitation of human reason, one which is inseparable from it, that we cannot think of any significant worth in the actions of a person without at the same time portraying this person or his expression in human guise, even though we do not thereby mean to say that this is how things are in themselves (κατ' ἀλήθειαν) for we always need a certain analogy with natural being to make supersensible characteristics comprehensible to us.

Where the discussion has led so far is to say that even if "symbolic" anthropomorphism is inevitable if we are to talk about God at all, we can avoid "dogmatic" anthropomorphism by restricting our interpretation of such anthropomorphic language in such a way that any claim that we make about God only tells us something about God's relation to the world and to humanity, and

---

the analogical relationship is, however, such that *all* that we could possibly know about that property is that it has the same kind of causal powers and effects as human intelligence. Saying that is quite compatible with saying that we remain completely agnostic about God's intrinsic nature.

[55] *Prolegomena*, p.145 (Ak. 4:355). What Kant says here implies that to represent, e.g., the claim that God was omniscient in the form $(\forall p)\ (p \to$ God knows that $p)$ would already be to be guilty of anthropomorphism, since it would ascribe propositional knowledge to God and hence a discursive understanding.

[56] *Religion within ...*, p.107 (Ak. 6:65).

nothing whatever about God's intrinsic properties, about God as He is "in Himself". What we have now to understand is the connection between this contention and the concept of analogy—how it is that the use of analogy succeeds in achieving this restriction.

Kant understands the concept of analogy in precisely the same way as Aristotle, namely as a four-term relation "A is to B as C is to D", and is adhering rigorously to that way of using the word "analogy". He emphasizes at the outset that no more is to be read into the claim that A and C are analogous than that such a four-term relation holds: that is to say, A and C are analogues, if and only if for some third and fourth terms (B and D), A is related to B as C is related to D: he will then insist that this in no way implies any further intrinsic similarities whatever between A and C:

> This type of cognition is cognition *according to analogy*, which surely does not signify, as the word is usually taken, an imperfect similarity between two things, but rather a perfect similarity between two relations in wholly dissimilar things.[57]

For Kant, then, if we are to use analogy to interpret the language we use in speaking about God, we need to find appropriate substitutions for the variables in "God is to X as human beings are to Y", and to interpret "God is F" ("wise", "loving") along the lines "God is to X as human beings that are F are to Y".[58] In the light of what has gone before, the "… is to …" in this formula will be spelled out in basically causal terms: it is here that the idea that the unschematized category of causality can be applied univocally to both phenomena and noumena becomes the crucial underpinning of Kant's account. The general pattern, then, of Kant's explanation of religious language will run along the lines: to say that God is F is to be interpreted as meaning that God produces the same kind of effects in the world as are ideally produced by human beings who are F. As I have already stressed, Kant wants this to be understood in such a way as to imply nothing about the nature of God as He is in Himself. In *Religion within* … Kant illustrates his conception as follows:

> I also want to remark incidentally that, in the ascent from the sensible to the supersensible, we can indeed *schematize* (render a concept comprehensible through analogy with something of the senses) but in no way infer by analogy that what pertains to the sensible must also be attributed to the supersensible (thus *expanding* the concept of the latter) … Thus I cannot say: Just as I cannot make the cause of a plant *comprehensible* to me (or the cause of any organic creature, or in general of the purposive world) in any other way than on the analogy of an

---

[57] *Prolegomena*, pp.146–147 (Ak. 4:357).

[58] This always allows for the possibility that we make the same substitutions for "X" and "Y" (*e.g.* with many examples, we may well substitute "the world" for the variable in both cases).

artificer in relation to his work (a clock), namely by attributing understanding to the cause, so too must the cause of the plant *have* understanding; *i.e.* attributing understanding to it is not just a condition of my capacity to comprehend but of the possibility of itself being a cause. But between the relation of a schema to its concept and the relationship of this very schema of the concept to the thing itself there is no analogy, but a formidable leap (μετάβασις εἰς ἄλλο γένος) which leads straight into anthropomorphism.[59]

And in *The Critique of Judgment*, he reinforces this conception by comparing this with the ways in which we talk in anthropomorphic terms about animals:

> when we compare the artful acts of animals with those of man, we do not know what basis in these animals gives rise to such effects, but we do know what basis gives rise to similar effects in the case of man (namely, reason); and hence we conceive of the basis for such acts in animals by means of the basis of such acts in man: *i.e.*, we conceive of the former basis as an analogue of reason. In doing so we wish to indicate at the same time that the basis of the artistic power in animals, called instinct, while indeed different in kind from reason, still has a similar relation to its effect (for example, if we compare the constructions of beavers with those of human beings). But that does not entitle me to infer that because man needs *reason* in order to construct things, beavers too must have it, and call this an *inference by analogy* … Similarly, though I can conceive of the causality of the supreme world cause when I compare its purposive products in the world with the works of art of man, by analogy with an understanding, I cannot by analogy infer that it has these same properties: for in this case the principle that authorizes such an inference is just what is lacking, *i.e.*, we do not have *paritas rationis* [sameness of grounds] for including the supreme being in one and the same general kind as man (as regards their respective causalities).[60]

---

[59] *Religion within* …, p.107 (Ak. 6:65). Martin Warner suggested to me that I amend the phrase in the di Giovanni translation from "the possibility itself to be a cause" to "the possibility of itself being a cause", which certainly seems to make Kant's meaning clearer.

[60] *CJ*, pp.356–357 (Ak. 5:464). It is instructive to compare and contrast this passage with Aquinas' discussion of the question "Can the human mind arrive at a knowledge of God?" in his commentary on Boethius' *De Trinitate* (Question 1, Article 2): "So the human mind advances in three ways in knowing God, though it does not reach a knowledge of what he is, but only that he is. First, by knowing more perfectly his power in producing things. Second by knowing him as the cause of more lofty effects which, because they bear some resemblance to him, give more praise to his greatness. Third, by an ever-growing knowledge of him as distant from everything that appears in his effects. Thus Dionysus says that we know God as the cause of all things, by transcendence, and by negation" (*Faith, Reason and Theology*, p.22). There are many obvious contrasts between Kant's account of religious language and that of Aquinas, reflecting broader differences in their respective theologies, but a major part of the explanation for the very different accounts of religious language we find in Kant from that which we found in Aquinas is attributable to the fact

We all of us talk anthropomorphically about animals, and in many contexts seem to have no alternative but to talk about them in anthropomorphic terms, apparently ascribing to them human emotions and intellectual powers.[61] We do this even if we believe that in reality they do not have such emotions or intellectual powers, or, at the very least, are agnostic as to the basis within the animal that gives rise to the behaviour that we find it natural to describe in these terms. The use of analogy of course does not *deny* that the emotions and inner life of animals are the same as those of humans: it neither affirms nor denies anything about such inner life. We may talk of monkeys as clever, spiders as ingenious, dogs as affectionate, mother bears as loving their cubs and so on. In so doing, we may actually be ascribing the same inner life to these animals as that of human beings, and thus *thinking* of them in human terms, and thus be involved, in Kant's terms, in *dogmatic* anthropomorphism. But we may not. We may only be using this language as a way of characterizing their behaviour and the nature of their interaction with the world. We then exploit a *symbolic* anthropomorphism, where we are talking *as if* they are human beings, but in fact are indirectly describing their behaviour by seeing it as the kind of behaviour that would be typical of a certain sort of human being. To describe the spider as ingenious will be to say nothing other than that the spider is to the web as the watchmaker is to the watch. We are talking of the spider as if it were a watchmaker, when what we are really doing is comparing the productions of the spider—its webs—with the productions of the watchmaker—the watches.

The core of Kant's position is that we can exploit *precisely the same* symbolic anthropomorphism in order to talk about God, and thereby talk significantly about God without any taint of dogmatic anthropomorphism. Just as we may use the language of human emotions and cognitive powers analogically to describe animals without begging any questions about the nature of their supposedly "lower" emotions and cognitive powers, so we may do the same for God, without begging any questions about the nature of His higher emotions and cognitive powers.

> if one only grants us, at the outset, the *deistic* concept of a first being as a necessary hypothesis (as does Hume in his *Dialogues* in the person of Philo as opposed to Cleanthes), which is a concept in which one thinks the first being by means of ontological predicates alone, of substance, cause, *etc.* … then nothing can keep us from predicating of this being a *causality through reason* with respect to the world, and thus from crossing over to theism, but without

---

that Kant's argument here shows that, of Aquinas' three stages in our knowledge of God, he would regard the second stage as involving an illegitimate inference, and as a consequence he sees us as obliged to construct an account of religious language in which only the first and the third stages of Aquinas' account are regarded as acceptable.

[61] For excellent discussions of the issues involved here, see Lorraine Daston, "Intelligences: Angelic, Animal, Human" and Sandra D. Mitchell, "Anthropomorphism and Cross-Species Modelling" (both in Lorraine Daston and Gregg Mitman, *Thinking with Animals*).

our being compelled to attribute this reason to that being in itself, as a property inhering in it. ... reason is not thereby transposed as a property onto the first being in itself, but only *onto the relation* of that being to the sensible world, and therefore anthropomorphism is completely avoided.[62]

Recapitulation

We may summarize Kant's philosophy of religion along the following lines. Reason obliges us to obey the categorical imperative, regardless of the consequences of our actions. But so that the moral stance required of us should not be undermined, morality must make sense. We must be able to see the world as one that is moving towards a final destination in which there is the *summum bonum*—a harmony between virtue and happiness. However, nature, of itself, contains no guarantee of there being any such harmony. We therefore postulate God as the guide and governor of the world moving it towards the ultimate arrival of the *summum bonum*.

We can make such a God and His activity comprehensible to ourselves, by talking of the world *as if* it were guided and governed by a human being, while at the same time rendering such a way of talking innocuous and free from any taint of anthropomorphism by interpreting everything we say analogically.

Discussion

The first comment on Kant's account of religion as I have presented it is that although Kant as an Enlightenment thinker is in many respects moving in a completely different thought world from the classical reformers, this account bears strong traces of his Lutheran and pietist heritage. There is the pietist emphasis on the practical life of the Christian, as opposed to theological speculation. There is the strong Lutheran emphasis upon divine transcendence. Despite the fact that Kant would vehemently reject the Reformation doctrine of the total depravity of man, his stress on the existence of "radical evil" in human beings that was so deeply at odds with so much Enlightenment thinking may also be symptomatic of this heritage. But above all, what we have just seen accords well with Melanchthon's principle "*Hoc est Christum cognoscere, beneficia eius cognoscere*".[63] Just as many have taken Melanchthon's principle as a justification for refusing to enter into metaphysical speculation in theology, so the account of religious language we have just seen not only makes such speculation idle, it makes it meaningless: the

---

[62]   *Prolegomena*, p.148 (Ak. 4:358–359).

[63]   "This is what it is to know Christ: to know His benefits". The Christology that Kant presents in *Religion within* ... may be seen as conforming exactly to Melanchthon's principle (see pp.103–108 [Ak. 6:60–66]).

only interpretation we can ever make of religious claims will always turn out to be claims about their repercussions for the religious life of the believer.[64]

The Ramseyfication of Theology

The account of religious language we have been looking at has at its core the following idea: when we say, *e.g.*, "God is wise" what we are saying, properly understood, amounts to saying "There is something, **X**, with some property **Φ**, where **Φ** is of such a nature that the activities of **X** with respect to the phenomenal world are such as to produce the kind of effects that one would expect of a wise human being". If we express his position in this somewhat cumbersome fashion, what this immediately suggests is a comparison with what later, twentieth century, philosophers have done, particularly in the philosophy of science, when they have proposed that we should "Ramseyfy" a theory.[65]

This is an idea first proposed by Frank Ramsey in "Theories". His concern was giving an account of a theory designed to explain observable phenomena, where the theory itself contained reference to theoretical entities. On his account you thought of there being a "primary" language in which the observable phenomena could be described and a secondary language—the language in which the theory was couched:

> The best way to write our theory seems to be this ($\exists \, \alpha, \, \beta, \, \gamma$) : dictionary . axioms.[66]

----

[64] One may also think of the old Lutheran hymn: "What God is we shall never know, but from His covenant He will never go."

[65] It is also instructive to compare Kant's account of religious language with the somewhat different, but related, account of scientific theories given by Norman Robert Campbell. The reason for mentioning him is that he explicitly posits the need for *analogy* into his account of his "dictionary"—a "dictionary" that plays the same role in his account as Ramsey's "dictionary", namely, that of relating the theory to the observable phenomena ("Laws and Theories", p.318): "But a theory cannot consist of a hypothesis alone; for if it did, it could not explain the physical part of laws and would have no relation to experiment. The relation to experiment is established by a 'dictionary', which (like everything that concerns experiment) is never stated formally. It consists of entries relating to measurable magnitudes certain combinations of the variables characteristic of the hypothesis ... In classical theories the dictionary entries usually are suggested immediately by the analogy on which the theory is based. In modern theories they are not so obvious; much of the technical discussion of relativity and wave mechanics concerns the appropriateness of proposed entries." For a fuller discussion of his conception of the need for analogy in one's account of scientific theories, see *What is Science?*, pp. 94–97, where he says, for example, on p.96, "The explanation offered by a theory ... is always based on an analogy, and the system with which an analogy is traced is always one of which the laws are known."

[66] Ramsey, "Theories", p.131.

We have here three components. Firstly, there is "($\exists\ \alpha,\ \beta,\ \gamma$)"—here we replace all theoretical terms mentioned in the theory by existential quantifiers that will typically be higher order quantifiers replacing the theoretical predicates. Secondly, there is the "dictionary"—this is the component of the theory linking the sentences of the primary language to sentences of the secondary language. And thirdly there are the axioms that specify the theory.

Although Kant's purpose is different from Ramsey's, we can see each of these three components in the version of religious language that I have just ascribed to him. The differences stem from the fact that whereas Ramsey was interested in giving an account of the way in which we should set out a scientific theory to explain the observable phenomena, Kant is trying to explain how we can use a phenomenal language to capture the significance of theological claims about a noumenal God. Hence, Ramsey's "axioms" will be replaced by the theological claims Kant needs to postulate in his philosophy of religion.

Ramsey's basic idea has been adopted, and adapted, for a variety of different purposes,[67] but the interesting question in the present context is whether Ramseyfication is put in the service of an "anti-realist" (reductionist) or a "realist" conception of theories. In the philosophy of science, "Ramsey sentence" accounts of scientific theories have been put forward both by those arguing for some form of scientific realism and by those arguing for a purely instrumentalist account of scientific terms. It is clearly important for Kant that he should still be regarded as having faith in a transcendent, noumenal, God. Therefore, if we view him as Ramseyfying theology, it can only be in a form that rebuts the charge that the effect of Ramseyfication is to reduce a theory to its empirical content, and thus, in Kant's case, retain a language that apparently talks about God, but actually has the effect of eliminating God from the picture. Kant's account apparently makes theological claims that have implications for the history of the phenomenal world. The question is: if, in the way that I have suggested, Kant is to be seen as Ramseyfying those theological claims, does the resultant account of religious language make any substantial claims over and above the claims that it implies for the phenomenal world?

There is, however, a crucial difference between what Kant is doing and what Ramsey does. Ramsey assumes that the theory is couched in a purely extensional language, and it is in versions of Ramseyfication in which there are no intensional terms in the theoretical language that Ramseyfication can most plausibly be seen as part of a reductionist strategy.[68] But Kant is assigning an essential role to "cause" in his account, and cause is a paradigmatically intensional notion. With this, Kant's theology remains committed to a transcendent deity, even if in the limited form of there being *something* behind the scene governing the phenomena.

How far, in introducing a twentieth-century idea like Ramseyfication into a discussion of Kant, is this anachronistic? It goes without saying that an eighteenth-

---

[67]   See, *e.g.*, David Lewis, "Psychophysical and Theoretical Identifications".

[68]   *Cf.* Joseph Melia and Juha Saatsi, "Ramseyfication and Theoretical Content".

century thinker could not have expressed himself in terms of quantification theory, let alone higher-order quantifiers. It is also clear that Kant's position can be perfectly expressed without this detour into the twentieth century. It is, however, I believe instructive and valuable to recognize that Kant is here adopting essentially the same strategy as was to be adopted in a very different context by later philosophers such as Ramsey.

"A Perfect Similarity between Two Relations"?

Kant has, it seems to me, presented us with a coherent account of religious language that, given his premises and given the limited aspirations of his theology, is fully adequate for his purposes. There is, however, another feature of his account of analogy that deserves discussion, since it gives rise to a number of questions that his discussion, at least as it stands, does not deal with adequately. This is his insistence in the *Prolegomena* that analogy "signifies,... *a perfect similarity [eine vollkomme Ähnlichkeit]* between two relations in wholly dissimilar things"[69] or in the *Critique of Judgment* that:

> **Analogy** (in a qualitative sense) is the *identity [Identität]* of the relation between bases and consequences (causes and effects), insofar as it is present despite what difference in kind between the things themselves (*i.e.*, considered apart from that relation), or between those properties themselves that contain the basis of similar consequences.[70]

1. What is meant by "perfect similarity" or "identity of the relation" in this context?
2. Can God enter into the *same* relation with the phenomenal world as a human being? Can we really say "in the way that a watch, a ship, and a regiment are related to an artisan, a builder, and a commander, the sensible world (or everything that makes up the bases of this sum total of appearances) is related to the unknown"?[71]
3. Does the fact that, even if God has no intrinsic properties in common with human beings, he is conceived as having relational properties in common with them re-introduce anthropomorphism into the account?

Such questions are inevitably prompted by Kant's discussion, but they have an importance that goes beyond the particularities of his account, since these questions or questions very like them can arise for any attempt to appeal to analogy to resolve the problem of religious language. Hence these questions will recur. But, in the

---

[69] *Prolegomena*, pp.146–147 (Ak. 4:357) (my italics).
[70] *CJ*, p.356 footnote (Ak. 5:464) (my italics).
[71] *Prolegomena*, p.146 (Ak. 4:357).

present context, I shall restrict my attention to Kant's own attempts to answer them.

The meaning of the phrase "*perfect* similarity" is far from clear, and what it is for relations holding in very different domains to be *identical* needs clarifying. It is clear why Kant needs to make these apparently strong claims about the relations: if he were to make weak claims, saying only that there was *some* resemblance between the relations, he would fail to secure the clear intelligibility of religious language that he is after, and if he were to say only that the relations were analogous, this would start to introduce an infinite regress into the account.

Kant illustrates his meaning with the following example:

> Such is an analogy between the legal relations of human actions and the mechanical relation of moving forces. I can never do anything to another without giving him the right to do the same to me under the same conditions; just as a body cannot act on another body with its motive force without thereby causing the other body to react just as much on it. Right and motive force are here completely dissimilar things, but in their relation there is nonetheless complete similarity.[72]

and in the *Critique of Judgment* comments on this example:

> by analogy with the law that action and reaction are equal when bodies attract or repel one another, I can also conceive of the community between the members of a commonwealth that is governed by rules of law. But I cannot transfer those specific characteristics (the material attraction or repulsion) to the community, and attribute them to the citizens so that these will form a system called a state.[73]

The example is not entirely convincing: it is doubtful whether the "similarity" of the relation is as complete as Kant claims, but, treated with caution, it can be seen as illustrating an idea that does indeed vindicate Kant's position. What Kant's example indicates is the possibility, which we already noted in Chapter 1 in the mathematical employment of analogy, of using analogy to treat one situation as a *model* of another situation, where despite the complete dissimilarity of the items in the two situations, the analogy sets up a network of corresponding relationships. At its simplest, we can think of a graph representing the profits and losses of a company, where the rising and falling of a line on the graph represents the varying financial health of a company: here there is clearly no intrinsic similarity between a point on the graph and the financial assets of the company, but the relations between the points map onto the relations between the financial state of the company at different times. Kant, however, clearly wants an example that

---

[72]   *Prolegomena*, p.147 (Ak. 4:357).

[73]   *CJ*, p.357 (Ak. 5:464–465).

goes beyond the simple mathematical "quantitative" relations given by such an example.

Although Kant's own example suggests the idea he has in mind, a clearer example would be that provided by Dedre Gentner and Donald R. Gentner, who explore the possibility of using analogy to provide models for an electrical circuit: either by water draining down pipes from a reservoir or by people moving down crowded corridors, where they are interested in the psychological question how far people can exploit such models in their understanding of electrical phenomena, by teaching basic laws of electricity to two different groups of people using one model for one group and the other for the other.[74] Here, the models require no intrinsic similarities between people and electrons, say, but only that the interactions between the people should mimic the interactions between the electrons.

The thought is that by abstracting from the specific content of the relationships, we can arrive at a relation that is indeed the same in both the model and the situation modelled, and do so in such a way that we can free religious language of every taint of anthropomorphism. Things are, however, not quite as straightforward as this would suggest. There is a difference between the way Kant applies analogy in the case of religious language and the way it is applied in these examples that needs commenting on. In both his example comparing legal relations between people with the mechanics of bodies and in the example comparing electrical current with flowing water, we have two different domains, **A** and **B**, where objects α_1, α_2 ... belong to **A**, and β_1, β_2 ... belong to **B** and where relations between the αs mirror relations between the βs. But in the main case that interests him, the analogy between God's relation to the world and human relations within the world, we have two domains **A** and **B**—the noumenal realm and the phenomenal world. However, Kant is not comparing relations within the noumenal realm with relations in the phenomenal world, but comparing a relation that crosses the two domains—the relation of God to the world—to a relation purely in the phenomenal world.

The question therefore that needs addressing if Kant's account is to work is "Can the relation between a noumenal being and a phenomenal being be the *same* relation as that between two phenomenal beings?" Here we need to bring in another aspect of Kant's thought: that the pure (unschematized) categories are equally applicable in both the phenomenal realm and the noumenal realm, and in particular, the pure concept of *cause*—the relation of ground to consequent ("If this, then necessarily that")—is so applicable. In this way, the full working out

---

[74] "Flowing Waters or Teeming Crowds: Mental Models of Electricity". Note that the point of the experiment is that one analogical model preserves one set of relations, the other a different set, so that the two groups reacted differently when asked to predict the consequences of Ohm's Law for different electrical circuits. What this illustrates is something I pointed out in Chapter 1: in analogical reasoning, one may only legitimately infer that the situation modelled will share with the model those properties that are invariant under modelling. Hence, if the modelling is set up in different ways, the properties that may be legitimately inferred may differ.

of Kant's position runs along the following lines: as Kant says, for him to talk of God's love is to say: "the promotion of the happiness of the children = a is to the love of the parents = b as the welfare of humankind = c is to the unknown in God = x, which we call love",[75] where we explicate the relation in purely causal terms. Kant will freely concede that we can form no definite conception of the workings of such divine causation, but even without any clear conception of the way such causation works, we may make sense of the claim that God brings about such effects in the world on behalf of humanity as we would expect loving parents to bring about on behalf of their children.

Here, at this level of abstraction we can indeed say that we are positing the *same* relation between God and humanity and parents and their children. What is more, if we insist, as Kant does, that the positing of this relation is *all* we mean when we talk of God as loving, we now have a programme for interpreting what we say about God, including our use of such human terms as "loving" or "father", without thereby introducing any trace of anthropomorphism into the account.

The Implications of Kant's Account of Religious Language

Kant has thus succeeded in producing a fully coherent account of religious language, given his framework: it is perhaps the simplest and most elegant account of religious language that anyone has offered. If there are difficulties with his account of religion they lie elsewhere, either with the "positive use of the concept of noumenon", or with the coherence of his defence of the need to postulate God. His account of the use of analogy succeeds in ridding religious language of every trace of anthropomorphism, while retaining an intelligible significance for that language. He has given us a way of talking about the transcendent without transgressing the boundary between the world of experience and what lies beyond that boundary. But he has done so at a cost: *every* claim about God is to be interpreted purely in terms of the implications of the existence of God for the religious life. This is a cost that Kant himself is only too willing to pay, but the question that this account of religious language raises is "If Kant were right about the implications of using analogy as the key to understanding language about God, how severe would the limits be that that places upon the nature of the claims we could make about God?"

Despite his evident deep respect, even reverence, for Jesus Christ, Kant cannot in any real sense be counted as an orthodox Christian. If he counts Christianity as the highest form of religion, it is only in a relative sense: each of Judaism, Islam and Christianity had as their core a "religion of morality", but Christianity approximated most closely to the idea of being such a religion. It is therefore no criticism of him if the account we have just seen places severe restrictions on the possibilities of significant claims about God. As he says,

[75] *Prolegomena*, p.147 (Ak. 4:358).

We determine the concept [of a supreme being] only with respect to the world and hence with respect to us, and *we have need of no more.*[76]

If, however, we wish to ask after the relevance of Kant's account of religious language to other, more orthodox, theologies, we must look at the question whether those restrictions are acceptable.

We can consider this question most simply if we consider a particular case: Kant's treatment of the doctrine of the Trinity in *Religion within the Boundaries of Mere Reason*:

> Now in accordance with this need of practical reason, the universal true religious faith is faith in God (1) as the almighty creator of heaven and earth, i.e. morally as *holy* lawgiver; (2) as the preserver of the human race, as its *benevolent* ruler and moral guardian; (3) as the administrator of his own holy laws, i.e. as *just* judge.
>
> This faith really contains no mystery, since it expresses solely God's moral bearing toward the human race. It is also by nature available to all human reason and is therefore to be met with in the religion of most civilized peoples.
>
> But, if this very faith (in a divine Trinity) were to be regarded not just as the representation of a practical idea, but as a faith that ought to represent what God is in himself, it would be a mystery surpassing all human concepts, hence unsuited to a revelation humanly comprehensible, and could only be declared in this respect as mystery. Faith in it as an extension of theoretical cognition of the divine nature would only be profession of a creed of ecclesiastical faith totally unintelligible to human beings or, if they think they understand it, the profession of an anthropomorphic creed, and not the least would thereby be accomplished for moral improvement.[77]

What Kant offers here clearly falls far short of anything that could seriously be described as a doctrine of the Trinity as has been traditionally conceived. The important point is that Kant is not merely arguing that this attenuated version of Trinitarian doctrine (which amounts to no more than assigning God three roles in His dealings with the world) is the most that we are justified in claiming as long as we remain "within the limits of mere reason". He is claiming that on his account of the way religious language is to be interpreted, this is the most anyone could

---

[76] *Prolegomena*, p.147 (Ak. 4:358) (my italics).

[77] *Religion within ...*, pp.165–167 (Ak. 6:139–142). Cf. *Conflict*, p.264 (Ak. 7:39): "The doctrine of the Trinity, taken literally, has *no practical relevance at all*, even if we think we understand it, and it is even more clearly irrelevant if we realize that it transcends all our concepts.—Whether we are to worship three or ten persons in the Deity makes no difference."

possibly *mean* by a doctrine of the Trinity, at least if they do not lapse into an anthropomorphic interpretation of it.

Kant has thus eliminated all possibility of any discussion of the nature of God as He is in Himself, and although his account of religion certainly contains a strong commitment to a belief in a transcendent God, *everything* that we say about God is always to be interpreted solely in terms of the repercussions for humanity of the existence and activity of God. In this way, Kant has succeeded in eliminating all traces of anthropomorphism from his "rational theology". But if he has sedulously avoided the Scylla of anthropomorphism, his account of religion is inevitably sucked into the Charybdis of extreme anthropocentrism. Kant would clearly not himself regard that as a criticism, but the most significant question posed by his account of the role of analogy in the interpretation of religious language is "Do appeals to analogy in our discussions of theology, if thought through to the end, inevitably lead to such anthropocentrism? And does religion inevitably turn in to no more than 'treating the law of morality as if it were a divine command?'"

Chapter 6
Karl Barth

Karl Barth's rich, complex and elusive discussion of religious language has received far less attention than other aspects of his theology. There has been a great deal of discussion of his treatment of analogy, and his contrast between an *analogia entis* and an *analogia fidei*, but this has for the most part been concerned with metaphysical questions concerning the nature of the analogy between God and the world, or the epistemological question whether that analogy gives us knowledge of God. But there has been far less written on the application of analogy in accounting for the language we use about God, which is our present concern. For a number of reasons, his account of religious language is far more difficult to interpret and discuss than that of either Aquinas or Kant. It is worth mentioning some of these reasons before looking in detail at aspects of Barth's theology and his treatment of analogy.

The most obvious consideration is the sheer vastness and rich complexity of the *Church Dogmatics*, making it impossible in our context to do more than indicate the theological themes that are most relevant to the topic of analogy. By comparison, Kant's theological concerns are relatively circumscribed, so that in his case the scale of the critical philosophy does not stand in the way of giving a full discussion of the role of analogy within his conception of religion. And even though, in the case of Aquinas, the *Summa Theologiae* is comparable in scope and richness to the *Church Dogmatics*, his actual treatment of the analogy of names can be treated in relative isolation from the subsequent parts of the *Summa* without falsification. However, even if Chapter 5 of *Church Dogmatics* II/1 is for our purposes the central text, what Barth says there cannot be properly understood except against the background of all that has led up that point. Equally, Chapter 5 cannot be treated as his definitive statement on the issues that concern us, but will be modified and clarified, for instance, by his treatment of analogy and the image of God in Volume III of the *Church Dogmatics*.

A second, equally important, consideration is Barth's conception of the nature of the project of theology and the implications of that conception for theological method. For Barth, the truth about God never is, and never becomes, a human possession, and dogma, as the definitive statement of a theological truth, is never to be attained in this lifetime:

> dogma differs from *doxa*. It is not something that is humanly established, posited, or maintained. It is something that is discovered, acknowledged, and promulgated. It is the statement underlying Christian statements, derived from the Word of God. But the dogma of which we say *this* is not given; it is sought.

Even acknowledged articles of faith are only an approximation to it. What is given is not unchangeable and infallible dogma but the dogma that in principle is changeable, reformable, and in need of supplementation.[1]

What this means is that there is no article of faith, no matter how deeply entrenched in the traditions of the Church, that cannot be challenged. As a result, theology has an essentially exploratory character, and theological work is to be regarded as a journey, a *theologia viatorum*:

We are on the way. This certainly indicates the limit, but it also indicates the positive possibility of our cognition. At best our theology is *theologia viatorum*. It is as such that it can and will be true. This concept was used in the older theology to designate the distinction of our present temporal from our future eternal knowledge of God, the distinction between faith and sight. In distinction to the former, the latter was described as *theologia comprehensorum* or *theologia patria*; the knowledge of those who are at home, who, no longer wandering on from one hour to another, from one decision to another, stand once for all at the goal of faith and know God face to face.[2]

Because of this, no statement in the *Church Dogmatics* can be regarded as Barth's definitive position on *any* theological issue. It is not simply that even his most passionately held convictions are always held with the proviso "until better instructed by the Word of God": the theological method that he evolved to correspond to his conception of theology as a *theologia viatorum* is such that every question will be revisited as the investigation progresses.

As a result, claims that Barth makes at one point in the *Church Dogmatics* may be revisited and then amplified, modified or even rejected. Thus, if we wish to present Barth's account of religious language, we have to engage in the far more complex task of integrating the various things he writes at different stages of his enquiry, and at the same time we have always to allow for the possibility that what he had written earlier might be something that he would no longer hold at a later stage of his discussion.

Barth's Theological Project

Before turning to Barth's treatment of language, I must first sketch some central themes from Barth's theology that provide the context for his explicit treatment of talking about God.

---

[1]   *Göttingen Dogmatics* I, p.39.

[2]   *CD* II/1, p.209.

"Dialectical Theology"

To understand what follows, we must consider Barth's break with liberal protestant theology at the beginning of the outbreak of the First World War. It was the insights that led to that break that were to inform the whole of his theology, and make him set theology in a wholly new direction. Barth had been an enthusiastic pupil of Wilhelm Herrmann, even if with a radically leftwing political agenda. There were undoubtedly a number of factors that were responsible for his gradual disillusionment with the theology that he had learnt. In the Preface to the second edition of his *Commentary on Romans*, he himself cites a number of reasons for his change of direction, of which we may mention two.

> I myself know what it means year in year out to mount the steps of the pulpit, conscious of the responsibility to understand and to interpret, and longing to fulfil it; and yet, utterly incapable, because at the University I had never been brought beyond that well-known "Awe in the presence of History" which means in the end no more than that all hope of engaging in the dignity of understanding and interpretation has been surrendered.[3]

He found that the form of theology that had seemed so exciting when he was at university left him empty-handed when it was put to the test in the parish pulpit.

First, and most important: the continued study of Paul himself.[4]

What Barth encountered in his reading of Paul was a way of talking and thinking about the relation of God to humanity that was completely different from that which he had encountered in his university studies, and he dared to transpose the complex Pauline dialectical presentation of the Law at the beginning of *Romans* into a complex dialectical presentation of all religious phenomena.[5] How far the resulting commentary is an interpretation of Paul and how far it is a theological meditation inspired by the reading of Paul we need not decide. What is decisive from our point of view is that religion, piety and morality are here displaced from their role as providing a foundation on which theology can be based, and placed instead under the judgment of God.

The event, however, that provided the occasion for Barth's decisive break with all forms of liberal Protestantism occurred at the outbreak of the First World War:

---

[3] *R2*, Preface to 2nd edition, p.9.

[4] *R2*, Preface to 2nd edition, p.3.

[5] For instance, in a typical passage, commenting on Rom. iii, 1, he writes: "What advantage then hath the Jew? He has an advantage. He possesses law—the impress of revelation—experience, religion, piety, perception, vision: in fact he has a Biblical outlook" (*R2*, p.90).

The actual end of the 19th century as the "good old days" came for theology as for everything else with the fateful year of 1914. Accidentally or not, a significant event took place during that very year. Ernst Troeltsch, the well-known professor of systematic theology and the leader of the then most modern school, gave up his chair in theology for one in philosophy. One day in early August 1914 stands out in my personal memory as a black day. Ninety-three German intellectuals impressed public opinion by their proclamation in support of the war policy of Wilhelm II and his counsellors. Among these intellectuals I discovered to my horror almost all of my theological teachers whom I had greatly venerated. In despair over what this indicated about the signs of the time I suddenly realized that I could not any longer follow either their ethics and dogmatics or their understanding of the Bible and of history.[6]

Although in time of war absurd militaristic propaganda on all sides is not uncommon,[7] the documents that Barth is referring to here are astonishing. Not only do they contain completely uncritical reproduction of imperial propaganda—including blatant falsehoods in defence of German actions—the thought runs through them that the war was a just war, because it was a war in defence of "German Culture".[8] In brief, these proclamations showed complete intellectual, moral and spiritual bankruptcy. As the war progressed there emerged a *"Kriegstheologie"*, in

---

[6]   "Evangelical Theology in the 19th Century", in *The Humanity of God*, p.14. Barth's memory seems to be slightly playing tricks with him here: it has often been noted that the proclamation by 93 German intellectuals was in October, not August, but I believe that Barth is actually conflating three separate proclamations: (1) *An die evangelischen Christen im Auslande*; (2) *An die Kulturwelt* and (3) *Erklärung der Hochschullehrer des Deutschen Reiches*. All three of these were signed by both Wilhelm Herrmann and Adolf von Harnack, but only (1) was published in August, only (2) was signed by "93 intellectuals" and only (3), with over 3,000 signatures, was signed by "almost all of my theological teachers". Of these, (1) is relatively innocuous, but (2) and (3) represent a real *trahison des clercs*. If I am right that Barth is running these three together in his mind, it explains the confusion that can be found in a number of commentators on Barth's development. Thus, Martin Rumscheidt, on p.202f. of *Revelation and Theology*, quotes (3) but describes it as "published in August 1914 by ninety-three German intellectuals"; and many commentators have queried Barth's claim that "almost all of my theological teachers" had signed the proclamation, when only three of the names (Harnack, Herrmann and Schlatter) among the 93 seem to fit that description. The point of mentioning this is that although Barth's memory might have misled him about the details, he was indeed right that "almost all of my theological teachers whom I had greatly venerated" had signed a "proclamation in support of the war policy of Wilhelm II and his counsellors".

[7]   For the sake of balance, I may quote Archdeacon Basil Wilberforce, preaching at the outset of the First World War: "To kill Germans is a divine service in the fullest acceptation of the term."

[8]   In von Harnack's case, he made it clear that he thought of the war as a defence of the Christian West against the threat of the Russian barbarians.

which not only was the war seen as a Christian war, but the experience of war was interpreted as a specific form of religious experience. Barth was thus confronted by a farrago of nonsense that was being subscribed to by almost all the teachers he had previously revered.

For Barth, the theology he had previously adhered to had been put to the test and found wanting. Instead of its leading exponents showing clarity and moral insight, they had been swept away into the crudest form of militaristic jingoism. How could these men, for all their seriousness and piety, have been led into, or at the very least not been protected from, this? Barth was led to question the foundations on which they had based their theology. Religion, religious experience, the moral sense and culture now appeared as no longer the data on which one could safely ground one's theological reflections, but deeply ambiguous and treacherous, as human, all too human, phenomena. Instead religion had to be seen as under God's judgment, justified, if at all, by the grace of God. Apart from God's grace, it was just a human phenomenon like any other, and can even be seen as unbelief, a defence that man erects against the true God.[10] The fundamental problem with liberal Protestantism is that it had regarded some human phenomenon, such as "the highest form of religion", as particularly close to God, and as providing a foundation for their theology. Whereas, what confronts us in the Bible is a God who cuts across all human phenomena, and never becomes a human possession. Above all, we could never regard God as at our disposal.[11]

Theology must therefore change direction and see itself as answerable to the Word of God, to God's revelation in Jesus Christ as witnessed in Holy Scripture alone, with the one task of measuring what we want to say about God by the Word of God. But with this, there enters the central paradox that Barth wishes to confront us with in his early theology. Theology itself now becomes profoundly problematic. It is not as if Barth was claiming to have found the true key with which to unlock the mysteries of God, and was opposing the false key espoused by liberal Protestantism, or that there was a "dialectical method" that was superior to the theological method of his teachers. Instead, he was demanding a radical recognition, of himself, every bit as much as of his opponents, that we were in no way in possession of the Word of God, and that God was and remained free to reveal Himself when and where He chose.

---

[9]   Barth is of course not denying that hearing the Word of God is a genuine human experience. But there is a deep difference between a theology that gives foundational significance to that experience as such, and one that seeks to concern itself purely with what that experience is experience of. *Cf.* Barth's critical discussion with Georg Wobbermin and Erich Schaeder in *CD* I/1, pp.209–214.

[10]   See *CD* I/2, pp.280–361. *E.g.* "Revelation does not link up with a human religion which is already present and practised. It contradicts it" (p.303).

[11]   In "Unsettled Questions for Theology Today" (p.70), Barth quotes from Franz Overbeck, *Christentum und Kultur*, p.268: "Theologians expect indeed 'to put God daily into their bag'."

How then was preaching as the declaration of the Word of God, or theology as the attempt to measure what we say about God against the Word of God?

> As ministers we ought to speak of God. We are human, however, and so cannot speak of God. We ought therefore to recognize both our obligation and our inability, and by that very recognition give God the glory. This is our perplexity.[12]

Erich Przywara saw in Barth's early theology "a genuine rebirth of Protestantism".[13] By this, he meant that he saw in Barth a stress on divine transcendence, a stress that would lead to a pure *theologia negativa*. Even though it is easy to see how he gained this impression, this seems to me to miss the essential point. What was principally at stake was whether we could in any way regard God and His Word as simply at our disposal. If there is such a thing as hearing the Word of God, or speaking in God's name, this was only by the grace of God, and never something that could be assumed to be under our control, or to which we could gain access by pointing to some human phenomenon that was seen as close to the divine. Of course, the Church lives by the promise that God is with them, but even so that promise is only fulfilled when and where God freely decides.

In such a context, the question "How was theology as a systematic and scientific attempt to measure what we wish to say about God by the Word of God?" became urgent, and on the face of it even impossible.

The Opposition to Natural Theology

Both of the accounts of religious language that we have looked at so far—those of Kant and Aquinas—were, even if in very different ways, exercises in natural theology. That is to say, at no point is appeal made to God's self-revelation in the development of the account. In Kant's case, this is explicitly because he is giving an account of "religion with the limits of reason alone", and also because of his scepticism about the possibility of a divine revelation that would be recognizable as such by us. In Aquinas' case, it looks very much as if his position is that we must first be able to establish the language we use to talk about God without appeal to revelation if a revealed theology is to be subsequently possible.[14]

Barth, however, is a staunch opponent of all forms of natural theology and this opposition will colour and condition the whole of his account of whether and

---

[12]   "The Word of God and the Task of the Ministry" (1922), in *The Word of God and the Word of Man.*

[13]   Quoted by Barth in *R2*, Preface to 4th edition, p.21.

[14]   *Cf.* Rudi te Velde, *Aquinas on God*, p.3: "If revelation is what it is said to be— a revelation of God, disclosing to man true knowledge concerning God—then the very intelligibility of this revelation-based discourse requires a prior ontological 'definition' of God, in reference to which the propositions of revelation have their truth."

how it is possible to use human language to speak about God. Because Barth is approaching the questions that confront us in this book in a radically different way from earlier writers, we need to understand the nature of his opposition to natural theology and some of its implications. This is particularly important since it seems to me that there is no aspect of Barth's theology that has been more widely misunderstood. Although it cannot be part of my present project to attempt a full defence of his stand, I shall begin by looking at some of the main criticisms of him at this point that I believe completely miss their mark.

The opposition moves into the foreground in the early 1930s at the beginning of the German Church Struggle, and Barth's insistence that theology had to be *exclusively* a theology of the Word of God provided him with a theological basis for a root and branch rejection of the "German Christian Movement" and their Nazi ideology.

> The Christian Church of all confessions and countries—I mention only two symptomatic examples—would have preserved a different attitude in 1914–18, and would have found a different word to speak at Stockholm in 1925, if it had not been sick.[15]

Although the opposition to all forms of natural theology is a natural development of his earlier dialectical theology, it is not until the German Church Struggle that it is presented as *the* enemy. In the different editions of the *Commentaries on Romans*, Barth had freely appealed to both Plato and Kant, and in the various writings in the 1920s there are occasional remarks against natural theology, but they are typically unelaborated and might easily be overlooked.[16] In the midst, however, of Barth's polemic against the Nazi ideology, document after document identifies natural theology as the basic error, even heresy, that must be opposed.[17] This has led some to claim that Barth's opposition to natural theology was primarily *politically* motivated. That, for example, is how Peter Winzeler presents matters in

---

[15] "Church and Culture", p.354.

[16] For instance in the Göttingen Dogmatics he brushes natural theology on one side ("For my part, although I am Reformed, I want no part of it" (p.91)), but the brevity of the discussion is such that it would be difficult to predict from these remarks the strenuous opposition that would come later.

[17] For example: "3. The protest against the heresy of the Deutschen Christen cannot begin with the Aryan paragraphs, with the rejection of the Old Testament, with the Arianism of the 'German Christian' Christology, with the naturalism and Pelagianism of the 'German Christian' doctrines of justification and sanctification, with the deification of the State in 'German Christian' ethics. It must fundamentally turn itself against the fact (as the source of all the particular errors) that the 'German Christians' declare the German nationhood [Volkstum], its history and its political present to be a second source of revelation alongside Holy Scripture as the unique source of revelation and thereby show themselves to be believers in 'another god'" ("Eccelsiastical Opposition 1933, Fundamentals", in *Lutherfeier* 1933, Section 4, p.20 *Theologische Existenz heute, heft* 4 (pp.1–24)).

Widerstehende Theologie. However to see Barth's opposition to natural theology as in any way a stance adopted opportunistically as a basis for an opposition to the "German Christians", or even as primarily a *political* stance would be a complete misunderstanding. It was always a theological stance, even if one that, in the circumstances, would have immediate political implications.[18] It is far more likely that it was through his recent discussions with Erich Przywara that it became clear to Barth that his opponent was natural theology in all its forms.

Approached in the wrong way, Barth's position can appear highly paradoxical. Beginning with the dispute between Barth and Emil Brunner,[19] Barth's position is most frequently presented as one in which Barth is *deducing* the impossibility of natural theology from a set of theological doctrines such as that

> Since man is a sinner who can be saved only by grace, the image of God in which he was created is obliterated entirely, *i.e.* without remnant. Man's rational nature, his capacity for culture and his humanity, none of which can be denied, contain no traces or remnants whatever of that lost image of God.[20]

We may leave on one side the fact that the "theses" that Brunner ascribes to Barth are a gross caricature of anything that Barth had ever said. Barth in his reply makes clear that he regards not only the attempt to derive the impossibility of natural theology from such theses as Brunner attributes to him but also *any* attempt to provide a theological deduction of the impossibility of natural theology as irrelevant to the point at issue.

> Real rejection of natural theology can come about only in the fear of God and hence only be a complete *lack* of interest in this matter.[21]

---

[18] This is the point of the often misunderstood opening of "Theological Existence Today" (p.9): "I endeavour to carry on theology, and only theology, now as previously, and as if nothing had happened." Significant political action in obedience to the Word of God could only stem from good theology.

[19] Translated by John Baillie as *Natural Theology*.

[20] Brunner, "Nature and Grace", p.20, where this is the first of six theses that Brunner ascribes to Barth. Out of countless other examples, one may compare with Brunner's approach the following passage from William Abraham (*Canon and Criterion in Christian Theology*, p.384): "Barth simply begged crucial questions about the nature of the grace of God working in creation and in the human subject. Engaging in natural theology can be interpreted as an activity made possible by God's common grace working in creation or as an expression of the image of God in the human mind without strain. It could equally well be expressed in terms of a doctrine of creation which speaks of the working of the Holy Spirit. Natural theology can well be interpreted as one means which the Holy Spirit uses to bring people to commitment to God. It is only if one is committed to a certain doctrine of sin or to a certain pneumatology that these claims will be called into question."

[21] "No!", p.76.

From Brunner's point of view, this must have appeared highly perverse. Confronted by fierce polemic against natural theology by Barth, Brunner had attempted to make sense of that polemic by ascribing to Barth a series of theological positions that would show natural theology to be impossible. Barth responds by not only rejecting those particular positions but by refusing to replace them with alternatives: he simply declares he is not interested in the question of natural theology.

A much better understanding of Barth's position can be gained however from his article "*Das erste Gebot als theologisches Axiom*" than from "*No!*" Although this is much less well known than the polemic against Brunner,[22] it is much clearer and more incisive. It becomes clear from this article why Barth can simultaneously engage in a fierce polemic against natural theology and declare "a complete *lack* of interest in this matter". There the central theme is not so much that natural theology is impossible as that it is forbidden. The First Commandment ("Thou shalt have no other gods before me"[23]) is interpreted as a prohibition laid upon the Church to listen to any other voice than that of God's self-revelation in Jesus Christ.

> The struggle against natural theology that is unavoidable in the light of the First Commandment is a struggle for true obedience in the Church. True obedience, good works in theology must consist in right thinking and speaking. It is right and good when it corresponds to and does not conflict with the First Commandment. Theology too has occasion to prove "what is that good, and acceptable, and perfect will of God" (Rom. 12, 2). In such proving we arrive at the result that theology today—we must today know better than the Reformers after 400 years and particularly after the last 200 years, what is at stake here—must say farewell to each and every natural theology, and dare to hang, in that constriction, in that isolation, solely on the God who has revealed Himself in Jesus Christ. Why? Because that and that alone is commanded us, because everything else is wilfulness, leading not to that God, but away from Him.[24]

The task of theology is to test the legitimacy of what we say about God against the one Word of God—Jesus Christ as he attested to us in Holy Scripture, prophetically in the Old Testament, apostolically in the New Testament. Any attempt to give a normative significance within your theology to some other source of knowledge alongside the Word of God, no matter how innocent sounding—whether the Word of God *and* religion, the Word of God *and* experience or the Word of God *and* Platonic metaphysics—would risk importing into your theology ideas that were alien to the gospel. All such "syntheses" carried with them the potential of turning away from the true God to "other gods".

Bruce McCormack presents Barth's rejection of natural theology as a: "theme learned at the feet of the great nineteenth-century liberal theologian,

---

[22]   To the best of my knowledge, it has not even been translated into English.

[23]   Deut. v, 7.

[24]   "*Das erste Gebot …*" pp.142–143 (my translation).

Wilhelm Herrmann".[25] Although Herrmann did undoubtedly have, and continue to have, a deep influence on Barth, the characteristic note of "*Das erste Gebot als theologisches Axiom*", that what is at stake is a question of *obedience*, is a specifically Barthian theme.[26]

Finally, a few clarifications are in order:

1. Barth is not denying the possibility of God addressing human beings when and where He chooses, or that there can be "Words of God" outside the scriptural witness. The crucial point here is the quotation Barth gives from the *Confessio Gallicana*: "*Non pas que Dieu soit attaché à telles aides ou moyen inferieurs, mais parce qu'ill luy plaist nous entretenir soubz telle charge et bride.*"[27] Barth comments on this: "If the question what God can do forces theology to be humble, the question what is commanded of us forces it to concrete obedience. God may speak to us through Russian Communism, a flute concerto, a blossoming shrub, or a dead dog. We do well to listen to Him if he really does. But, unless we regard ourselves as the prophets and founders of a new Church, we cannot say we are commissioned to pass on what we have heard as independent proclamation."[28]

2. It is important not to confuse natural theology and a theology of nature—an attempt to gain a theological understanding of the world of nature. James Barr, for example, sees Barth as softening his stance on natural theology, quoting him as saying: "Later I brought natural theology back in by way of Christology. Today my criticism would be all you have to do is say it differently, and that means Christologically."[29] Whereas his earlier opposition was to regarding any natural phenomenon as providing a source of knowledge of God apart from God's self-revelation, what he is concerned with in a passage such as this is a theological interpretation of the world of nature in the light of God's self-revelation. In fact, when we come to look at the central concern of this chapter—the language we use to talk about God—one of the best ways of regarding what Barth is doing is offering a theological interpretation of the natural phenomena of human language.

---

[25]   *Karl Barth's Critically Realistic* ..., p.466.

[26]   *Cf.* Barth's article, "The Principles of Dogmatics according to Wilhelm Herrmann", where Barth acknowledges his debt to Herrmann, but the latter part of the article is largely devoted to what Herrmann might have meant, but "Alas! Herrmann did not so mean it" (p.263). Barth's rejection of natural theology goes way beyond what he would have found in Herrmann.

[27]   "Not that God is bound to such aids and subordinate means, but because it pleases him to govern us by such restraints" (Confessio Gallicana, art. 25).

[28]   *CD* I/1, pp.54–55.

[29]   Quoted by James Barr in *Biblical Faith and Natural Theology*, p.13.

"Christologische Engführung"

Most criticisms of Barth's stance on natural theology seem to me to rest on misunderstandings of what Barth's opposition is and why he takes the stand he does. However, before leaving the topic of natural theology, it is worth introducing a criticism that Hans Urs von Balthasar made of Barth's position. Although I believe Barth's stance to be fully tenable, this is to my mind the most significant challenge that it has to meet. This is when Balthasar accuses Barth of *"Christologische Engführung"*.[30] This criticism has often been misunderstood, and possibly even by Barth himself. Balthasar is not saying that Barth is treating the whole of creation as of little account when compared with Jesus Christ. Such a criticism would be absurd. The point is, rather, methodological or epistemological. The point here depends on a correct understanding of the word *"Engführung"*. As Balthasar says, he intended a metaphor from the theory of the fugue,[31] and it should therefore be translated "stretto"—a passage in a fugue where the subject and counter-subject are made to overlap with each other. Because of Barth's rejection of all forms of natural theology, and his daring to base his whole theology on the biblical prophetic and apostolic witness to Jesus Christ, he will seek to develop his whole theology in the form of a reflection upon the person and work of Jesus Christ, "the one Word of God which we have to hear and which we have to trust and obey in life and in death".[32] He will for instance begin Volume III of the *Church Dogmatics*:

> The insight that man owes his existence and form, together with all the reality distinct from God, to God's creation, is achieved only in the reception and answer of the divine self-witness, that is, only in faith in Jesus Christ, i.e., in the knowledge of the unity of Creator and creature in Him.[33]

In Barth, the doctrines of creation, of reconciliation, of God, of theological anthropology and of election are all to be established by reflection on the person and work of Jesus Christ. Balthasar, who, like Barth, wishes to develop a radically Christocentric theology, is asking "Is this possible?" "Can all these doctrines be developed on the basis of *one* text?" If Jesus Christ is the answer to the question posed by the creation, can we hear both the question and the answer in the one text?

> Yes, it may well be true that meaning ultimately comes from Christ, that we can say nothing conclusive about the (provisional) meaning of creation until we have considered Christ. Yes, it may well be true that this ultimate meaning is the ontological ground for the presence of every other (provisional) meaning. But it remains no less true that this very relationship requires us to preserve

---

[30]   *The Theology of Karl Barth*, p.242.

[31]   Ibid., p.393.

[32]   *Theological Declaration of the Synod of Barmen.*

[33]   *CD* III/1, p.3.

scrupulously all relative meanings as proper to themselves and to avoid any appearance of *deducing* them from their ultimate meaning.[34]

It is here that the metaphor of "stretto" has its point: if Christ is the answer to the question posed by the creation, then for Balthasar, we must be able to hear first the question and then the answer, whereas he sees Barth as making question and answer overlap in the one text. For Balthasar, separating out the question and the answer requires a natural theology as a preparation for the gospel.

This is not the place to develop a full reply to Balthasar, but it does serve to set in relief the nature of Barth's theological project. I shall just say that from Barth's point of view, it is only in the light of Jesus Christ that we have any chance of understanding what is meant by seeing the world as God's creation at all.

Anselm: Fides Quaerens Intellectum

> Only a comparatively few commentators, for example Hans Urs von Balthasar, have realized that my interest in Anselm was never a side-issue for me or—assuming I am more or less correct in my historical interpretation of St Anselm—realized how much it has influenced me or been absorbed into my own line of thinking. Most of them have completely failed to see that in this book on Anselm I am working with a vital key, if not the key, to an understanding of that whole process of thought that has impressed me more and more in my *Church Dogmatics* as the only one proper to theology.[35]

Barth's little book on Anselm is of particular relevance to our concerns, because at the beginning of Chapter 5 of *CD* II/1, which will form one of the central texts for the present study, he writes:

> I believe I learned the fundamental attitude to the problem of the knowledge and existence of God which is adopted in this section—and indeed in the whole chapter—at the feet of Anselm of Canterbury, and in particular from his proofs of God set out in *Prosl.* 2–4.[36]

This book has been the subject of controversy. On the one hand, von Balthasar saw the book as a key moment in Barth's development, in which Barth turned from "dialectic" to "analogy".[37] On the other hand, Bruce McCormack insisted there

---

[34]   *The Theology of Karl Barth*, p.242.
[35]   *FQA*, p.11.
[36]   *CD* II/1, p.4.
[37]   *The Theology of Karl Barth*, p.137.

was no change of direction. In this McCormack was undoubtedly right. Balthasar had mistaken a change in style for a change in substance.[38]

However, McCormack is led by his disagreement with Balthasar to play down the significance of Anselm for Barth:

> In his enthusiasm for his work, everything was new to him every day. This alone would be enough to account for an exaggeration here and there.[39]

This seems to me as serious a mistake as the error he is seeking to correct. The fact that it does not constitute the kind of turning point envisaged by Balthasar does not diminish its significance, and there is every reason to take seriously the stress that Barth himself places on his engagement with Anselm. Barth does not himself claim that there is a change of direction here.[40] And it is only if it is seen as such a change that there is any reason to see Barth as exaggerating.

What, then, was the significance for Barth of his study of Anselm?[41] Barth's account of the *Proslogion* is completely at variance with standard accounts that see Chapters 2–4 as initiating what is now called the "ontological argument". This is not the place to decide between these differing interpretations.[42] The main

---

[38]   *Cf. CD* I/1, p.xi: "I could still say what I had said. I wished to do so. But I could not do it in the same way."

[39]   *Karl Barth's Critically Realistic* ..., pp.442–443.

[40]   *Cf.* Barth, *FQA*, p.7: "But of course my love for Anselm goes back much further than that [1930]."

[41]   An excellent treatment of Barth's understanding of Anselm is Gordon Watson, "Karl Barth and St. Anselm's Theological Programme". My only quarrel with this article is Watson's claim that "this understanding evinces a characteristic weakness in Barth's own theological project". Watson does nothing to substantiate this claim, and, as far as I can see, all he can mean is that he disagrees with Barth.

[42]   At least it should be said that Barth's reading respects the actual text of the Proslogion in a way that more standard readings do not. On the "rationalist" interpretations of the argument of Proslogion 2–4, statements such as "For this also I believe, that unless I believed I should not understand" turn out to be empty rhetorical flourishes.

I believe that Barth's interpretation of Proslogion 3–4 can be summarized as follows: (1) "we believe that You are something than which nothing greater can be conceived"; (2) "it is possible to conceive of a being that cannot be conceived not to exist; and this would be greater than one that can be conceived not to exist"; therefore, (3) You cannot be conceived not to exist; therefore, (4) Whatever the Fool meant when he said in his heart "There is no God" he was not denying the existence of the God in whom we believe. ("So, then, no one who understands what God is can conceive that God does not exist; although he says these words in his heart, either without any, or with some foreign, signification.") This is a valid argument. Premise (1) is an affirmation of faith and not a definition of the word "God". The only point at which the argument can be challenged is premise (2). But although it is a valid argument, it is important to recognize what it does and does not establish. This is not a "proof of the existence of God" in the sense that has become traditional since Aquinas. If

point for our purposes is that for Barth, Anselm is to be regarded as a theologian rather than a philosopher and the *Proslogion* seen as a work of theology and not a philosophical exercise.[43]

It is hard to point to any specific doctrines that Barth learnt from Anselm, and *pace* Balthasar there is nothing about analogy in the book on Anselm. Barth, however, does not talk of specific doctrines, but of "that whole process of thought that has impressed me more and more in my *Church Dogmatics* as the only one proper to theology".[44] As I understand Barth, the central problem of theology was that the task of the theologian was to measure what one said about God by the Word of God, while respecting the fact that the Word of God never was and never became at the disposal of the theologian.[45] How could one both remain true to that task and respect the fact that God and God alone chose when to reveal Himself to the believer?[46] What I believe Anselm showed Barth was how it was possible to undertake disciplined, systematic, "scientific" theology without ever leaving the ground of faith, and in a way that respected the fact that the object of that science—God and His Word—was not a possession of the theologian and could not be counted on to be available at will, but only became manifest as and when it was pleasing to God Himself.

Anselm's theological method is most clearly expressed in the preface to *Cur Deus Homo*: there he writes that in order to understand the necessity of the Incarnation, he will, for the purpose of the enquiry, suspend all knowledge of the

read as such, it will either be misread as the "ontological argument", or dismissed as a *petitio principii*. If it is not a "proof of the existence" of God in the sense in which that phrase is normally understood, what is it, and what does it seek to prove? The answer, I believe, is that the conclusion of the argument is that if God has revealed Himself as something than which nothing greater can be conceived, He has revealed Himself in such a way that it is impossible to doubt His existence: "I now so understand by your illumination, that if I were tempted to believe that you did not exist, I should not be able not to understand that you do." Barth's own version of what I take to be this conclusion is at *CD* II/1, p.7: "True knowledge of God is not and cannot be attacked: it is without anxiety and without doubt."

[43] *FQA*, p.59: "Instructive though it may be from a technical point of view to refer to his inevitable philosophical background (Augustine, Plotinus, Plato), there is absolutely no good reason against and a great many reasons for understanding him right across the board as a theologian" (my translation). It should be noted that the only English translation available of *Fides Quaerens Intellectum* is highly unreliable, and the translation of this sentence in particular is one of its worst blunders, converting what Barth wrote into almost its exact opposite.

[44] *FQA*, p.11.

[45] *Cf. Proslogion*, Chapter 1: "Nor do I seek to understand so that I can believe, but rather I believe so that I can understand. For I believe this too, that 'unless I believe I shall not understand'" (Isa. 7:9).

[46] *Proslogion*, Chapter 1: "Teach me to seek you, and reveal yourself to this seeker. For I cannot seek you unless you teach me how, nor can I find you unless you show yourself to me."

fact that God became man and seek to prove the necessity of the Incarnation on the basis of other doctrines of the faith, such as the justice and mercy of God. In this way, we come to understand one doctrine of the faith by seeing how it fits with the other doctrines. This goes beyond seeing how the doctrines are interrelated, since we gain a deeper understanding of the doctrine we are concerned with in virtue of the need to understand it in such a way as to fit with the rest of the faith.[47]

As McCormack has emphasized,[48] this method needs modification if it is to fit Barth's own theological method. Unlike Anselm, for Barth all the doctrines that we accept are only accepted provisionally "until better instructed by the Word of God". Therefore while Anselm could start from premises that were to be regarded as incontestable premises, Barth's premises could only represent the best understanding of the Church in the light of past revelation and were therefore in principle as much subject to modification as a result of the enquiry as the doctrine he is currently investigating. Because of this, theology becomes essentially a *theologia viatorum*, with every subject needing to be revisited as the enquiry progresses, giving the appearance of repetitiousness that is one's initial impression of the *Church Dogmatics*.

Analogia Entis vs. Analogia Fidei

> I can see no third alternative between that exploitation of the *analogia entis* which is legitimate only on the basis of Roman Catholicism, between the greatness and misery of a so-called natural knowledge of God in the sense of the *Vaticanum*, and a Protestant theology which draws from its own source, which stands on its own feet, and which finally liberates us from this secular misery. Hence I have no option but to say No at this point. I regard the *analogia entis* as the invention of Antichrist, and I believe that because of it it is impossible ever to become a Roman Catholic, all other reasons for not doing so being to my mind short-sighted and trivial.[49]

This must be one of the most famous passages in all Barth's writings, yet its precise significance is far from clear. What does Barth understand by the "*analogia entis*"? Is there a specific form of the doctrine of the *analogia entis* to which one is *ipso facto* committed in becoming a Roman Catholic? What makes it "the invention of Antichrist"? What is Barth's alternative doctrine of analogy (which he will subsequently call the "*analogia fidei*")? We can gain a preliminary answer to these questions if we consider a passage from one of his earlier writings, *The Holy Ghost and the Christian Life*:

---

[47] This may perhaps be part of what Barth has in mind when he talks of the *analogia fidei*. Originally, that meant interpreting an obscure passage of scripture in the light of clear passages. Here we are interpreting one doctrine of the faith in the light of others.

[48] *Karl Barth's Critically Realistic Dialectical Theology*, p.434.

[49] CD I/1, p.xiii.

If the creature is to be strictly understood as a reality willed and placed by God in distinction from His own reality: that is to say, as the wonder of a reality, which, by the power of God's love, has a place and persistence alongside of His own reality, then the continuity between Him and it (the true *analogia entis*, by virtue of which He, the uncreated Spirit, can be revealed to the created spirit)—this continuity cannot belong to the creature itself but only to the Creator *in His relation* to the creature. It cannot be taken to mean that the creature has an original endowment in his makeup, but only as a second marvel of God's love, as the inconceivable, undeserved, divine *bestowal* on His creature. Man as *creature* is not in a position from which he can establish and survey (for example, in a scheme of the unity of like and unlike) his relation to God, and thereby interpret himself as "open upwards," as Erich Przywara says, and consequently describe his own knowledge as if it meant that God's revealedness were within the compass of his own understanding by itself.[50]

The first point to note about this passage, which seems to be the first place in which he sketches what he will later call the *"analogia fidei"*, is that Barth is prepared to use the phrase "the true *analogia entis*" to describe his position, implying that it would be rash to use *the phrase* "the *analogia entis*" as a Shibboleth in this discussion.

There seem to be a number of different concerns at work here, one or other of which will move into the foreground in the various later discussions of analogy. Although these concerns are interconnected in Barth's mind, they are distinguishable and capable of being discussed independently of each other. In the first instance, Barth was concerned to oppose his Roman Catholic critics who advocated a doctrine of the analogy of being that provided a basis for natural theology, and it is the supposed connection between a doctrine of the *analogia entis* and natural theology to which he recurs with great frequency.[51] Next, there is the thought that is the most difficult to interpret: there is no analogy between God and the world considered in itself and apart from its relation to God, but God in His revelation does not find but creates an analogy between Himself and the believer.[52] Finally, Barth in Volume III of the *Church Dogmatics* will develop a contrast between an *analogia entis* and an *analogia relationis*.[53] In what follows,

---

[50]   *The Holy Ghost and the Christian Life*, pp.14–15.

[51]   It is noteworthy that when in *CD* II/1 (pp.81–82) he discusses Gottlieb Söhngen's advocacy of a version of the *analogia entis* that does not carry with it any implication of a knowability of God apart from God's self-disclosure ("analogia fidei", *Catholica* 1934), he writes "naturally I must withdraw my earlier statement that I regard the analogia entis as 'the invention of anti-Christ'". This is despite the fact that in other respects Barth's doctrine of analogy diverges from that of Söhngen.

[52]   This idea is developed most emphatically by Eberhard Jüngel in *God as the Mystery of the World*.

[53]   In *CD* III/3, Barth will use the phrase "analogia fidei sive relationis".

I will be looking most closely at this last way of looking at the contrast, since I believe it provides the key to understanding the other ways.

The Language used to Talk about God

When we looked at the accounts of religious language offered by Aquinas and Kant, it was easy to gain the impression that we were dealing with something of great technical importance, but which had few repercussions for the religious life of the believer. When we look at the account that Barth presents, whatever else may be said for or against it, the whole topic comes to life, as he shows how our understanding of the words used to talk about God is transformed by our encounter with the Word of God. This is not only true of the theory of religious language that concerns us directly, but also of the whole treatment of the divine perfections in Chapter 6 of *CD* II/1, with its remarkable freedom from a priori speculation about the nature of omnipotence, omniscience and so on.

However, before looking in detail at Barth's explorations of the language we use to talk about God, there are some warnings to be made about the way in which to approach the text of the *Church Dogmatics*.

1. Whatever we think of their accounts of the relation of analogy to talk about God, Kant and Aquinas both show considerable conceptual clarity in the ways that they discuss analogy; Barth clearly shows at times that he was not at home in the technicalities of discussions of analogy. In fact when he explains what he means by the word "analogy", he gives a completely informal account that does not obviously relate to traditional discussions of analogy: "In distinction to both likeness and unlikeness "analogy" means similarity [*Ähnlichkeit*], i.e. a partial correspondence and agreement (and, therefore, one which limits both parity and disparity between two or more different entities)."[54]

2. It may look as though Barth gives a more technical clarification of what is meant in the long footnote in *CD* II/1 discussing Quenstedt's account of analogy.[55] This footnote *looks* as if it ought to be the place where Barth most directly addresses the question that concerns us in this book. However, even apart from the fact that, at least to judge by Barth's account of what he says, Quenstedt is hardly the best representative of earlier theories of analogy and religious language, Barth's explanations show that he has simply misunderstood many of the key terms in the debate, such as the *analogia proportionalitatis*.[56] Hence, it is virtually impossible to know

---

[54] *CD* II/1, p.225.

[55] *CD* II/1, pp.237–243.

[56] Barth's gloss on what is meant by this term—"the similarity which exists in the agreement when some determinations of two objects agree but at the same time others

how to assess his commitment in that footnote to an *"analogia attributionis extrinsicae"*: the texts surrounding that footnote suggest that Barth is not concerned with what, following Cajetan, would have been understood by this phrase at all, and has merely misinterpreted the terminology involved in the debate.[57]

Hence, in the light of all this, we must gather what Barth understands by "analogy" from an interpretation of his detailed discussions rather than from his initial statements on his use of the word.

Church Dogmatics *II/1* Chapter 5

The scriptural basis for Barth's account of language about God

One of the central themes of CD II/1 Chapter 5, and the one that is most directly relevant to this present study, is the idea that the words we use in talking about God have their primary, or proper, meaning and use in talking about God, and not in their everyday use in talking about worldly phenomena. This inevitably recalls Aquinas' similar claim in the *Summa Theologiae*. This gives rise to the question, "How far are they saying the same thing?" At least one major difference is that whereas Aquinas' doctrine was best seen as a development within Neo-Platonic metaphysics, Barth's position is unequivocally presented as a response to the scriptural witness to divine revelation,[58] and in particular to the radical discontinuity between the ideas of this world—whether religious, ethical or political—and what we encounter in Jesus Christ. Before turning to Barth himself, we may consider one representative passage:

> For Christ did not send me to baptize but to preach the gospel, and not with eloquent wisdom, lest the cross of Christ be emptied of its power. For the word of the cross is folly to those who are perishing, but to us who are being saved it is the power of God. For it is written, "I will destroy the wisdom of the wise, and the cleverness of the clever I will thwart." Where is the wise man? Where is the scribe? Where is the debater of this age? Has not God made foolish the wisdom of the world? For since, in the wisdom of God, the world did not know God through wisdom, it pleased God through the folly of what we preach to save those who believe. For Jews demand signs and Greeks seek wisdom, but we preach Christ crucified, a stumbling block to Jews and folly to Gentiles, but to those who are called, both Jews and Greeks, Christ the power of God and the wisdom of God. For the foolishness of God is wiser than men, and the weakness of God is stronger than men.

---

disagree" (ibid. pp.237–238) has nothing to do with what the phrase actually meant, which was simply what Aristotle understood by "ἀναλογία".

[57] *Cf.* a good discussion in John McIntyre, "Analogy", pp.15–17.

[58] Barth indicates such a basis in the footnote on *CD* II/1, pp.229–230.

For consider your call, brethren; not many of you were wise according to worldly standards, not many were powerful, not many were of noble birth; but God chose what is foolish in the world to shame the wise, God chose what is weak in the world to shame the strong, God chose what is low and despised in the world, even things that are not, to bring to nothing things that are, so that no human being might boast in the presence of God. He is the source of your life in Christ Jesus, whom God made our wisdom, our righteousness and sanctification and redemption; therefore, as it is written, "Let him who boasts, boast of the Lord".[59]

The revelation of God in "Jesus Christ and Him crucified" is seen not as a confirmation or refinement of the world's religion and values. Instead, Paul is presenting us with a contrast between the wisdom and power of God and what the word reckons to be wise and powerful.[60] In Christ, there is manifest a "revaluation of all values".

We may best regard the account that follows as Barth's attempt to make sense of this situation, and to draw out its implications for our understanding of the phenomena of language.

"The homecoming of concepts"

Barth's position can initially appear highly paradoxical, and, indeed, some commentators have regarded him as committed to absurdities.[61] What we have to examine is not only his claim that the words that we use to talk about God have their primary or "proper" use in talking about God, but also that our everyday secular use of those words involves a kind of misuse of those words:

> We use our words improperly and pictorially—as we can now say, looking back from divine revelation—when we apply them within the confines of what is appropriate to us as creatures.[62]

The first of these claims we have already met in Aquinas, but the second claim is far more radical and gives the air of paradox to Barth's position, at least if we assume that the meanings of the words we use supervenes on the use we make of those words. If the way we use words determines what those words mean, how can our everyday use constitute a kind of misuse? I believe, however, that Barth is presenting a subtle and fully coherent position. At the same time, despite Barth's

---

[59] I Cor. I, 17–31.

[60] *Cf.* Luther, Sermon on Acts 1–13, quoted by Barth in *CD* I/1, p.151: "That is the New Testament and kingdom of Christ that cometh home with as little might, and yet with almighty power and might which none can withstand. It appeareth to be foolish that Christ doth set up the New Testament in this wise."

[61] See, *e.g.*, Jay Wesley Richards, "Barth on the Divine 'Conscription' of Language".

[62] *CD* II/1, p.229.

usual prolixity, he expresses the core of that position in a remarkably compressed form in *CD* II/1 pp.227–229. Our task is to try to spell out his train of thought in those pages.

"Semantic externalism"   The crucial point to appreciate in order to understand Barth's account is that, like Aquinas,[63] he is arguing for a form of what is now called "semantic externalism". The basic idea here, which was introduced into contemporary philosophical debate by the works of Saul Kripke[64] and Hilary Putnam,[65] is that there is a large range of cases of words, where we use those words to designate features of the world and where the meanings of those words are to be explained in terms of those actual features of the world, rather than our ideas of those features.

Thus, influenza is a viral disease, caused by RNA viruses of the Orthomyxo-viridae family. On this conception, people who use the word "influenza" use it as the name of a viral disease, and the correct explanation of the meaning of the word as they are using it is as the name of a certain type of viral disease, even if the majority of the users of the word do not know that it is a viral disease, and may not even know what a virus is. What makes it plausible to say this is not the dubious "twin earth" thought experiment introduced by Putnam,[66] but rather that our interest and concern—why we have the word in the language at all—is in the actual disease itself, and not simply, say, in a certain range of symptoms— symptoms that might have been also caused by a range of other diseases. To the extent that, as here, our interest is in the things that lie out there in the world, and not in our idea of those things, it makes sense to think of the words designating those things as having their meanings defined in terms of the actual natures of the things, even if the typical speaker of the language has only a limited knowledge of those natures.

> Creatures who are the suitable object of our human views, concepts and words are actually His creation. But our thought and our language in their appropriateness to this object are also His creation. Therefore the truth in which we know this appropriate object in the way appropriate to us is His creation, His truth.[67]

Although Barth is here presenting a form of semantic externalism, in which the "truth" of our "views, concepts and words" is measured by "their appropriateness to this object", there are clear differences from the position of Putnam, say, that give to Barth's position a specifically theological content.

---

[63]   See *ST*, 1a 13, 2 and my discussion of the passage above.

[64]   See *Naming and Necessity*.

[65]   See "The Meaning of 'Meaning'".

[66]   The reason that the thought experiment is dubious is that it relies heavily on highly fallible intuitions as to what we would say in certain counterfactual situations.

[67]   *CD* II/1, p.228.

The differences all stem from the fact that Barth is viewing the world as God's creation. For Putnam if water is H_2O, and what we mean by the word "water" is H_2O, then it is seen as the business of the "scientist" to discover the real meaning of the word. For Barth, however, viewing the world as God's creation opens up the possibility that it is God alone who knows the real meanings of the words we use. What this does is create a way of looking at language in which we can make sense of two of Barth's apparently most paradoxical claims: that "Our words are not our property but [God's]",[68] and that our everyday secular use of our words is an "improper and merely pictorial use".[69]

Language as God's creation "But our thought and our language in their appropriateness to this object are also [God's] creation."[70]

What does it mean here to talk of language as God's creation? One might think that Barth is here thinking of language as having arisen as a direct act of special creation on God's part. That is how Graham Ward seems to read him.[71] On this reading there was an original language which was fully suited to talking about God and His relation to the world, but this language has been corrupted ("The Tower of Babel"), so that now the language we speak stands in need of restoration by God to return it to its uncorrupted state.

However, not only is there no need to read what Barth says in this way, this completely misses the subtlety of Barth's position and would not serve Barth's purposes. What Barth writes here is fully compatible with a "naturalistic" account of the evolution of language, and makes best sense in terms of such an account. Also, the idea that the language we speak is a "fallen" language is equally wide of the mark. The mistake Ward makes comes out in the following passage:

> Barth seems to write as if God spoke an idealized German—a German sounding and appearing the same to both God and human beings, but which each employs, reads and understands differently. He writes as if German were related to some primary *Ursprache*.[72]

The idea of such an "*Ursprache*" has no place in Barth's thought. The thought instead is that God speaks not an "idealized German", but our everyday language— a language that, however, He uses properly, where we use it improperly.

The sense in which we are to think of our language as God's creation is clarified by the sentence immediately preceding the one we quoted in which Barth makes this claim:

---

[68] *CD* II/1, p.229.
[69] *CD* II/1, p.229.
[70] *CD* II/1, p.228.
[71] See *Barth, Derrida and the Language of Theology*, pp.35–36.
[72] Ibid., p.28.

Creatures who are the suitable object of our human views, concepts and words
are actually His creation.[73]

Our language has evolved in such a way that we can talk about ourselves, our
relations with each other and the world we find ourselves in. In that way it will
be a language that is appropriate for talking about such a world, and the concepts
we designate in our language will be the concepts that reflect the concerns and
interests of beings living in such a world. But this world, whether we know it or
not, is God's creation.

In this way, language is "God's creation" in two senses. It is God's creation
simply as one of the phenomena of this world, all of which is God's creation. But,
secondly, and for Barth's purposes more importantly, it is God's creation in the
sense that language has evolved among human beings as a way of talking about
God's creation and their place in that creation. It is therefore a language that is
appropriate for talking about God's creation. Its vocabulary will contain the words
appropriate for talking about the world, and in that sense reflect God's creation.
God who knows the world as His creation is in that way the true master of the
language that we have evolved. It is in this way that Barth is inviting us to see
God, and not ourselves, as having the true knowledge and understanding of the
language we use.

In *CD* II/1 Barth does not discuss why or in what way a language that is
appropriate for talking about God's creation should also be a language that
is appropriate for talking about God Himself. To see why in Barth's terms that
should be so, we have to wait for the account of analogy that Barth develops in his
doctrine of creation in Volume III of the *Church Dogmatics*.

 If this can be regarded as a form of semantic externalism, it nevertheless differs
in fundamental respects from the form of semantic externalism proposed by Kripke
and Putnam. In the first instance, and most obviously, for Putnam given the name
of a chemical compound such as water, it is a matter of empirical investigation on
the part of scientists to discover for us the meaning of the word for us; for Barth,
it is God, and those to whom God reveals it, who know the true meaning of the
words with which we are concerned in our talk about God.[74]

The major difference is however in the range of words that come into
consideration in the two accounts, and the reasons offered for supposing in these
cases that speakers of the language may make significant use of these words
without full knowledge of what these words mean. For Kripke and Putnam, there
are "natural kinds", such as chemicals or animal species, which the normal speaker
can identify by their characteristic appearances. They use the words, however,
not as names for those appearances but as names of the natural kinds that give

---

[73]   *CD* II/1, p.228.

[74]   Barth makes it clear that for him, apart from revelation, we cannot know the true
meanings of these words: "Now, it certainly does not lie in our power to return our words
to their proper use" (*CD* II/1, p.230).

those appearances, even though they do not necessarily know the precise nature of what they are thus naming. If, however we consider the list of examples that Barth gives—"being, spirit, sovereign, creator, redeemer, righteousness, wisdom and goodness but also ... such words as eye, ear and mouth, arm, hand, love, wrath, mercy, patience"[75]—not one of these words would come into consideration for Kripke and Putnam. What grounds the "externalist" account of these words is that they all contain a normative element. They refer to a standard that things approach to a greater or lesser degree.[76] God is the archetype, or perfect realization of the concepts designated by these words, while the objects in this world that are appropriately described by these words are ectypes of their divine original. We use these words to describe things that *appear* to us to meet the standards set by these words, which we can do even if we do not *know*, or have misconceptions as to, what those standards actually are. So far, this seems to agree with Aquinas' conception, with, however, the major difference that Aquinas is ultimately basing his conception on a form of Platonic metaphysics, while Barth will base his upon the doctrine of creation.

Where, however, Barth apparently diverges from Aquinas, and certainly from Kripke and Putnam, forms the subject of our next section. The appearances of water that Putnam had in mind were *faithful* appearances of water. His idea required that we should be adept at recognizing samples of water, even without knowing what chemical compound these samples were samples of. Unless we were able to recognize water when we encounter it, we would be unable to fix the meaning of the word as a word for a certain chemical compound. For Barth, however, apart from God's self-revelation, we are massively in error, and profoundly mistaken in our application of the words we use in talking about God.

Our "improper and pictorial" use of words   "In the first instance, whatever is said by us was, is and will be said truly in Him ... It will be said in Him infallibly, by us (for we are not only creatures but sinful creatures who have fallen from Him) always in error, and yet in such a way that even in error, doubly hidden from ourselves (by our creatureliness and our sin), and therefore in a double sense without any possibility of reclamation, we live by His infallible truth."[77]

Throughout this discussion Barth contrasts the "proper" (*eigentlich*) and "improper" (*uneigentlich*) use of our words. There is a difficulty in interpreting this since he appears to be running together two distinct contrasts. In some contexts, he

---

[75]   *CD* II/1, p.225.

[76]   As Barth's discussion makes clear this is true of the names of the bodily parts he lists. He is thinking of words such as "hand" and "eye" in functional terms. ("Only God has hands—not paws like ours.") His reason for including such words is in part to protest against the assumption that these words are more anthropomorphic than "spiritual" words in talking about God, and partly to do justice to the free use made of these words throughout scripture.

[77]   *CD* II/1, pp.228–229.

seems clearly to be talking in terms that we have already looked at in our discussion of Aquinas, of a contrast between a primary and secondary use of words:

> For example, the words "father" and "son" do not first and properly have their truth at the point of reference to the underlying views and concepts in our thought and language, i.e., in their application to the two nearest male members in the succession of physical generation of man or of animal creation generally. They have it first and properly at a point to which, as our words, they cannot refer at all ... in their application to God, in the doctrine of the Trinity.[78]

Here, there does not seem to be anything to imply that it is *wrong* to call a male biological parent a father: it is instead to be seen as a secondary use of the word.

In other contexts, however, Barth clearly wishes to say that our everyday use of words is mistaken: that, apart from God's revelation we call things "*F*" that are not *F* at all, so that in "Peace I leave with you; my peace I give to you; not as the world gives do I give to you"[79] not only does Jesus give his disciples peace, but shows them that what the world calls "peace" is not true peace at all.

I shall postpone until the final discussion in this chapter the question whether the idea of a universal error in the meanings of the words we use can be accommodated in a theory of meaning for our language, and for now take an example to indicate the kind of possibility Barth has in mind.[80]

Consider "king"—the word for a sovereign ruler over his people. In I Samuel viii there is a remarkable description of the inauguration of kingship in Israel. The judges have become corrupt, and the people ask Samuel to appoint a king for them "to govern us like all the nations". In the situation described, this is a humanly intelligible request, but is seen by God as an act of apostasy: "they have not rejected you, but they have rejected me from being king over them". Samuel then warns the people in grim detail of the ways in which they will be exploited and oppressed by a king: "and in that day you will cry out because of your king, whom you have chosen for yourselves; but the Lord will not answer you in that day". The people persist in their request, and the history of the kings of Israel begins.

Despite the high price that they have to pay, the decision to have a king can seem humanly inevitable. A king provides a stable context in which people can live out their lives. The king gives his people a rule of law, even if that law can be grossly unjust and even if it is to be enforced by the king demanding the right of life and death over his subjects. But only the most incompetent tyrant will fail to ensure that his people are fed. The benefits of having a king can easily appear to outweigh all its obvious disadvantages.

---

[78]   *CD* II/1 p.229.

[79]   John xiv, 27.

[80]   I also analysed this example earlier in my article "Notes on Analogical Predication and Speaking about God".

The kings of the Gentiles exercise lordship over them; and those in authority over them are called benefactors. But not so with you; rather let the greatest among you become as the youngest, and the leader as one who serves. For which is the greater, one who sits at table, or one who serves? Is it not the one who sits at table? But I am among you as one who serves.[81]

At the beginning of His ministry, one of the temptations confronting Jesus is the temptation to become a king of this world:

And the devil took him up, and showed him all the kingdoms of the world in a moment of time, and said to him, "To you I will give all this authority and their glory; for it has been delivered to me, and I give it to whom I will. If you, then, will worship me, it shall all be yours."

Why not become a king, with the clear power to become an obvious benefactor of mankind: to build roads, hospitals and schools? The achievements of the kings of this world are real and tangible. By comparison, following Jesus' chosen path of an itinerant preacher can seem something very small indeed. But the temptation is rejected as satanic.

Yet while rejecting earthly kingship, Jesus claims for Himself a kingship "not of this world".[82] The precise nature of the contrast perhaps stands out most clearly if we look at the Johannine account of the confrontation between Jesus and Pilate.[83] Negatively, Jesus renounces all use of violence to enforce His rule:

If my kingship were of this world, my servants would fight, that I might not be handed over to the Jews, but my kingship is not from the world.[84]

But, positively, He defines His kingship:

You say that I am a king. For this I was born, and for this I have come into the world, to bear witness to the truth. Every one who is of the truth hears my voice.[85]

Pilate can make nothing of this, and warns Jesus that he has power of life and death over him. To which Jesus replies:

---

[81] Luke xii, 25–27.

[82] It almost goes without saying that a "theocracy" that uses the weapons of this world to enforce its laws is just another "kingdom of this world".

[83] John xviii, 29–xix 11.

[84] John xviii, 36.

[85] John xviii, 37.

You would have no power over me unless it had been given you from above.[86]

There is here an ambiguity that is typical of John's Gospel. This can mean either that all earthly power is only there as ordained by God, or, more mundanely, that Pilate's power derives solely from the fact that he is Caesar's delegate. The latter reading points to the contingency of all human power—the kings, magistrates and those in power in general are only in power insofar as other people permit them that power. *Their* sovereignty is a legal fiction maintained only while it is accepted and respected by their subjects, and while they can muster the force necessary to enforce that acceptance and respect.

What this entails is an unremitting need to compromise with political realities, and, in the event, despite his repeated expressing the wish to release Jesus, Pilate is manipulated into doing what he does not wish to do.

By contrast, Jesus' sovereignty is absolute. He makes no compromise, and rules simply by His word—his "bearing witness to the truth" and "every one who is of the truth hears His voice". Here we have a sovereign power that is absolute and that needs no resort to violence or threats to bolster its vulnerability. And it is here that we learn what true kingship is like.

"Analogia Relationis" and the Image of God

We may begin with an informal account that Barth gave in a question and answer session after lectures given at Princeton Theological Seminary in 1962:

> Question: How can we explain the covenant of God with man analogically, and what type of analogy would you consider appropriate for an evangelical theology?

> Answer: What is meant in theology by analogy? I would say an analogy is a created picture, an image, which involves both similarity and dissimilarity. In the picture or image—if we have eyes to see—the original is itself mirrored. The "original" of Scripture is the covenant between God and man—this relation, this story, this happening between God and man. Are there analogies to this central Biblical content? One can only say there are more or less enlightening, more or less adequate analogies. For example, the relation of man and his neighbour is an analogy of God and man in the covenant. This is not *my* invention for the Bible tells us so! Husband and wife and their togetherness is such an image. They are created together, and in their togetherness they reflect something of the relation between God and man. Man is not God. Certainly not! But in his relation to woman, he reflects,—Paul says it not I, something of the glory of Christ and of God himself ... There are many more which may help us to understand, but there is no such analogy which can explain or reveal the original itself unless we

---

[86]   John xix, 11.

already know something of the original, for example, of Jesus Christ. Then we may detect him also in such reflections, such mirroring, Please do not say, "Now he is going to erect a natural theology." It has nothing to do with it.[87]

Our task is to discover the theological basis that legitimizes for Barth the use of such analogies, and to replace his talk of images and pictures by something that is theoretically more precise.

In fact, in the doctrine of analogy that Barth develops throughout Volume III of the *Church Dogmatics*, there are two different sorts of analogy at stake, which although related are quite distinct. There are analogies between the relation of the Father to the Son within the Trinity and the relation of God to the world, and analogies between the divine and the human—between either relations within the Trinity or the relation of God to His creation and relations between human beings. I shall look briefly at the first sort of analogy.

> As the Father, God procreates Himself from eternity in His Son, and with His Son He is also from eternity the origin of Himself in the Holy Spirit; and as the Creator He posits the reality of all things that are distinct from Himself. The two things are not identical. Neither the Son nor the Holy Spirit is the world; each is God as the Father Himself is God. But between the two, i.e., the relationship in God Himself and God's relationship to the world there is obviously a *proportion*.[88]
>
> The eternal fellowship between Father and Son, or between God and His Word, thus finds a correspondence in the very different but not dissimilar fellowship between God and His creature.[89]

And:

> there is disparity between the relationship of God and man and the prior relationship of the Father to the Son and the Son to the Father, of God to Himself.
>
> But for all the disparity—and this is the positive sense of the term "image"—there is a correspondence and similarity between the two relationships. This is not a correspondence and similarity of being, an *analogia entis*. The being of God cannot be compared with that of man. But it is not a question of this twofold being. It is a question of the relationship within the being of God on the one side and between the being of God and that of man on the other. Between these two relationships as such—and it is in this sense that the second is the image of the first—there is correspondence and similarity. There is an *analogia relationis*. The correspondence and similarity of the two relationships consists in

---

[87] "A Theological Dialogue".

[88] *CD* III/1, p.49.

[89] *CD* III/1, p.50.

the fact that the freedom in which God posits Himself as the Father, is posited by Himself as the Son and confirms Himself as the Holy Ghost, is the same freedom as that in which He is the Creator of man, in which man may be His creature, and in which the Creator-creature relationship is established by the Creator.[90]

As we can see from the first of these two quotations Barth is here appealing to Aristotelian analogy—the *analogia proportionalitas* that he had apparently rejected in *CD* II/1: the Father is to the Son as God is to His creature. This immediately gives us purchase as to the significance of the contrast that Barth draws in the third of these quotations between an *analogia entis* and an *analogia relationis*. The point at stake (though Barth would not have liked my putting it this way) is a highly Aristotelian one. Aristotle had stressed throughout his discussions of analogy that analogy permitted comparisons between things that were "remote". Two things, *A* and *B*, that were too different in kind to permit any direct comparison between them could nevertheless be compared if *A* was related to other things in its domain in the same way that *B* was related to other things in its domain. In this way, although God's being is completely unlike the being of His creation, an indirect comparison by analogy between Him and His creation is still possible.

However, it is the second group of applications of analogy that is most directly of relevance to our concerns. These are built upon comparisons between the human and the divine: either comparing relations between human beings with relations within the godhead, or comparing relations between human beings with the relation of God to His creation—and specifically the relation of God to His covenant people. The particular relevance of this second use of analogy to the problem of talking about God is as follows: if relations between human beings can be seen as mirroring divine relationships, then it becomes clear how it is for Barth that the language that we have evolved for talking about those relations should find its most proper employment in talking about God: it is the divine relationships that set the standard for the human relations—that tell us how those relations ought ideally to be.

These analogies all rest ultimately upon Barth's conception of the image of God—on his reading of Genesis i 26–27:

> Then God said, "Let us make man in our image, after our likeness; and let them have dominion over the fish of the sea, and over the birds of the air, and over the cattle, and over all the earth, and over every creeping thing that creeps upon the earth." So God created man in his own image, in the image of God he created him; male and female he created them.

The image of God

In the light of the fierce controversy with Brunner in which the image of God had played such a central role, it may seem surprising to find Barth himself giving such

---

[90]   *CD* III/2, p.220.

a crucial position to the doctrine of the image of God. Earlier he had, for instance, written:

> as a possibility which is proper to man *qua* creature, the image of God is not just, as it is said, destroyed apart from a few relics; it is totally annihilated.[91]

Does what we find in *CD* III/1 represent a recantation? It is important to recognize that the answer to this question is "No". Although he almost certainly would not yet have developed his later understanding of the image of God when he was in dispute with Brunner, what he says in Volume III is wholly consistent with his earlier position. In the earlier confrontation, he had been concerned with Brunner's use of the idea of the image of God as the basis for a particular kind of natural theology, and also for his brand of apologetics—that there remained in man a "point of contact" (*Anknüpfungspunkt*) that implied that there was already a receptivity to the gospel on the part of natural man. Barth wanted nothing to do with this, at any stage of his work.

One thing is however clear: Barth would not accept that the image of God was a known datum such as human rationality or a moral sense: it would only be in the light of divine revelation that we could know what it meant to talk of the image of God at all.

Barth's starting point for his doctrine of the image of God is to take the words "male and female He created them" as a gloss on "God created man in his own image": to be in the image of God is to exist as male and female.

> "He created them male and female." This is the interpretation immediately given to the sentence "God created man." As in this sense man is the first and only one to be created in genuine confrontation with God and as a genuine counterpart to his fellows [*seinesgleichen*], it is he first and alone who is created "in the image" and "after the likeness of God. For an understanding of the general biblical use of this concept, it is advisable to keep as close as possible to the simple sense of "God-likeness" given in this passage. It is not a quality of man. Hence there is no point in asking in which of man's peculiar attributes and attitudes it consists. It does not consist in anything man is or does ... For the meaning and purpose of God at his creation were as follows. He willed the existence of a being which in all its non-deity and therefore its differentiation can be a real partner; which is capable of action and responsibility in relation to Him; to which His own divine form of life is not alien; which in a creaturely repetition, as a copy and imitation, can be a bearer of this form of life ... In God's own being and sphere there is a counterpart [*Gegenüber*]: a genuine but harmonious self-encounter and self-discovery; a free co-existence and co-operation; an open confrontation and reciprocity. Man is the repetition of this divine form of life; its copy and

---

[91]   *CD* I/1 p.238.

reflection ... Thus the *tertium comparationis*, the analogy between God and man is simply the existence of the I and the Thou in confrontation.[92]

> ... this plurality, the differentiation of sex, is something which formally he has in common with the beasts. What distinguishes him from the beasts? According to Gen. I, it is the fact that in the case of man the differentiation of sex is the only differentiation. Man is not said to be created or to exist in groups and species, in races and peoples, etc. The only real differentiation and relationship is that of man to man, and in its original and most concrete form of man to woman and woman to man. Man is no more solitary than God. But as God is One, and He alone is God, so man is one and alone, and two only in the duality of his kind, i.e., in the duality of man and woman. In this way he is a copy and imitation of God. In this way he repeats in his confrontation of God and himself the confrontation in God.[93]

For our purposes, what is crucial in this is that the image of God in humanity is seen in terms of human *relationships*, that human beings exist in specifically human relations to one another (paradigmatically as man and woman), mirroring relationships within God Himself.

> God created man in His own image, in correspondence with His own being and essence. He created Him in the image which emerges even in His work as the Creator and Lord of the covenant. Because He is not solitary in Himself, and therefore does not will to be so *ad extra*, it is not good for man to be alone, and God created him in His own image, as male and female ... We need not waste words on the dissimilarity in the similarity of the similitude. Quite obviously we do not have here more than an analogy, i.e., similarity in dissimilarity. We merely repeat that there can be no question of an analogy of being, but of relationship. God is in relationship, and so too is the man created by Him. This is his divine likeness.[94]

For Barth, we could say, the *essence* of being human lies in the fact that human beings are the creatures of whom God said "It is not good that the man should be alone",[95] and that it is existing in relation to other human beings that constitutes their being in the image of God, reflecting the life of God as Father, Son and Holy Ghost.[96] Although the paradigm is man and woman, it is clear as the discussion progresses that Barth sees this as extending to all human relationships, all relations

---

92   *CD* III/1, pp.184–185.

93   *CD* III/1, p.186.

94   *CD* III/2, p.324.

95   Gen. ii, 18.

96   To the dismay of many Old Testament scholars, Barth sees a Trinitarian significance in the unusual use of the plural: "Let us ..." in Gen i, 26. Such an interpretation has ancient precedent: see, *e.g.*, Augustine, *The Literal Meaning of Genesis*, I, Chapter 19, "The Blessed

in which I confront another human being as one both like myself and different from myself—all that constitutes life together.

It is therefore among the personal and social relationships that are constitutive of human life-together that analogies with God and His relation to the world are to be found—husband and wife, parent and child, king and his people.[97]

What this way of conceiving of the image of God implies is that it is inappropriate to look for any attributes of human beings that may be directly compared with divine attributes. Instead, we have a series of analogies of proportionality, comparing either the relations within the Godhead, or the relation of God to the world, with human relations—the Father is to the Son as a human father is to a son; God is to mankind as a king is to his people; and so on.

In the light of this, when Barth talked of "a created picture, an image",[98] the best way to think of what is meant is in terms of an analogical *model*—the model that results from extending those basic analogies. In this way, having said that God is to the covenant as a king is to his people, we may develop this analogy by describing the relations between God and His people as if we were talking about a king and his subjects.

Of course, such models need careful interpretation: taken in themselves they could lead to the most perversely idolatrous conceptions of God. For Barth, the crucial point here is that the models must be interpreted in the light of what they are models of and not vice versa. Quite apart from the finite creatureliness of the model, the human relations as we in practice encounter them are relations between sinful human beings. Although for Barth the fact of our being in the image of God is untouched by sin, the relations that we form as part of our life together are perversions of what those relations were intended to be.

> This human activity is the sign of the genuine creaturely confrontation in open differentiation and joyful relationship which is the image and likeness of the divine form of life. In itself and as such their activity is no doubt a denial of their divine image and likeness, and laden with all the mortal sickness which is

---

Trinity is implied in God's Decree to Create Man". I believe Barth's way of conceiving the image can be defended without reading an allusion to the Trinity into Genesis.

[97]   Perhaps it is worth commenting on Barth's adherence to "male" bases for analogies such as "father" and king, that has led to protests from feminist theologians such as Sallie McFague, who writes: "The classic models of the Christian tradition have been and still are hierarchical, authoritarian ones which have been absolutized. As feminist theologians have become increasingly aware, the orthodox tradition did a thorough job of plumbing the depths of one such model, the patriarchal, as a way of being articulate about God" (*Metaphorical Theology*, p.29). Obviously, from Barth's point of view, the important point is that it is these analogies that have scriptural warrant. But equally, it must be stressed that for Barth, calling Jesus the one and only true king carries with it a radical critique of the human, all too human, phenomena of the kings of this world.

[98]   "A Theological Dialogue".

a consequence of this denial, but this does not in any way alter the fact that this activity is the sign of hope given to man; the sign of the Son of Man and of His community.[99]

If, then, we are to interpret these analogies correctly, then we have to understand them in the light of God's self-revelation—and that means, Christologically:

it is this relationship in the inner divine being which is repeated and reflected in God's eternal covenant with man as revealed and operative in time in the humanity of Jesus.

We now stand before the true and original correspondence and similarity of which we have to take note in this respect. We have seen that there is factual, materially necessary, and supremely, as the origin of the factual and materially necessary, an inner divine correspondence and similarity between the being of the man Jesus for God and His being for His fellows. This correspondence and similarity consists in the fact that the man Jesus in His being for man repeats and reflects the inner being or essence of God and this confirms His being for God. We obviously have to do here with the final and decisive basis indicated when we spoke of the ontological character, the reality and the radical nature of the being of Jesus for His fellow-men. It is from this context that these derive their truth and power. The humanity of Jesus is not merely the repetition and reflection of His divinity, or of God's controlling will; it is the repetition and reflection of God Himself, no more and no less. It is the image of God, the *imago Dei*.[100]

It is at this point that the contrast I drew earlier between a natural theology and a theology of nature comes into its own. Barth develops these analogies, and insists that the use of such analogies is vital to theology. However, it is only in the light of God's self-revelation that we can see these analogies as legitimate analogies, and it is only in the light of God's self-revelation that we can interpret such analogies correctly.

Jesus Christ as very God and very man, the basis and fulfilment of the history of the covenant, is certainly not to be found again in general creaturely occurrence. This cannot then be more than a mirror and likeness. And everything thus takes place differently for all the similarities. Yet there are similarities. The contrast and connexion of heaven and earth, of the inconceivable and the conceivable world, is not the same as that of God and man in Jesus Christ; but it is similar. The antitheses of above and below, of light and darkness, of beautiful and ugly, of becoming and perishing, of joy and sadness, which are obviously to be found in creaturely occurrence, are certainly not the same as the true antitheses of

---

[99]   *CD* III/1, p.191.

[100]   *CD* III/2, pp.218–219. *Cf.* "the Humanity of God", p.51: "In the mirror of this humanity of Jesus Christ the humanity of God enclosed in His deity reveals itself."

grace and sin, deliverance and destruction, life and death in the history of the covenant; but they are at least similar. . . .

"The heavens declare the glory of God; and the firmament sheweth his handywork. Day unto day uttereth speech, and night unto night sheweth knowledge. There is no speech nor language, where their voice is not heard. Yet their line is gone out through all the earth, and their words to the end of the world" (Ps. 19 1f.). What can be known of God is manifest (φανερόν) among men because God "hath shewed it unto them" (ἐφανέρωσεν). His invisible being, namely His eternal power and Godhead from the creation of the world, may well be understood as seen in his works (νοούμενα καθορᾶται, Rom. 1, 19f.). But is this image really seen, this reflection recognised, this likeness understood? Are there necessary seeing eyes to see it? The original must obviously be known to make this possible. But to know the original we need faith in God's Word and revelation to have a part in the history of the covenant, and then genuinely in creaturely history. If we are children of the Father, we certainly recognise His house in more and more likenesses.[101]

Discussion

The main point to return to from the point of view of the present study is Barth's commitment to the ideas that, apart from revelation, we do not know, and cannot know, the meanings of a large number of the words we use, and also that this carries with it the implication that the use of those words involves a widespread misuse of those words:

> We use our words improperly and pictorially—as we can now say, looking back from God's revelation—when we apply them within the confines of what is appropriate to us as creatures.[102]

These two ideas appear highly contentious and to fly in the face of basic intuitions in the philosophy of language. In fact, Barth's account here may be seen precisely as a challenge to those intuitions.

Putnam's version of semantic externalism would already challenge the idea that we fully know the meanings of the words we use—in the case of a term such as water it is a matter of empirical, scientific, discovery that "water" is used to designate H_2O, and this discovery might not be known to many of the people who nevertheless *use* the word correctly. That correct use would, however, rest upon the possibility that they were able to identify, with a high degree of accuracy, specimens of water by its characteristic, readily recognizable, *symptoms*. Such correct identifications of specimens of water would serve to fix the reference and

---

[101]   *CD* III/3, pp.49–50.
[102]   *CD* II/1, p.229.

meaning of the word "water", even without the speakers of the language knowing what precisely the reference and meaning was that they were thereby fixing.

Such a picture of the way language and meaning are established may be disputable, but it is at least highly intelligible. Barth's position is, however, more radical than that. It implies a widespread misuse of our words—a widespread misidentification of what are and what are not instances of *F*. It is this contention that can appear outrageous, and which explains the hostile reaction that Barth's position has encountered. Barth is here contradicting the intuition that lay behind what used to be called the "Paradigm Case Argument". According to that, we would explain the meaning of a word such as "king" by picking out Henry VIII, and possibly a range of other exemplars, and saying "Henry VIII is a king, and so is …, and so are other people who resemble them in relevant respects". If that is so, how could we subsequently turn round and say "Henry VIII wasn't really a king"? How could someone learn the meaning of the word "king" in a world where the word was always used "improperly or pictorially"? Is the idea that the meanings of our words supervene on the use we make of those words compatible with the idea that there is a universal, or near universal, misuse of those words?

What these questions betray is an oversimplified conception of the ways in which we learn complex words. We can make no sense of the hypothesis that people are almost universally in error in their classification of things as red, or as dogs. Here, we may assume that a major part of fixing the meanings of such words as "red" or "dog" consists in people describing things as "red" or as "dogs" when confronted by appropriate samples.

However, if we think of a word like "beautiful" this simple picture no longer applies. Learning the meaning of a word like beautiful certainly does not consist in showing someone beautiful things and being told that they are beautiful. It is a much more subtle process. To greatly simplify what actually happens, we may imagine the following. Suppose a child is shown a variety of things which he is told are beautiful. (The mother says "listen to the beautiful music", and so on.) Through this the child catches on to the word "beautiful". What does he learn? That these *are* all examples of beautiful things? Not necessarily. The mother might have appalling taste, and the examples for the most part be examples, not of beauty, but of sentimental kitsch. What will then be the case will be examples that *appear* to the mother to be beautiful. But it will also be apparent that the mother values these things and values them because she finds them beautiful. As the boy grows older, he may come to think that the things that his mother told him were beautiful were valueless, certainly by comparison with the things he now values. But he also recognizes those things that he had earlier been told were beautiful were caricatures of the real thing. That is to say, he learns the meaning of the word "beauty" from the fact that the things he was introduced to *seemed* to his mother to be beautiful, not that they were. In learning a word like "beauty", we can learn to see that those who use the word are putting forward things as meeting a certain standard—even if the things that they put forward fall far short of anything that is truly beautiful.

In the same way, we can learn the use of words such as "justice", "mercy", "judge" and "king" from their application to worldly phenomena, and only subsequently, in the light of divine revelation, come to realize that these apparent exemplars were just caricatures of true justice, mercy, judgment and kingship.

The final question to discuss in Barth's discussions of analogy is the following: the treatment of the language we use to talk about God in *CD* II/1 is most aptly expressed in terms of the analogy of attribution, but the treatment of the analogy between God and His creation in the Doctrine of Creation (*CD* III) in terms of Aristotelian analogy—the analogy of proportionality. How are these two accounts to be reconciled? I leave that question until the next chapter.

analogy of attribution
vs
analogy of proportionality
- reconciliation

Chapter 7
Final Reflections

We have now looked at three very different accounts of religious language, each of which contains deep insights into the problems that confront us here. However, the differences between these accounts are such that, at least as they stand, they cannot all be correct. It is also clear that the differences between these accounts reflect the different theological perspectives and presuppositions of Aquinas, Kant and Barth. It is the aim of the present study neither to adjudicate between them, nor even to offer my own theory of religious language. Properly to fulfil either of those two aims would be a *theological* task, whereas my aim is purely *philosophical*—an exploration of the question how far the different ideas that we have encountered offer a viable account of religious language.

A viable account would be one that satisfied three conditions: (1) it would provide a coherent account of talk about God, both of its meaningfulness and of its meaning; (2) it would show how the use of such language did not involve us in anthropomorphism; and (3) it would avoid agnosticism—that is to say, it would give an account of the meaning of such language in such a way that there could be a genuine phenomenon of a human being understanding what was being said.

Analogy of Proportionality or Analogy of Attribution?

Two ideas have recurred in the preceding chapters—that of the "analogy of proportionality" or Aristotelian analogy on the one hand, and that of the "analogy of attribution" or "focal meaning" on the other. My first questions are: "How far is either of these two ideas capable of providing solutions to the problems that confront us?" and "Is there any way of incorporating the insights that have led to these two apparently very different ideas into a single coherent account?"

Analogy of Proportionality

We must consider the real or apparent difficulties confronting the attempt to use the analogy of proportionality in our account of the language we use to talk about God. I shall start by looking at various objections to the use of this form of analogy from within the Thomist tradition. In the recent reaction against Cajetan's championing of the analogy of proportionality, a number of commentators have sought to show, not only that in this Cajetan was misinterpreting Aquinas, but that this use of analogy could not possibly be applied to the problem of understanding the divine perfections.

1. David Burrell

> Thus "good" said of a citizen and a train robbery is justified by recourse to the paradigm $a:b::c:d$—"good:citizen::good:robbery"—which reminds us strongly of 2:4::3:6. Now the mathematical example is useful to clarify what language leaves ambiguous: $good_1$, said of a citizen, must be distinguished from $good_2$, said of the robbery. For generally, if b differs from d, so must a from c to preserve a proportion. Yet from this point on the mathematical proportion ceases to be useful and becomes misleading. For ordered couples can be unequivocally expressed—as in our case 1:2—and so form equalities: 2:4 = 3:6. But all attempt to find an element (like the 1:2) common to the ratios "good:citizen" and "good:robbery" have failed. Such efforts must fail since the very search for a schema to regularize the usage of terms like good sprang initially from want of a formula to express the conditions for their use. This failure to conform to an account which will not vary from one context to another is precisely what merits such terms being classified as "systematically ambiguous" or "analogous". So the commentary must point out that the "::" relating $a:b$ with $c:d$ may not be interpreted as "=", and this discrepancy signals the limit of any promise of systematic clarity. Since we know how to operate with = but have no idea what to do with ::, the schema $a:b::c:d$ becomes itself an analogy, at once useful and misleading, for analogous use.[1]

Although I believe this passage to be completely misguided, I shall begin with this quotation from David Burrell, both because his views have been widely influential and because the way in which he goes wrong here is instructive. We can see that he must have gone astray, since if his argument were good, it would rule out not only the problem cases such as the word "good" but also the unproblematic cases of words said by analogy such as "wing" said of birds and of butterflies.

Burrell's thought seems to be that people who have thought that a word like "good" was said by analogy were claiming that there were different sorts of good, and that this good was to citizens as that good was to train robberies. That way of interpreting the claim does indeed lead to virtually unintelligible results. But this is not what Aristotle or Archytas had in mind. If we return to the example that I examined in Chapter 3, the idea was not that there were different sorts of calm and that this calm was to the sea as that calm was to the air. The idea was, rather, that because windlessness was to the air as wavelessness was to the sea, we could use this analogy to introduce a concept, *calm*, which covered both these cases. When we compare Burrell's account with what Archytas did, we can see where Burrell has gone wrong. When we introduce a concept F, and say that the word "F" that designates that concept is said by analogy, we do not use the word "F" in the specification of the underlying analogical scheme. If we were to attempt

---

[1]   David Burrell, *Analogy and Philosophical Language*, p.10.

to apply analogy in the way suggested by Burrell, the circularity in the account would inevitably result in the kind of unintelligibility that he finds.

2. E. Jennifer Ashworth

> In his *De veritate*, he [Aquinas] argues that the analogy of attribution involves a determinate relation, which cannot hold between God and creatures, and that the analogy of proportionality must be used for the divine names. We must compare the relation between God and his properties to the relation between creatures and their properties. This solution was deeply flawed, given that the problem of divine names arises precisely because the relationship of God to his properties is so radically different from our relation to our properties.[2]

Here Ashworth is envisaging a different but related application of the analogy of proportionality, according to the pattern "God's wisdom is to God as human wisdom is to human beings". Certainly a number of authors have offered such an application, although it should be noted that Ashworth goes beyond what Aquinas actually says in ascribing this conception to *de Veritate*. The key point, which I shall return to below, is that Ashworth's criticism here is not so much directed against the use of the analogy of proportionality in the account of religious language, but only a particular application of the analogy—and as we saw in the case of Kant, say, that application is by no means the only possible one. My difficulty here with this application of analogy is, however, different from Ashworth: the issue is not whether the relationship between God and His properties is the same as, or different from, our relation to our properties, but one of interpreting the formula at all: what "relationship" can possibly be meant here.

3. Réginald Garrigou-Lagrange

> The Agnostics insist with the objection that, if the similarity of analogy is to be found only between the two relations God/His being = creature/its being, then the concept of analogous being is no more than that of a relation, and how are we then to avoid the Agnostic schema $\infty/\infty = a/b$ which means $?/? = a/b$? At least it seems we have but a purely negative and relative knowledge.[3]

Unlike the previous two authors, Garrigou-Lagrange advocates the use of the analogy of proportionality, and is here presenting a criticism that he will go on to offer his own reply to. The objection raised is, however, important in its own right. If two of the terms in the analogical schema are "unknowns", how can we solve it in such a way as to give us genuine knowledge? The question can be put in the form: "How informative is this application of analogy?" "Do we really learn what

---

[2]   E. Jennifer Ashworth, "Medieval Theories of Analogy".

[3]   Réginald Garrigou-Lagrange, *God, His Existence and Nature*, Volume II, p.218.

it means to say that God is wise by being told that God's wisdom is related to God as human wisdom is to a wise human being?"

The main point to make about all three of these criticisms of the use of the analogy of proportionality is that they are not criticisms of the analogy per se, but only criticisms of a particular way of applying it. It is not an application of the analogical formula that finds a precedent in any of Aristotle's explorations of analogy. Equally it does not correspond to the use of the analogy of proportionality made by either Kant or, on my interpretation, Barth in Volume III of the *Church Dogmatics*.

My own difficulty with this way of applying analogy is more radical than any of those cited above: I simply do not understand what is meant. If we take Garrigou-Lagrange's version—"God/His being = creature/its being"—I do not know how to understand what it means to talk of the relation of God to His being.

Be that as it may, there is a serious issue confronting the use of the analogy of proportionality that needs discussing. Aquinas does not, to my knowledge, ever say why he in his later writings rejects the analogy of proportionality in favour of the analogy of attribution, but I believe it is this.[4] The analogy of proportionality is a symmetric relation—if *A* is analogous to *B*, then *B* is analogous to *A*. How then can we do justice to the priority and superiority that we wish to ascribe to God by appeal to this analogy?

Analogy of Attribution

There are two questions that need addressing when we consider the analogy of attribution. The first question is "Does using the analogy of attribution give us an account of religious language that makes it possible for human beings to grasp what is said when we talk about God?" I argued above that when Aquinas and Barth adopted the analogy of attribution they both relied on an "externalist semantics", according to which we could use words significantly, without necessarily knowing the meanings of the words we use. The primary sense of the words used is in their application to God, and He alone can master that primary use. Thus Aquinas writes:

> "God is living" does not mean the same as "causes life"; the sentence is used to
> say that life does pre-exist in the source of all things, though in a higher way than
> we can understand or signify.[5]

If we talk here of a "a higher way than we can understand or signify", does that mean that we use such words without knowing what it is we are saying? It is right to stress how little we are able to grasp of the nature of God, and how far short

---

    [4]   One may also compare Barth's explanation of his advocacy of the analogy of attribution in *CD* II/1, p.238.

    [5]   *ST*, 1a 13, 2.

any of our thoughts fall when thinking about God. However, it must still be the case that if there is to be such a thing as informed faith, it must be possible that we should have some understanding of what it is we mean when we profess that faith.

The second question concerns the scope of the application of the analogy of attribution in religious language. At least as used by Aquinas in the *Summa Theologiae* and by Barth in *CD* II/1, it was primarily appealed to in order to explain the "names of God", in which we ascribe perfections to God, such as "God is wise" or "God is living". But such sentences only form a part of what we need to understand when we talk about God. In addition, in the Bible God is presented as creating, speaking and acting—in one way or another interacting with His creatures and His creation. It looks very much as though Aquinas will appeal to the analogy of proportionality to explain *such* ways of talking, but only to explain them as *metaphorical* ways of speaking. Is there any way that the analogy of attribution can be appealed to in the explanation of more than a fraction of what we need to say in talking about God?

Analogy of Proportionality and *Analogy of Attribution?*

Eberhard Jüngel writes of a "factual intermingling of [the analogy of attribution and the analogy of proportionality]",[6] and proposes that we need to employ some sort of synthesis of the two analogies to give a proper account of talk about God, but it is not clear how he would envisage this being carried through. In fact, he ascribes such "intermingling" to both Kant and Aquinas, but in the case of Kant that seems a straightforward misreading: the fact that, for instance, Kant explains the analogy between God and the world in causal terms does not imply that he is appealing to an analogy of attribution, but only that the "is to" in "God is to the world as a watchmaker is to a watch" is always a causal relation.

In the case of Aquinas, matters are more complicated. If I follow Jüngel's train of thought, it goes along the following lines. According to the doctrine of causal participation, earthly life is caused by God's communicating something of His life to creatures. The analogy of attribution would tell us that when we say that God is the living God, what we mean is that God is the cause of life in others. Aquinas is, however, insistent that that is not what we mean: when we ascribe life to God, we are referring to the superabundant life in God that he communicates to others, the life with which we are familiar being a reflection of that life. The analogy of attribution cannot of itself capture the resemblance that Aquinas claims between earthly justice and its divine original. Hence we have to give a different account of the nature of that resemblance. Since God is not in a genus, and cannot share any properties with creatures, we have to appeal to the analogy of proportionality, which was specifically introduced as a way to compare beings that were too remote to be compared directly.

---

[6]   *God as the Mystery of the World*, p.276.

However, I know of no text in which Aquinas himself takes the final step of appealing to the analogy of proportionality, being content to talk of some sort of resemblance between God's justice and terrestrial justice. The introduction of the analogy of proportionality into the account seems to be one made by subsequent commentators. But the major mistake in the above train of thought is the assumption that an analogy of attribution *must* be spelled out in causal terms. Although Aquinas does indeed hold that divine justice is the cause of all created justice, *linguistically* the priority that is assigned to the meaning of the word "just" as applied to God is explained in terms of God's being justice itself—the standard according to which all created justice is measured. At this point Aquinas seems content to talk of a likeness without further explanation. This seems the wisest course, since if we say God's justice is to God as human justice is to human beings then we lose what was vital to Aquinas' account, namely the asymmetry of the situation: that it is appropriate to compare earthly justice to divine justice but not vice versa.

However, in the case of Barth we do encounter such "factual intermingling": a term such as "lord" is treated in *CD* II/1 in a way that is clearly best expressed in terms of an analogy of attribution with the first and proper use of the term being found in its application to Jesus Christ,[7] but in *CD* III the term is treated in a way that is equally best expressed in terms of an analogy of proportionality.[8] It is not immediately obvious how these two accounts are to be reconciled. Certainly this needs handling in a different way from those we have just been looking at. The main aim of this chapter is to argue for the right way to coordinate the two analogies, and thereby draw together many of the threads that have emerged throughout this book.

Analogical Models and Alternation

One of the chief strengths of the analogy of attribution is that it gives an interpretation of religious language that respects the qualitative superiority of God over His creation. It allows us to understand what it means to say of God that He is just, say, but does so in such a way that we are not thereby simply including God in a class that also includes just human beings. By contrast, it is a prima facie difficulty for the analogy of proportionality—Aristotelian analogy—that it seems to do so. Analogy is a symmetric relation: if A is analogous to B, then B is analogous to A, and if situation X is used as an analogical model of situation Y, then we can automatically use situation Y as an analogical model of situation X. The question is, then, "Can we use Aristotelian analogy in such a way as to respect the qualitative superiority of God to His creation?" "Are we not inevitably putting God and creatures on a level and thus led into overt or covert anthropomorphism?"

---

[7]   p.230.
[8]   See, *e.g.*, *CD* III/2, p.324.

Such questions may be directed to Kant, whose chief aim was to give an account of religious language that avoided anthropomorphism, when he writes:

> If I say that we are compelled to look upon the world *as if* it were the work of a supreme understanding and will, I actually say nothing more than: in the way that a watch, a ship, and a regiment, are related to an artisan, a builder, the commander, the sensible world (or everything that makes up the basis of this sum total of appearances) is related to the unknown.[9]

Does this positing of the same relation obtaining in both the phenomenal and noumenal worlds really avoid anthropomorphism? Is it really less anthropomorphic to ascribe to God the same relational properties as human beings than to ascribe the same intrinsic properties? Or, again, how are we to reconcile Barth's insistence in Volume II/1 of the *Church Dogmatics* that the words we use to talk about God have their only proper use in talking about God with his appeal to analogical models in Volume III?

The answer to such questions may be found if we return to one of the most basic features of analogy—*that analogies alternate*. That is to say, if A:B::C:D, then A:C::B:D. The best way to understand how this provides the key to the solution of our problems is by illustration—by looking at some examples.

There is a form of argument that recurs in the Bible in which a human situation is described, and then the analogous divine situation is introduced by the phrase "How much more". We may consider a particularly clear case.

> What father among you, if his son asks for a fish, will instead of a fish give him a serpent; or if he asks for an egg, will give him a scorpion?. If you then, who are evil, know how to give good gifts to your children, how much more will the heavenly Father give the Holy Spirit to those who ask him![10]

We start with a familiar human situation—that of a father giving to his son what the son asks for, provided that what the child asks for is something truly beneficial. On the basis of the analogy: God is to mankind as a human father is to his children, that situation is then used as an analogical model for God's giving the Holy Spirit to those who ask for it. This yields the analogy envisaged in the parable: God is to the gift of the Holy Spirit as a human father is to his gifts to his children. But now ("how much more") we alternate this analogy: if God is to the gift of the Holy Spirit as a human father is to his gifts to his children, then God is to a human father as the gift of the Holy Spirit is to a human father's gifts to his children. That is to say: the greater the giver, the greater the gift.

---

[9]   Kant, *Prolegomena*, p.146 (Ak. 4:357).

[10]   Luke xi, 11–13.

In this way, despite the fact that analogical modeling is a symmetric relation, we can use such modeling in such a way that an inferior situation can be used as a model of a superior situation, and vice versa.

We can see what happens here in detail if we consider another, secular, example.[11] In *The Origin of Species* Charles Darwin wishes to argue along the following lines: that there is a process of natural selection; that natural selection can be responsible for evolutionary change in animals; and that change could be sufficiently great to allow for speciation—the emergence of new species. The central argument for these claims is an argument by analogy from what happens under artificial selection: there is variation in the farmyard, and farmers by selecting which of their stock they permit to breed can successfully modify the characteristics of that stock. There are in nature processes that similarly discriminate among animals in the wild, promoting the reproductive success of animals with favourable traits and frustrating the reproductive success of animals with unfavourable traits. Hence, by analogy, natural selection can successfully modify animals in the wild.

Here the argument runs into an apparent difficulty: the problem of reversion. Artificial selection appeared never to be capable of effecting *irreversible* changes in animals. If an animal had been bred under domestication and then returned to the wild, its offspring would eventually revert to their feral state. How then could you argue by analogy that natural selection could be responsible for speciation? You are now arguing by analogy from what happens on the farm to something happening in nature that never happens on the farm.

Because of this the argument of the *Origin* takes the following form. In the opening chapter Darwin examines what happens in domestic settings, where artificial selection operating upon variations in the animals under domestication produces major modifications in the farmer's stock, leading to new varieties. In the next two chapters he will argue that there is an analogy between what happens on the farm and what happens in the wild: firstly that, just as on the farm, there is variation in the wild and secondly that the struggle for existence will lead to natural selection—a process analogous to artificial selection. This enables Darwin to treat the farm or pigeon loft as an analogical model for the world of nature, based on the analogy: as artificial selection is to the modification of traits in animals under domestication, natural selection is to the modification of traits in animals in the wild.

But then in Chapter 4, Darwin seeks to establish, not only that natural processes can act selectively, but that it is possible that they should achieve something that artificial selection apparently could not—namely the kind of irreversible change constituted by the emergence of a new species. The key passage in the argument is the following where he seeks to show that natural selection will be an altogether more powerful and efficient process than artificial selection: ·

----

[11]   Jonathan Hodge, Gregory Radick and I are preparing an extended article on Darwin's use of analogy.

As man can produce and certainly has produced a great result by his methodical and unconscious means of selection, what may not nature effect? Man can act only on external and visible characters: nature cares nothing for appearances, except in so far as they may be useful to any being. She can act on every internal organ, on every shade of constitutional difference, on the whole machinery of life. Man selects only for his own good; Nature only for that of the being which she tends. Every selected character is fully exercised by her; and the being is placed under well-suited conditions of life. Man keeps the natives of many climates in the same country; he seldom exercises each selected character in some peculiar and fitting manner; he feeds a long and a short beaked pigeon on the same food; he does not exercise a long-backed or long-legged quadruped in any peculiar manner; he exposes sheep with long and short wool to the same climate. He does not allow the most vigorous males to struggle for the females. He does not rigidly destroy all inferior animals, but protects during each varying season, as far as lies in his power, all his productions. He often begins his selection by some half-monstrous form; or at least by some modification prominent enough to catch his eye, or to be plainly useful to him. Under nature, the slightest difference of structure or constitution may well turn the nicely-balanced scale in the struggle for life, and so be preserved. How fleeting are the wishes and efforts of man! how short his time! and consequently how poor will his products be, compared with those accumulated by nature during whole geological periods. Can we wonder, then, that nature's productions should be far "truer" in character than man's productions; that they should be infinitely better adapted to the most complex conditions of life, and should plainly bear the stamp of far higher workmanship?

It may be said that natural selection is daily and hourly scrutinising, throughout the world, every variation, even the slightest; rejecting that which is bad, preserving and adding up all that is good; silently and insensibly working, whenever and wherever opportunity offers, at the improvement of each organic being in relation to its organic and inorganic conditions of life. We see nothing of these slow changes in progress, until the hand of time has marked the long lapses of ages, and then so imperfect is our view into long past geological ages, that we only see that the forms of life are now different from what they formerly were.[12]

Here Darwin surveys a number of respects in which, in addition to the obvious consideration that nature has a much longer time at her disposal, nature will prove to be a superior selector to a human being. For instance, "nature cares nothing for appearances": whereas the farmer has no alternative but to select for a characteristic that *appears* to be favourable, out in the wild, if a characteristic is favourable, it *will* confer an advantage on the animal possessing it, and so on.

From this Darwin will conclude that the superiority of Natural Selection over Artificial Selection is such that much more will be achieved in the wild than could

---

[12]   Charles Darwin, *Origin*, Chapter 4.

be achieved on the farm. From our point of view, we can see the structure of this argument as taking the following form. We start by establishing that we can use the farm as an analogical model of nature in the wild, based on the analogical formula: Artificial Selection (AS) is to modifications achieved on the farm as Natural Selection (NS) is to modifications achieved in nature. We then establish that Natural Selection is a more powerful and efficient selector than the farmer. We alternate the analogy: if NS is to modifications achieved in nature as AS is to modifications achieved on the farm, then NS is to AS as modifications achieved in nature are to modifications achieved on the farm. That is to say, the superiority of Natural Selection over Artificial Selection will be reflected in the superiority of the effects it can achieve. So that if, by selective breeding, farmers produce new varieties, it is possible than natural processes, by natural selection, should produce new species.

In both cases, what we do is to take a familiar everyday situation and show that we can use analogy to make that situation a model for a target situation. We then argue by analogy that since this happens in the model the same thing will happen in the target. But then pointing out the superiority of the elements in the target to the elements in the model, we alternate the analogy to argue that what will happen in the target will be correspondingly superior to what happens in the model. It is important to note that this style of argument does not argue that *despite* the fact that the model is inferior to the target, we may nevertheless use it as an analogical model. Instead, the argument depends essentially upon the fact that the model is inferior to the target, which is why in both cases that inferiority is stressed ("you then, *who are evil*" and "How fleeting are the wishes and efforts of man! how short his time! and consequently how *poor will his products be*").[13]

What we are concerned with in these two examples is *argument* by analogy, but the same considerations may be adduced *mutatis mutandis* for the use of language in describing the model and its target. We may, say, use the analogy of proportionality to make the familiar situation of an earthly king and his subjects into a model for God's relation to His covenant people. We then argue that the primary sense of the words used in the descriptions of the two situations is that in which we apply them to God—that He alone is truly king, is truly sovereign, His justice alone is true justice, and that earthly kingship, sovereignty and justice are only so in a derivative sense. In this way, we may take earthly kingship as a model for divine kingship, however defective and corrupted such a model may be. If, however, the primary use of the words is when they are used to talk about God's kingship and not the kings of this world, the earthly model has to be interpreted in the light of what it is a model of, and not vice versa.

---

[13]   It is in this connection striking how many of Jesus' parables involve disconcertingly incongruous comparisons, in which, *e.g.*, God is compared to a man who will not get up out of bed to help a friend (Luke xi, 5–8), "a judge who neither feared God nor regarded man" (Luke xviii, 3) and "a hard man, reaping where you did not sow, and gathering where you did not winnow" (Matth. xxv, 26).

A man that looks on glass,
On it may stay his eye;
Or it hé pleaseth, through it pass,
And then the heav'n espy.[14]

Metaphor and Religious Language

The "way of analogy" that I have been exploring throughout this book is a way of explaining how it is possible to use human language to speak about God, in such a way that we may make claims that are *literally* true of God, while yet respect the fundamental difference between God and His creation. It is worthwhile looking, at least briefly, at the widespread claim that this is impossible, and that, instead, we should treat all claims that we may make about God as no more than metaphors, indicating but not stating the truth about God. We may consider here a representative passage from Jüngel:

> If language about God is only appropriate if it speaks of the fundamental difference between God and the world, then the question arises: how is such language possible? Our language is worldly language, and has only worldly words which refer to and are predicated of worldly beings. All predication is worldly; even the word "God" belongs to worldly language and therefore—as Luther showed in his exposition of the first commandment—can only say that it transcends the world from within that horizon: "That to which your heart clings and entrusts itself is, I say, really your God".[15] And obviously this can be an idol, a piece of the world. Consequently, no word which speaks of God can of itself designate the difference between God and the world. It must be transferred from other states of affairs. The difference between God and the world, and indeed God himself, can only come to speech metaphorically. God is only properly spoken about when we speak of him metaphorically.[16]

Clearly, even if it is a more difficult task than might initially appear to distinguish the literal and the metaphorical in the Bible, on any understanding there are a large number of passages where metaphors are used in talking about God—"Our God is a consuming fire",[17] "The Lord is my shepherd, I shall not want",[18] or "'I am the Alpha and the Omega,' says the Lord God, who is and who was and who is to come, the Almighty".[19] My present concern is not that, but only with the thesis that

---

[14] George Herbert,"The Elixir".
[15] Martin Luther, *The Large Catechism*.
[16] Eberhard Jüngel, "Metaphorical Truth", pp.59–60.
[17] Heb. xii, 29.
[18] Psalm xxiii, 1.
[19] Rev. i, 8.

the *only* way in which we can talk about God is metaphorically, and that all claims about God are so to be understood.

There are three points to make here, of which the third is the most fundamental.

1. The proposal is only to be taken seriously if it is accompanied by an account of what is involved in understanding such metaphors. This is not a criticism of Jüngel, but all too frequently the proposal is made without any real indication of how such "metaphors" are to be understood. Saying that these metaphors are "irreducible" is irrelevant here. One is not asking for a translation of the metaphors into equivalent literal propositions, but the onus is on the proponents of this idea to indicate a theory of metaphor according to which it is possible for human beings to interpret and understand such metaphors.

2. Metaphor is essentially a parasitic use of language. The point is not just that we can make no sense of the idea of a word that could only be used metaphorically, and never literally, but that it is arguable that we can make no sense of the idea that there was something that could only be talked about metaphorically. It would take us too far afield to argue this in detail,[20] but the basic point is that if there were an entity X for which we could construct no literal propositions, and concerning which every sentence containing the name "X" was to be interpreted metaphorically, we would lack the means for fixing the reference of the name "X", and so would not have any way of knowing what we were talking about.

3. One of the major concerns of those who have advocated a purely metaphorical account of religious language has always been to avoid anthropomorphism or, in Jüngel's phrase, to respect "the fundamental difference between God and the world". In fact, however, it is precisely "metaphorical theology" that leads directly to a form of anthropomorphism.

It is instructive to note that Jüngel, who usually follows Barth closely, takes a diametrically opposed stand to Barth. Barth avoids saying what Jüngel says here precisely because it involves us in construing what is meant by ascribing kingship to God by extrapolation from human kingship. On Jüngel's proposal, confronted by a verse such as

> But the Lord is the true God; He is the living God and the everlasting King. At
> His wrath the earth quakes, and the nations cannot endure His indignation[21]

---

[20]   I offer an account that shows the way in which talking about A metaphorically is only possible if it is already possible to talk about A literally in *The Structure of Metaphor*.

[21]   Jer. x, 10.

we understand this use of the word "king", by "transference from other states of affairs". That is to say, we take our understanding of the worldly phenomenon of kingship, and in some way purify or refine it, to arrive at an appropriate interpretation of the metaphor. But that involves us in interpreting divine kingship in terms of human kingship, and hence in a subtle form of anthropomorphism.

The point comes out clearly if we consider Sallie McFague who writes:

> The Protestant tradition is, I would suggest, "metaphorical", having just cited Barth as an example … in an extreme form Karl Barth's concept of *analogia fidei*, which insists that our language refers to God only as God from time to time causes our words to conform to the divine being.[22]

McFague is rightly concerned to oppose a kind of flatfooted "literalism" in which when we talk of God as king we should conceive Him as some kind of oriental despot. Her book is a useful warning against the dangers inherent in a simplistic approach to religious language.

But the opposition between what she suggests—that we see such talk as metaphorical—and what Barth had argued runs deep. For Barth, there was nothing metaphorical about calling God a king. On the contrary, this was *the* literal, proper, use of the word. It would be closer to the spirit of Barth's position to say that it is our everyday use of the word "king"—our calling Nebuchadnezzar, David or Henry VIII "king"—that is metaphorical.[23] I have been arguing that, paradoxical as it sounds, it is Barth's approach and not McFague's, that is the right way to safeguard her concerns.

Anthropomorphism and Agnosticism

I shall return finally to the question with which I began: "How far does appeal to the concept of analogy permit us to understand religious language in such a way as to avoid anthropomorphism on the one hand, and complete agnosticism on the other hand?"

Anthropomorphism

Narrowly conceived anthropomorphism consists in thinking of God as possessing properties that could only be possessed by a finite embodied human being. By a natural extension the term can apply to thinking of God in ways that imply he has material properties or can be located in space and time, or is spatially related to His creation, so that creating the universe would be like a magician taking a rabbit out of an empty hat.

---

22 *Metaphorical Theology*, p.13.
23 *CD* II/1, p.229: "We use our words improperly and pictorially".

It is, however, important that we should extend the concept yet further to prevent a more insidious and dangerous form of anthropomorphism. We should include the ascription to God of human values and attitudes:

> You leave the commandment of God, and hold fast the tradition of men.[24]

> For my thoughts are not your thoughts, neither are your ways my ways, says the Lord. For as the heavens are higher than the earth, so are my ways higher than your ways and my thoughts than your thoughts.[25]

Once we do include *all* thinking of God in human terms within the scope of anthropomorphism, we realize that avoiding anthropomorphism cannot be a matter of avoiding one sort of vocabulary in speaking of God—vocabulary ascribing physical characteristics to God, and regarding another kind of vocabulary— "spiritual", "moral" or "metaphysical"—as safe. One can be thinking just as anthropomorphically when one talks of His aseity or His impassibility as of His eyes or hands.

However, as I said in the Preamble to this book, we have no alternative but to use the everyday language we use for talking of human beings and their relationships in talking about God, and it would be a delusion to suppose that we could devise a special way of talking that escaped our human limitations.

> A papal decree condemns the Anthropomorphites for speaking about God as if they were speaking about a human being, and for ascribing to Him eyes, ears, arms, etc. However, the condemnation is unjust. Indeed, how could men speak otherwise of God among men? If it is heresy to think of God in this manner, then a verdict has been rendered concerning the salvation of all children, who think and speak of God in this childlike fashion. But even apart from children: give me the most learned doctor—how else will he teach and speak about God?[26]

We are obliged to use our human language just as it stands:

> For it is the God who said, "Let light shine out of darkness," who has shone in our hearts to give the light of the knowledge of the glory of God in the face of Christ. But we have this treasure in earthen vessels, to show that the transcendent power belongs to God and not to us.[27]

The issue therefore is not the vocabulary we use in speaking of God, but the way in which we interpret and understand that vocabulary. Here we may contrast two

---

[24]   Mark vii, 8.

[25]   Isaiah lv, 8–9.

[26]   Luther, *Lectures on Genesis*, Volume I, pp.14–15.

[27]   2 Cor. iv, 6–7.

approaches, the first of which is seductive but fails to appreciate the depth of the problem that we face.

First, one may think that the problem is one of using our everyday vocabulary and "purifying" it—ridding it of its unwanted anthropomorphic implications. We can take William Alston as a representative of this approach. He insists that we should understand the language of the Bible "literally", which is really not the issue—the writers who adopt the opposite approach, such as Aquinas or Barth, will equally understand religious language "literally". The issue is what that amounts to. What it amounts to for Alston can be seen by considering the following representative passage:

> Suppose that "Comfort *H*" or "Forgive *H*", or "Command *H* to do *A*", as applied to human beings, does mean something like "bring about effect *E* by some movements of one's body". In that sense we cannot use any of these terms of God in just that sense. But not to worry. We can simply lop off the requirement of the effects being brought about by movements of the agent's body, thereby constructing a less specific derivative sense: *produce effect E in some way or other*. The term with that sense, which is surely intelligible if the original sense was, can then be applied univocally to God and to man.[28]

So, when we apply a word to God that we also apply to humans, the meaning of the word is its human meaning minus such elements as imply human limitations or infirmities. It is not clear whether this can be carried through in detail—whether there is in all cases a concept that can coherently be defined by this kind of subtraction—I do not know what the relevant concepts corresponding to "remember" minus ... or "father" minus ..., say, would be. But be that as it may, it is clear that this, if followed through, would give us a conception of God as an idealized human being. (This already sounds suspiciously like Feuerbach.) One would be talking of God "simply by talking of man in a loud voice".[29] We are here not escaping anthropomorphism at all, but seeing God in man's image from the very outset.

Second, it is, however, clear that if we are to talk of God at all the language we all speak and understand must be in some way appropriate to the task. That surely implies the possibility of some sort of comparison between God and His activities and human beings and their activities. Here we may take our cue from Aquinas who emphasized that "... is an image of ..." is an anti-symmetric relation. Therefore although it is correct to say that God created man in His image, we may not say that God is in the image of man. Anthropomorphism is then a matter of making that illegitimate transition.

If we then insist that we may only compare humans to God and not vice versa, that entails taking the further step, taken by both Aquinas and Barth, of saying

---

28 William Alston, "How to Think about Divine Action", p.67.
29 Barth, "The Word of God and the Task of the Ministry", p.196.

that the primary, or proper, meanings of the words that we use in talking about God is in their application to God, and that their application to humans involves a secondary meaning. So that God alone is merciful, and when we call a human being merciful we mean that they approximate to the mercy of God as the standard by which all mercy is measured. I argued in the chapters on Aquinas and Barth that despite its counterintuitive appearance, this was a fully coherent position. What I did not, however, discuss was whether this position would entail a certain kind of agnosticism: we have guaranteed the meaningfulness of religious language, but not in such a way that we can grasp what that meaning is.

Agnosticism

In our context, agnosticism does not mean a profession of ignorance concerning the existence of God, but scepticism concerning our ability to grasp the meaning of what is said when we talk about God. My final concern is to ask how far the three accounts of analogy and religious language I have looked at give accounts of that language in such a way that we can really understand what is meant when we talk about God.

Kant is the most straightforward case. He has offered us an account of religious language that fully safeguards God's transcendence, and where the claims made by such language are fully comprehensible. However, he has done so in such a way as to severely restrict the significance of such claims. When we make a claim about God, *all* that we are claiming is something about the nature of the effects He brings about in the world. Apart from knowing that the "ontological predicates" such as substance are applicable to God, Kant is, and is content to be, completely agnostic as to God's intrinsic nature. We have no knowledge or understanding of what God is in Himself, and no insight into how he achieves his effects.

With both Aquinas and Barth the situation is more complicated, since the way in which they have secured the meaningfulness of talk about God does not in itself carry with it any implication that the users of the language know what that meaning is. In its primary sense, the word "wise" refers to the wisdom of God, and not to the pale reflection of God's wisdom that we find among men. Both stress how little comprehension we can have of the nature of God in this life, but neither will wish to deny the possibility of *some* understanding of what we believe.

To understand what I take to be the core disagreement between them, I may return to the quotation from Rudi te Velde that I cited in the last chapter:

> If revelation is what it is said to be—a revelation of God, disclosing to man true knowledge concerning God—then the very intelligibility of this revelation-based discourse requires a prior ontological "definition" of God, in reference to which the propositions of revelation have their truth.[30]

---

[30]   *Aquinas on God*, p.3.

Barth could not possibly agree with the position that te Velde here ascribes to Aquinas. It is indeed at the heart of his disagreement with Roman Catholicism. The implications of this for the question that now confronts us run deep. If, for Aquinas, for revelation to be possible we must already have an account of what God is and how to talk about Him, then it must be possible to establish the meaning of claims made about God independently of, and prior to, God's self-revelation. (Put simply: "How could we understand the Word of God, unless it was couched in a language that we already understood?") For Barth, however, apart from divine revelation we misunderstand the language that is used in that revelation and God Himself in His revelation teaches us how to interpret His Word.

What they agree on is that the primary use of the words we use to talk about God is in their application to God and not to creatures. When we apply those words to creatures it is in virtue of the fact that they bear some resemblance to their divine original. In Aquinas' case, this resemblance is a consequence of causal participation; in Barth's case ultimately because man is created in the image of God. Because of the primacy of God's justice—the fact that divine justice is the measure whereby earthly justice is measured and not vice versa—there is no backward route from the human to the divine, no straightforward way of inferring what divine justice is like from our acquaintance with what we call justice on earth.

Aquinas is developing his account against a background of Neo-Platonic theologies. Such theologies have always tended towards a purely apophatic theology, ultimately reflecting Plato's own scepticism about the possibility of there being human knowledge of the Form of the Good. Aquinas too will emphasize the extent of our ignorance in such a way that he can write as if all that is possible to us is a *theologia negativa*:

> When the existence of a thing has been ascertained there remains the further question of the manner of its existence, in order that we may know its essence. Now, because we cannot know what God is, but rather what He is not, we have no means for considering how God is, but rather how He is not.[31]

In this way, when we say that God is simple, we are not claiming to have any conception of what such simplicity would be like, but only to deny any composition in God. Although elsewhere he will claim that such negative knowledge gives us some genuine knowledge of God: "For we know each thing more perfectly the more fully we see its differences from other things."[32] What we have to consider is the question "How far does Aquinas' 'way of analogy' take him beyond complete agnosticism?"

On Aquinas' account when I say "God is wise", I am using the word "wise" in its primary sense, and when I say that Solomon is wise I am using the word in a secondary sense, to mean that Solomon approaches to some degree the standard set

---

[31] *ST* I, 3 prol.
[32] *SCG* I, Chapter 14.

by the wisdom of God. But the wisdom of God itself is something of which we can form no positive conception, beyond the fact that Solomon's wisdom bears some resemblance to it. In this way, it is impossible for us to gain full understanding of what we mean when we say God is wise, and are restricted to the knowledge that the wisdom of Solomon is a faint reflection of God's wisdom. This does go beyond a purely apophatic theology, but only just. The extent of our knowledge is that God's wisdom is the standard whereby all wisdom is to be judged, without our being able to form a positive conception of what such wisdom is like.[33]

Barth's position is in one way more negative than Aquinas', in another way more positive. The basis for his account is the idea that "our thought and our language are ... [God's] creation",[34] in that it is a language that has evolved for us to talk about the world and our place in it, and that world, whether we know it or not is God's creation. In that way, our language reflects God's creation, and because God has created us in His image, our language reflects God Himself—contains the vocabulary that is most appropriately used for talking about God.

However, his position is more negative than Aquinas', in that natural man, without divine revelation, does not know and has deep misconceptions of what wisdom, peace and mercy are. We radically misuse and misunderstand the language we use, unless that language is restored for us by God. Given that misunderstanding and misuse, any backward route from our language and the world is completely blocked.

Barth is also far more positive than Aquinas. The world is and remains God's good creation, and man is and remains in God's image. Therefore the world contains, particularly among human relationships, images and analogical models of God—both God as He is in Himself, and God in His relation to the world, however defective those images and models might be—defective both because of our finitude and creatureliness and our sinfulness. Therefore, when in God's revelation, in His Word to us, words are restored to their proper meanings, those who have ears to hear can hear something of those meanings. We are now enabled to see those images as images of God, and to interpret them correctly.

> because it is God's revelation, it is correct and trustworthy revelation. It is the will, but also the power of this object, to make Himself know to us.[35]

What this means is that it is above all in Christ that we can learn something of the true meanings of "peace", "love", "mercy" and "power". We can take the worldly phenomena that we are accustomed to call "peace", "love", "mercy" and "power", in all their perversion and inadequacy, as images of their divine originals.

---

33   *ST*, 1a 13, 2: "the sentence ['God is living'] is used to say that life does pre-exist in the source of all things, though in a higher way than we can understand or signify".

34   *CD* II/1, p.228.

35   *CD* II/1, p.210.

For it is the God who said, "Let light shine out of darkness," who has shone in our hearts to give the light of the knowledge of the glory of God in the face of Christ.[36]

He is the image of the invisible God, the first-born of all creation.[37]

To have all the riches of assured understanding and the knowledge of God's mystery, of Christ, in whom are hid all the treasures of wisdom and knowledge.[38]

And:

And the Word became flesh and dwelt among us, full of grace and truth; we have beheld his glory, glory as of the only Son from the Father.[39]

---

[36] 2 Cor. iv, 6.
[37] Col. i, 15.
[38] Col. ii, 2–3.
[39] John i, 14.

Bibliography

Abraham, William J., *Canon and Criterion in Christian Theology: from the Fathers to Feminism*, Oxford, Clarendon Press, 1998.

Alston, William, "How to Think about Divine Action", in Hebblethwaite and Henderson, 1990, pp.71–91.

Anselm, *Proslogion*, 1077–1078.

————, *Cur Deus homo*, 1099.

Aquinas (Thomas), *Commentary on the Sentences of Peter Lombard*, 1256.

————, *Commentary on Boethius's "de Trinitate"* [1256–1261] (Questions I–IV translated by Armand Maurer as *Faith, Reason and Theology*, Toronto, Pontifical Institute of Mediaeval Studies, 1987).

————, *Quaestiones Disputatae de Potentia Dei* [1259–1268].

————, *Quaestiones disputatae de Veritate* [1256–1259] (translated from the Definitive Leonine text by Robert W. Mulligan as *Truth*, Chicago, H. Regnery Co., 1952).

————, *Summa contra Gentiles* [1261–1263] (translated by Anton C. Pegis F. R. S. C. as *On the Truth of the Catholic Faith*, Garden City, NY, Image Books, 1955).

————, *Summa Theologiae* [1265–1272] (Volume II, *Existence and Nature of God* [1a. 2–11], translated by Timothy McDermott O. P., London, Blackfriars, 1964; Volume III, *Knowing and Naming God* [1a. 12–13], translated by Herbert McCabe O. P., London, Blackfriars, 1964; Volume IV, *Knowledge in God* [1a. 14–18], translated by Thomas Gornall S. J., London, Blackfriars, 1964).

Aristotle, *Categories*.

————, *Categories, and De Interpretatione* (translated with notes by J. L. Ackrill), Oxford, Clarendon Press, 1963.

————, *de Anima*.

————, *de Anima* (translated with an introduction and notes by R. D. Hicks), Cambridge, Cambridge University Press, 1907.

————, *de Generatione et Corruptione*.

————, *Eudemian Ethics*.

————, *History of Animals*.

————, *Historia Animalium* (I, translated by A. L. Peck, 1965; II, translated by A. L. Peck, 1970; III, translated by D. M. Balme, 1991) Cambridge, MA, Harvard University Press.

————, *Metaphysics*.

————, *Metaphysics I–IX* (translated by Hugh Tredennick), London, Loeb Classical Library, William Heinemann Ltd., 1933.

————, *Metaphysics Books Γ, Δ, and E* (translated with notes by Christopher Kirwan), 2nd edition, Oxford, Clarendon Press, 1993.

————, *Metaphysics, Books Z and H* (translated with a commentary by David Bostock), Oxford, Clarendon Press, 1994.

————, *Meteorologica*.

————, *Nicomachean Ethics*.

————, *Nicomachean Ethics* (edited and translated Rackham H.), London, Loeb Classical Library, Heinemann, 1926.

————, *Parts of Animals*.

————, *De partibus animalium I and De generatione animalium I (with passages from II.1–3)* (translated with notes by D. M. Balme), Oxford, Clarendon Press, 1972.

————, *Poetics*.

————, *Politics*.

————, *Posterior Analytics*.

————, *Posterior Analytics* (translated with notes by Jonathan Barnes), Oxford, Clarendon Press, 1975.

————, *Rhetoric*.

————, *Topics*.

[School of Aristotle], *Magna Moralia*.

Ashworth, E. Jennifer, "Medieval Theories of Analogy", in *The Stanford Encyclopedia of Philosophy*, 2004.

Augustine, *The Literal Meaning of Genesis*, I (translated by J. H. Taylor), New York, Newman Press, 1982.

Baillie, John (ed.) *Natural Theology*, Geoffrey Bles: The Centenary Press, 1946 (translations by P. Fraenkel of Emil Brunner, "Nature and Grace" and Karl Barth "No!").

Balthasar, Hans Urs von, *Karl Barth, Darstellung und Deutung seiner Theologie*, Cologne, Verlag Jakob Hegner, 1951; E.T. *The Theology of Karl Barth* (translated by Edward T. Oakes), San Francisco, Ignatius Press, 1992.

Barker, Andrew, "Archytas Unbound", in Sedley, 2006, pp.297–321.

Barnes, Jonathan, "Homonymy in Aristotle and Speusippus", in *The Classical Quarterly*, New Series, Vol. 21, No. 1 (May, 1971), pp.65–80.

Barr, James, *Biblical Faith and Natural Theology*, Oxford, Clarendon Press, 1993.

Barth, Karl, "Unsettled Questions for Theology Today" [1920], in *Theology and Church*, pp.55–73.

————, *Der Römerbrief*, (2nd edition, Munich, 1922, 6th edition, Munich, 1928); E.T. *The Epistle to the Romans* (translated by Edwyn C. Hoskyns), London, Oxford University Press, 1933.

————, "The Word of God and the Task of the Ministry" [1922], in *The Word of God and the Word of Man*.

————, *The Word of God and the Word of Man* (translated by D. Horton), London, Hodder & Stoughton, 1928 (*Das Wort Gottes und die Theologie*, Munich, Chr. Kaiser, 1925).

————, *The Göttingen Dogmatics: Instruction in the Christian Religion*, Vol. I [1924–1925] (ed. Hannelotte Reiffen, translated by G. W. Bromiley), Grand Rapids, MI, W. B. Eerdmans, 1991.

————, "The Principles of Dogmatics according to Wilhelm Herrmann" [1925], in *Theology and Church*, pp.238–271.

————, "Church and Culture" [1926], in *Theology and Church*, pp.334–354.

————, *Die christliche Dogmatik im Entwurf: Erster Band: Die Lehre vom Worte Gottes, Prolegomena zur christlichen Dogmatik*, Munich, Christian Kaiser Verlag, 1927.

————, *Theology and Church: Shorter Writings 1920–1928* (translated by Louise Pettibone Smith), London, SCM Press, 1962.

————, *The Holy Ghost and the Christian Life* [1929] (translated by R. Birch Hoyle), London, F. Muller, 1938.

————, *Fides Quaerens Intellectum: Anselms Beweis der Existenz Gottes im Zusammenhang seines theologischen Programms* [Zurich, 1931]; E.T. *Anselm: Fides Quaerens Intellectum* (translated by Ian W. Robertson), London, SCM, 1960.

————, *Kirchliche Dogmatik*, E.T. *Church Dogmatics*:

————, *(Die Lehre vom Wort Gottes) I/1* [Munich, 1932]; E.T. *Church Dogmatics I/1 (The Doctrine of the Word of God)* (translated by G. W. Bromiley), 2nd edition, Edinburgh, T. &. T. Clark, 1975.

————, *Theological Existence To-Day!* [1933] (translated by R. Birch Hoyle), London, Hodder and Stoughton, 1933.

————, *Das erste Gebot als theologisches Axiom, Zwischen den Zeiten*, 1933, pp.297–314 (reprinted in *Theologische Fragen und Antworten*, pp.127–143).

————, *Theologische Existenz heute, heft* 4, 1933: *Lutherfeier* 1933, pp.1–24.

————, *Theological Declaration of the Synod of Barmen.*

————, *Nein! Antwort an Emil Brunner, Theologische Existenz Heute*, 1934 (translated in John Baillie, 1946, pp.67–128).

————, *Kirchliche Dogmatik*, E.T. *Church Dogmatics*:

————, *(Die Lehre von Gott) II/1* [Zurich, 1940]; E.T. *Church Dogmatics II/1 (The Doctrine of God)*, (translated by G. W. Bromiley and T. F. Torrance), Edinburgh, T. &. T. Clark, 1957.

————, *(Die Lehre von Schöpfung) III/1* [Zurich, 1945]; E.T. *Church Dogmatics III/1 (The Doctrine of Creation)* (translated by J. W. Edwards, O. Busey and Harold Knight), Edinburgh, T. &. T. Clark, 1958.

————, *(Die Lehre von Schöpfung) III/2* [Zurich, 1948]; E.T. *Church Dogmatics III/2 (The Doctrine of Creation)* (translated by Harold Knight, G. W. Bromiley, J. K. S. Reid and R. H. Fuller), Edinburgh, T. &. T. Clark, 1960.

————, *(Die Lehre von Schöpfung) III/3* [Zurich, 1950]; E.T. *Church Dogmatics III/3 (The Doctrine of Creation)* (translated by G. W. Bromiley and R. J. Ehrlich), Edinburgh, T. &. T. Clark, 1961.

————, *(Die Lehre von Versöhnung) IV/3* [*Erste Hälfte*] [Zurich, 1959]; E.T. *Church Dogmatics IV/3* [*First Half*] *(The Doctrine of Reconciliation)* (ed. T. F. Torrance; translated by G. W. Bromiley), Edinburgh, T. &. T. Clark, 1961.

————, *Dogmatics in Outline*, translated by G. T. Thompson, SCM 1949 (*Dogmatik im Grundriss*: Zurich, EVZ-Verlag, 1947).

————, *Theologische Fragen und Antworten*, Zollikon, Evangelischer Verlag AG., 1957.

————, "The Humanity of God", in *The Humanity of God*, pp.37–65.

————, "Evangelical Theology in the 19th Century" [1957], in *The Humanity of God*, pp.11–36.

————, *The Humanity of God* (translated by John Newton Thomas and Thomas Wieser), Richmond, John Knox Press, 1960.

————, "A Theological Dialogue", in *Theology Today*, Vol. 19, No. 2, 1962.

Berkeley, George, *A Treatise Concerning the Principles of Human Knowledge* [1710], Oxford philosophical texts, edited by Jonathan Dancy, New York, Oxford University Press, 1998.

Black, Max, "Metaphor", in *PAS* 55, 1954, pp.273–294 (reprinted in *Models and Metaphor*, pp.25–47).

————, "Models and Archetypes" [1958], in *Models and Metaphor*, pp.219–243.

————, *Models and Metaphor*, New York, Cornell University Press, 1962.

Brown, Stephen J., S. J., *The World of Imagery: Metaphor and Kindred Imagery*, London, K. Paul, Trench, Trubner & Co., 1927.

Brunner, Emil, *Nature and Grace* [1934] (translated by Peter Fraenkel in *Natural Theology*, with an introduction by John Baillie, London, Geoffrey Bles: The Centenary Press, 1946).

Burrell, David, *Analogy and Philosophical Language*, New Haven and London, Yale University Press, 1973.

Byrne, Peter, *Kant on God*, Aldershot, Ashgate, 2007.

Cajetan (Thomas de Vio), *The Analogy of Names* [*de Nominum Analogia*] and *The Concept of Being* (literally translated and annotated by E. A. Bushinski and Henry J. Koren), Pittsburgh, Duquesne University, 1959.

Campbell, Norman, *What is Science?*, London, Methuen, 1921.

————, "Laws and Theories", in *Philosophy*, Vol. 13, No. 51 (July, 1938), pp.313–320.

Clarke, W. Norris, S. J., *The Philosophical Approach to God: A Contemporary Neo-Thomist Perspective*, Winston-Salem, Wake Forest University Press, 1979.

Confessio Gallicana, 1559.

Cross, Richard, "Idolatry and Religious Language", in *Faith and Philosophy*, Vol. 25, No. 2 (April, 2008), pp.190–196.

Darwin, Charles, *On the Origin of Species* [1859], a facsimile of the first edition with an introduction by Ernst Mayr, Cambridge, MA, Harvard University Press, 1964.

Darwin, Francis, *The life and letters of Charles Darwin, including an autobiographical chapter*, London, John Murray, 1887.

Daston, Lorraine, "Intelligences: Angelic, Animal, Human", in Daston and Mitman, 2005, pp.37–58.

Daston, Lorraine and Mitman, Gregg (eds), *Thinking with Animals, New Perspectives on Anthropomorphism*, New York, Columbia University Press, 2005.

Dedekind, Richard, "Continuity and Irrational Numbers" [*Stetigkeit und irrationale Zahlen*, 1872], in *Essays on the Theory of Numbers* (translated by W. W. Beman), Chicago, The Open Court Publishing Company, 1909.

de Haas, Frans and Mansfield, Jaap (eds), *Aristotle: On Generation and Corruption, Book I, Symposium Aristotelicum*, Oxford, Clarendon Press, 2004.

Euclid, *Elements* (ed. Isaac Todhunter), London, J. M. Dent & Sons Ltd, 1933.

Frede, Dorothea, "*On Generation and Corruption* I.10: on Mixture and Mixables", in de Haas and Mansfield, 2004, pp.289–314.

Frege, Gottlob, "Boole's Logical Calculus and the Concept-script", in Frege, 1979, pp.9–46.

———, "Comments on Sense and Meaning", in Frege, 1979, pp.118–125.

———, *Posthumous Writings* (ed. H. Hermes, F. Kambartel and F. Kaulbach; translated by P. Long and R. White), Oxford, Blackwell, 1979.

Garrigou-Lagrange, Réginald, *God, His Existence and Nature: A Thomistic Solution of Certain Agnostic Antinomies* [1914] (translated from the 5th French edition by Bede Rose, London, B. Herder book Co., 1934–1936).

Gentner, Dedre and Gentner, Donald R., "Flowing Waters or Teeming Crowds: Mental Models of Electricity", in D. Gentner and A. L. Stevens (eds), *Mental Models*, Hillsdale NJ, Lawrence Erlbaum Associates, 1983, pp.99–129.

Gill, Marie Louise, *Aristotle on Substance: the Paradox of Unity*, Princeton, Princeton University Press, 1989.

Gotthelf, Allan, "Darwin on Aristotle", in *Journal of the History of Biology*, Vol. 32 (1999), pp.3–30.

Gunderson Keith (ed.), *Language, Mind and Knowledge*, Minneapolis, University of Minnesota Press, 1975.

Hart, John W., *Karl Barth vs. Emil Brunner, the Formation and Dissolution of a Theological Alliance, 1916–1936*, New York, Peter Lang, 2001.

Hebblethwaite, Brian and Henderson, Edward (eds), *Divine Action: Studies Inspired by the Philosophical Theology of Austin Farrer*, Edinburgh, T. & T. Clark, 1990.

Hebblethwaite, Brian L. and Sutherland, Stewart R. (eds), *The Philosophical Frontiers of Christian Theology*, Cambridge, Cambridge University Press, 1982.

Hesse, Mary, "Aristotle's Logic of Analogy", in *Philosophical Quarterly*, Vol. 15, No. 61 (1965), pp.328–340.

Hodge, M. J. S., Radick, Gregory and White, Roger M., "The Analogical Character of Darwin's Argument for Natural Selection", in preparation.

Huffman, Carl A., *Archytas of Tarentum: Pythagorean, Philosopher, and Mathematician King*, Cambridge, Cambridge University Press, 2005.

Isocrates, *To Philip* [346 BC] (translated by George Norlin), in Loeb Classical Library, *Isocrates*, Vol. I, London, William Heinemann Ltd., 1928, pp.244–342.

Jüngel, Eberhard, *God as the Mystery of the World: on the Foundation of the Theology of the Crucified One in the Dispute between Theism and Atheism* (translated by Darrell L. Guder), Edinburgh, T. & T. Clark, 1983.

————, "Metaphorical Truth. Reflections on Theological Metaphor as a Contribution to a Hermeneutics of Narrative Theology" [1974], in *Theological Essays*, pp.16–71.

————, *Theological Essays* (translated by J. B. Webster), Edinburgh, T. & T. Clark, 1989.

Kant, Immanuel, *The Cambridge Edition of the Works of Immanuel Kant: Religion and Rational Theology* (ed. Allen Wood and George di Giovanni), Cambridge, Cambridge University Press, 1996:

————, *Religion within the Boundaries of Mere Reason* [1793] (translated by George di Giovanni), pp.39–216.

————, *The Conflict of the Faculties* [1798] (translated by Mary J. Gregor and Robert Anchor), pp.233–327.

————, *Lectures on the Philosophical Doctrine of Religion* (ed. K. Pölitz, 1817, delivered 1791?, trans. Allen W. Wood), pp.335–451.

————, *Theoretical Philosophy after 1781*, ed. Henry Allison and Peter Heath, Cambridge, 2002.

————, *Prolegomena to any Future Metaphysics that will be able to come forward as Science* [1783] (translated by Gary Hatfield) (in *Theoretical Philosophy after 1781*, pp.29–169).

————, *Practical Philosophy* (ed. and translated by Mary J. Gregor), Cambridge, 1996:

————, *Groundwork of the Metaphysic of Morals* [1785], pp.41–108.

————, *Critique of Practical Reason* [1788], pp.137–271.

————, "Toward Perpetual Peace" [1795], pp.315–351.

————, *The Metaphysic of Morals* [1797], pp.353–603.

————, "On a Supposed Right to Lie from Philanthropy" [1797], pp.609–615.

————, *Critique of Judgment* [2nd edition, 1793], translated by Werner S. Pluhar, Indianapolis, Hackett Publishing Company, 1987.

————, *Critique of Pure Reason* [2nd edition, 1787], translated by Norman Kemp Smith, London, Macmillan, 1933.

Klubertanz, George Peter, S. J., *St. Thomas Aquinas on Analogy: a Textual Analysis and Systematic Synthesis*, Chicago, Loyola University Press, 1960.

Kneale, William, *Probability and Induction*, Oxford, Clarendon Press, 1949.

Kripke, Saul, *Naming and Necessity*, 1972 revised edition, Oxford, Blackwell, 1981.

Lakoff, George and Johnson, Mark, *Metaphors We Live by*, Chicago and London, University of Chicago, 1980.

Le Blond, Jean-Marie, *Logique et Methode chez Aristote*, Libraire Philosophique, Paris, J. Vrin, 1939.

————, *Aristote, philosophe de la vie. Le livre premier du traité sur les parties des animaux* (*Texte et traduction, avec introduction et commentaire par J.-M. Le Blond*) Paris, Éditions Montaigne, 1945.

Le Guyader, Hervé, *Étienne Geoffroy Saint-Hilaire 1772–1844: A Visionary Naturalist* (translated by M. Grene), Chicago, University of Chicago Press, 2004.

Lennox, James G., "Aristotle on Genera, Species, and 'the More and the Less'", in *Journal of the History of Biology*, Vol. 13, No. 2 (September, 1980), pp.321–346.

————, *Aristotle: On the Parts of Animals I–IV* (translated with an introduction and commentary), Oxford, Clarendon Press, 2001.

————, *Aristotle's Philosophy of Biology: Studies in the Origins of Life Science*, Cambridge, Cambridge University Press, 2001.

Lewis, David, "Psychophysical and Theoretical Identifications", in *Australasian Journal of Philosophy*, Vol. 50, No. 3 (December, 1972), pp.249–258.

Lloyd, G. E. R., *Polarity and Analogy: Two Types of Argumentation in Early Greek Thought*, Cambridge, Cambridge University Press, 1966.

Luther, Martin [1529] *The Large Catechism*, Philadelphia, Fortress Press, 1961.

————, [1534] *Sermon on Acts 1–13.*

————, [1535] *Lectures on Genesis Chapters 1–5* (translated by George V Schick) in *Luther's Works*, edited by Jaroslav Pelikan, Vol. I, St. Louis Missouri, Concordia, 1958.

Lyttkens, Hampus, *The Analogy between God and the World; an Investigation of its Background and Interpretation of its Use by Thomas of Aquino*, Uppsala, Uppsala universitets arsskrift, 1953.

MacKinnon, D. M., "Kant's Philosophy of Religion", in *Philosophy*, 50 (1975), pp.131–144.

Maxwell, James Clerk, "On Faraday's Lines of Force" [1855–1856], in *The Scientific Papers of James Clerk Maxwell*, Vol. 1 (ed. W. D. Niven), New York, Dover, 2003.

McCarthy, Mary, "American Realist Playwrights", in *On the Contrary: Articles of Belief, 1946–61*, New York, Farrar, Straus and Cudahy, 1961.

McCormack, Bruce L., *Karl Barth's Critically Realistic Dialectical Theology*, Oxford, Clarendon Press, 1995.

McFague, Sallie, *Metaphorical Theology: Models of God in Religious Language*, London, SCM, 1983.

McGrath, Alister E., *A Scientific Theology*, Vol. 3 "Theory", London, T & T Clark, 2002.

McInerny, Ralph M., *The Logic of Analogy: an Interpretation of St. Thomas*, The Hague, Martinus Nijhoff, 1971.

McIntyre, John, "Analogy", in *Scottish Journal of Theology*, Vol. 12 (1959), pp.1–20.

Melia, Joseph and Saatsi, Juha, "Ramseyfication and Theoretical Content", in *British Journal for the Philosophy of Science*, Vol. 57, No. 3 (2006), pp.561–585.

Mitchell, Sandra D., "Anthropomorphism and Cross-Species Modelling", in Daston and Mitman, 2005, pp.100–117.

Overbeck, Franz, *Christentum und Kultur* (ed. C. A. Bernoulli), Basel, Benno Schwabe u. Cie, 1919.

Owen, G. E. L., "Logic and Metaphysics in Some Earlier Works of Aristotle", in *Aristotle and Plato in the Mid-Fourth Century*, ed. I. Düring and G. E. L. Owen, Gothenburg, 1960, pp.163–190.

Plato, *Phaedo* [ca. 360 BC].

————, *Gorgias* [ca. 360 BC].

————, *Republic* [ca.360 BC].

————, *The Republic of Plato* (translated with an introduction and notes by Francis M. Cornford), London, Oxford University Press, 1941.

————, *Philebus*.

————, *Sophist*.

————, *Statesman*.

Przywara, Erich, *Polarity: A German Catholic's Interpretation of Religion* (trans. A C. Bouquet), London, Oxford University Press, 1935 (translation of "Religionsphilosophie Katholischer Theologie" from the *Handbuch der Philosophie*, Vol. II, ed. A. Baeumler and A Schroeter, Munich, 1927–1930).

————, *Analogia Entis [Schriften 3]*, Einsiedeln, Johannes Verlag, 1962.

————, *In und Gegen; Stellungnahmen zur Zeit*, Nuremberg, Glock und Lutz, 1955.

Putnam, Hilary, "The Meaning of 'Meaning'", in Gunderson, 1975, pp.131–193.

Ramsey, F. P., "Theories" [1929], in *Philosophical Papers*, ed. D. H. Mellor, Cambridge, Cambridge University Press, 1990.

Reid, Thomas, *Essays on the Intellectual Powers of Man*, Edinburgh, 1785.

Richards, Jay Wesley, "Barth on the Divine 'Conscription' of Language", in *Heythrop Journal*, 38, Issue 3 (1997), pp.247–266.

Ross, James F., *Portraying Analogy*, Cambridge, Cambridge University Press, 1981.

Rumscheidt, H. Martin, *Revelation and Theology, an Analysis of the Barth-Harnack Correspondence of 1923*, Cambridge, Cambridge University Press, 1972.

Sedley, David N. (ed.), *Oxford Studies in Ancient Philosophy. Vol. XXXI*, Winter 2006, Oxford, Oxford University Press, 2006.

Smith, Adam, *An Inquiry into the Nature and Causes of the Wealth of Nations*, Vol. I [1776] (eds R. H. Campbell, A. S. Skinner and W. B. Todd), Oxford, Clarendon Press, 1976.

Söhngen, Gottlieb, "*Analogia fidei*", *Catholica* 1934, *Heft* 3 and 4.

Velde, Rudi te, *Aquinas on God: The 'Divine Science' of the Summa Theologiae*, Farnham, Surrey, Ashgate, 2006.

Waerden, B. L. van der, *Science Awakening* (translated by A. Dresden), Groningen, P. Noordhoff, 1954.

Ward, Graham, *Barth, Derrida, and the Language of Theology*, Cambridge, Cambridge University Press, 1995.

Watson, Gordon, "Karl Barth and St. Anselm's Theological Programme", in *Scottish Journal of Theology*, Vol. 30 (1977), pp.31–45.

Whately, Richard, *Elements of Rhetoric*, London, 1828.

White, Roger M., "Notes on Analogical Predication and Speaking about God", in Hebblethwaite and Sutherland, 1982, pp.197–226.

————, *The Structure of Metaphor: the Way the Language of Metaphor Works*, Oxford, Blackwell, 1996.

Winzeler, Peter, *Widerstehende Theologie: Karl Barth 1920–35*, Stuttgart, Alektor Verlag, 1982.

Index